a
ticket
to the
Circus

THE CIRCUS STREET PARADE. Pictured is the No. 1 band chariot, a gleaming red wagon with gold-leafed carvings. It was pulled by ten perfectly matched red-plumed Percherons. Following were cages of ferocious beasts, herds of elephants, droves of camels, and beautiful ladies picturesque and charming in their attire, and all elegantly mounted. Gone forever is this pageant which captured the eye, and spirited away the hearts of the youngsters on the curb.

(John M. Kelley Collection)

a ticket to the Circus

A Pictorial History of The Incredible Ringlings

BY

CHARLES PHILIP FOX

BRAMHALL HOUSE · NEW YORK

This edition published by Bramhall House,
a division of Clarkson N. Potter, Inc.,
by arrangement with Superior Publishing Company

(B)

PRINTED IN THE UNITED STATES OF AMERICA

DEDICATION.

TO THE ARMY OF PEOPLE WHO CONSTITUTED THE GREAT
FAMILY THAT LIVED FOR SEVEN MERRY MONTHS
UNDER THE WHITE TENTS OF THE

Ringling Brothers' World's Greatest Shows

THIS VOLUME IS RESPECTFULLY
DEDICATED, WITH THE HOPE THAT IT MAY, IN A
MEASURE, FULFILL THE SENTIMENTS OF THE POET, WHO SAID:

" There are moments in life that are never forgot,
Which brighten and brighten, as time steals away;
They give a new charm to the happiest lot,
And they shine on the gloom of the loneliest day."

Dedication from the
Ringling Route Book Season of 1894

Table of Contents

Preface

August 15, 1958

Dear "Chappie" Fox:

I have just finished reading the manuscript of your fine chronicle of the Ringling Circus, and of the lives of the men who dreamed it and built it. The men who, in your words, were the *Incredible Ringlings*, but to me were just *Papa* and *Uncle Al* and *Uncle Alfred*, and *Uncle Otto*, and *Uncle John*, and not at all incredible, but just the ordinary *folks* who made the world go round, for a little Wisconsin girl who lived among them and loved them in the early days of the century. These five were, of course, the members of the firm, but to me not more interesting, nor more loved than the other two brothers, Uncle Gus and Uncle Henry, who at first were not members of the firm, but later came to be a very important part of the circus.

It is good to hear these seven men spoken of as if they were real people, and not figments of someone's imagination—and sometimes so inaccurately—as, for example, when one writer of circus annals spoke of my father's *piercing blue eyes,* when he had eyes of the deepest brown, which could never have seemed *piercing* to anyone who really knew him.

Of course, the things I remember best are not the factual things of the growth and development of the circus, with its dates, and details of time and place. Much that you have recorded, I could not have done, for it all seemed so *every-day* to me at that time that I would have given it little thought and could not have remembered it with any accuracy. So there is much in your book that clarifies and revivifies my memories, and serves as a background for my vivid personal impressions of it all, as it was in those long past days, and of the men who gave it its aura—the true aura of sawdust and stardust, which was part of the daily living of my early days.

In your book, the men live again for me, undistorted by any straining after the sensational spectacular. I see again the benign and gentle face of Uncle Al, the oldest of the brothers, who was always warm and kindly and told us funny little stories, and cherished his gay-nineties moustache longer than did any of the others. And Uncle Alfred, who to me as a young child, was always "Uncle Appers," who loved books and music, as most of them did, was sometimes entertainingly absentminded—one day sending us into spasms of strangled merriment when he acknowledged an introduction to some man whose name I no longer remember by saying, "How do you do, Mr. Ringling"; and often asked for another cup of tea when he had just consumed a cup of coffee. And Uncle Otto—such a special one to me—who never married and was perhaps the *unclest* of them all, since he had no children of his own. Uncle Otto, of the rich warm chuckle for all our foolishness—who brought my first real grief when he died while still so much too young. And then there was Uncle Gus, whom I always remember as the most charming of men—a little austere, and very erudite, who also died when I was still quite young. And Uncle Henry, the youngest of them all—the baby—and such a big one—more than six feet tall, with a massive leonine head—a quiet man, immersed in books, and I thought then somewhat aloof, though I found out later that he was just as warm and responsive as any of them, but a little diffident. And Uncle John—the one of them all who was perhaps the most like the commonly dreamed-up pictures of what a circus man should be—who went to Europe for long months, to bring back glamour from the old world, and suddenly appeared at long intervals in our little rural town of Baraboo, always handsomely dressed, if with a shade more showiness than the others ever indulged in, carrying a gold-headed cane, arriving in a European car, driven by a liveried chauffeur, and impressing us all with his splendor.

They are all gone now, but I see them again in the light of your book, and they come alive, and I hear once more the rich male laughter, and the warm vigorous voices of five men working harmoniously together to build something that became a part of the American tradition, and which in those days of no television, and no cinema, and no radio, gave much of stimulation and color and delight, and even of education, to lives which were hungry for it all.

So, dear "Chappie" Fox, I am glad for your book, and grateful to you for letting me read it, and I wish it and you well.

(Signed) Hester Ringling Sanford
Sarasota, Florida

a
ticket
to the
Circus

RINGLING BROS
BARNUM & BAILEY
AFTERNOON AND NIGHT
MILWAUKEE LAKE FRONT
FRI. AUG. 18
SAT. AUG. 19
RINGLING BR
AND
BARNUM & BAIL
AFTERNOON AND NIGHT
MILWAUKEE LAKE FRONT
FRIDAY AUG. 18
SATURDAY AUG. 19

THE RINGLING CIRCUS has effected the lives of many Americans in varying degrees. The noted cartoonist, J. R. Williams, has nostalgically captured a few of these fleeting moments in his unforgettable drawings reproduced here. (NEA Service)

Ringling Beginning

This is the story of seven incredible brothers named Ringling, but in the broader sense it is the story of the Circus itself . . . that gaudy, glittering, glamorous institution that weaves so stout a thread through the fabric of happy memories. This is so because to generations of Americans, Ringling Brothers has *meant* the Circus. The very sound of the name conjures up the brazen voice of the calliope, the spine-chilling rumble of the lions, the enchanting smell of sawdust and popcorn and wild animals, the brave flutter of bright flags above the Big Top.

Almost lost in oblivion are such great circus names as Hagenbeck-Wallace, Sparks, Dan Rice, John Robinson, Christy Brothers, W. W. Cole, Sells-Floto, Adam Forepaugh, W. C. Coup, Al G. Barnes, Gollmar Brothers and Gentry Brothers. But the great name of Ringling Bros. lives on, based on the genius of the most amazing aggregation of circus brains in the history of American show business . . . the seven original brothers[1] and the younger members of the Ringling family who entered the firm in later years.

------

[1] The seven Ringling Brothers were: Albert Charles (Al) Ringling, 1852-1916, Charles August (Gus) Ringling, 1854-1907, William Henry Otto (Otto) Ringling, 1858-1911, Alfred Theodore (Alf T.) Ringling, 1861-1919, Charles Edward (Charley) Ringling, 1864-1926, John Nicholas (John) Ringling, 1866-1936, Henry William George (Henry) Ringling, 1868-1918. The Ringling family included one sister, Ida Loraina Wilhelmina Ringling, 1874-1950, and an eighth brother, George C., who was born in 1856, but died at the age of six months.

Ida Ringling, who married Henry Whitestone North, was the mother of the latest generation of this great circus family. Her sons, John Ringling North and Henry Ringling North have guided the Greatest Show on Earth during most of its history since 1937.

The parents of the Ringling Brothers were August Frederick and Marie Salome Ringling[2]. August was a harness-maker who did his work with Teutonic skill and thoroughness, but he appears to have been possessed of the same wanderlust that led his sons to a long career of one-night stands. The family fortunes were seldom above the level of honest poverty. Al, the oldest brother, was born in Chicago in 1852. It was here that August changed his German name, Rüngeling to the Americanized version, Ringling. The second brother, Gus, was born in Milwaukee, where August felt the harness-making business might be better. Apparently it wasn't, for by 1855 the Ringling family was in Baraboo, where Otto was born.

The family remained there for five years before August was overcome again with the desire for greener pastures. The move this time was to McGregor,

------

[2] The life span of August Ringling was from 1826 to 1898; that of his wife, Marie, from 1833 to 1907.

1884 WAS THE FIRST SEASON for the Ringling Brothers' Circus. At this time Al was 32 years old; Otto 26; and Alf. T. 23. Chas. had reached 20 years of age; while John was only 18. This lithograph was one of their first posters and was probably printed when the circus was 2 or 3 years old. (Wis. Hist. Soc.)

1857.

THE ONE HORSE HARNESS

"ESTABLISHMENT" will now, good friends pass
for a

DOUBLE HORSE

Concern. Call and see if it is not so.

The subscriber has just returned from the
East, with a full assortment of every thing necessary to SPEED to the horse or ornament him
for the task—such as

Whips Harnesses, Saddles, Fly-Nets,
Curry Combs, Brushes, Raw Hides,
&c., &c.

No, I am no longer the "One Horse Establishment," but am now as large as any of them.
Call and see if I am not a man of truth.

n10   A. RINGLING.

Baraboo, May 27, 1856.

THIS ADVERTISEMENT appeared in the "Baraboo
Republic" (Wis.) on April 30, 1857. The wording used
in this ad has the real circus flavor — a flourish of
words, thinking big.   (Walter Scholl, Collection)

Iowa, on the banks of the Mississippi River. Although
August's prosperity did not increase, his family did.
During a twelve-year stay in Iowa, Alf T., Charles,
John and Henry were born.

Lost in history is the spark that kindled the flame
of circus enthusiasm in the five brothers. It is known
that in the early morning hours of a summer day in
1870, Al, then 18 and the eldest, took his brothers
down to the river to watch a side-wheeler unload Dan
Rice's Circus onto the docks. This same day, Father
Ringling received a family pass to the performance
for work he did in repairing some leather trappings
for the circus.

Perhaps it was their collective ingenuity and close
companionship that caused childish panorama and
pin shows to develop. Their pin show was preceded
by a parade with all boys marching and carrying banners. A goat by the name of Billy Rainbow pulled
a red cart. Their tent was made out of borrowed rugs
hung over a clothesline. Admission was 10 pins and
the Ringlings sang, danced, and played with great
enthusiasm. Next, they raised their admission charge
to a penny, and with their first profits bought a bolt
of cotton fabric to make a tent.

All of this lore is related in a book, *The Life Story
of the Ringling Bros.* by Alf. T. Ringling[1]

The legend goes on to say the boys gathered together all of their prize possessions, a silver watch,

a skiff, and jackknives and traded them off for a decrepit swaybacked horse and a dilapidated democrat
wagon. The wagon they refurbished with seats and
a coat of red paint, and called it their "bandwagon".
The band was made up of an accordian, Jews harp,
mouth organ, an old army trumpet and a brass drum.

While all these enterprises were developing, August Ringling in 1872 again moved his family, this
time to Prairie du Chien, Wiconsin. Ida, his only
daughter, was born there . In the spring of 1875 the
family moved to Stillwater, Minnesota, for a three-
month period, but by summer the Ringling family
was back in Baraboo. August Ringling, Sr., and his
wife moved again, this time without their boys, to
Rice Lake, Wisconsin. They stayed there until their
sons prospered with their circus, at which time the boys
brought their parents back to Baraboo and settled
them in a comfortable home.

Not much is known about the early teen age days
of the brothers. They probably led commonplace and
hardworking lives up until they organized their circus. From that point forward, however, there was
nothing commonplace in their lives ever again. Al, who
was the eldest of the brothers, at the age of 20, set
out on his own. In the spring of 1872 he landed in
Brodhead, Wisconsin, where he secured a job as fin-
isher and trimmer with Laube & Durner Carriage &
Wagon Works. While in Brodhead he lived in a
third floor room of the Exchange House where he was
known to have spent all of his spare time in the development of his acrobatic skill. During the summer
of 1874, according to the *New York Clipper,* Al found
work with the Yankee Robinson Circus where, no
doubt, sawdust and spangles got in his blood. By
1876 he had mastered juggling and had become an expert on the bars and balancing.

During the era of 1878-79 Al was the idol of all
the kids in Brodhead, Wisconsin. Joe Laube, for whose
father Al worked, remembered how the boys followed
Al around town. He was always up to some trick
or act, soon joining up with a fellow by the name
of Frederick (Bob) White, who operated a puppet
show called *Babes In The Woods.* Al did juggling
and acrobatic stunts as a side attraction for the puppet show. He never made much money and when he
was broke he would come back to John Laube for his
job. As rough as they were, these days were undoubtedly the beginning of Al Ringling's professional
career.

While in Brodhead, Al had often boasted, when

---

[1] Published in 1900 in book form and put on sale in June
1901 in their menagerie tent where, according to the route
book, "they went like hot cakes." Excerpts from the story
had been previously published in their 1894 and 1896
route book.

he had to defend his juggling and acrobatics, that he would some day own a circus. To make good on his boast, ten years later when he did have his own circus, Al brought it to this town for all to see. Then, to really make good his boast to his friends, he routed his railroad circus into Brodhead in 1891. People of Brodhead now say Al not only made good, but many residents claim their town to be the birthplace of the Ringling Circus.

Many are the rumors that emanated from this town that Al was able to walk the tight rope. At least two of the village oldsters insist they saw Al walk on a tight rope that was stretched across the street from one building to another. It is probable that Al did this trick, but it is also probable he never became very proficient at it. If he had he surely would have included tight rope walking in his repertoire when the boys started their circus and were so desperate for acts. Henry North says he never remembers any of his uncles even mentioning Al's ability to walk the tight rope, which would indicate that if Al did accomplish this trick, it was nothing he did consistently, or with any degree of expertness.

In 1882, when Al came back to Baraboo, Wisconsin, he and four of his brothers organized the *Ringling Bros. Classic & Comic Concert Co.* In this effort they collectively put on one or two-act plays and skits. They also sang, danced and played musical instruments. They toured during the winter months only, playing opera houses and concert halls in scores of small towns throughout the Midwest and Manitoba. At this point in their lives Al was 30 years old, Otto 24, Alf. T. 21, Chas. 18, and John 16.

In these years, when their winter theatrical season was finished, all of the brothers worked in Baraboo except Al, who went to work for circuses. These included the J. W. Parson's Great Grecian Circus and Yankee Robinson Circus. (Eventually Al hired both his former bosses, Yankee Robinson and J. W. Parsons, when he and his brothers formed their own circus).

Although the Ringlings started their summer tented circus in the spring of 1884, they continued their Carnival of Fun theatrical efforts during the winter months until the close of the season in the spring of 1887. Their circus by then had grown to such proportions as to require all their attention.

It is often said of old August Ringling that nothing slip-shod ever came from his hands. Perhaps the Ringling boys were not "born in sawdust," yet their father's character must have left its imprint on his seven sons — thoroughness of execution, honesty of purpose, and devotion to an ideal — which resulted eventually in "The Greatest Show On Earth".[3]

MR. & MRS. AUGUST RINGLING SR., whose sons founded the circus.   (Mrs. Hester Ringling Sanford)

[3] An interesting footnote to circus history is the fact that two sisters of the Ringling brother's mother also married men who became closely associated with the circus business in Baraboo. Mary Magdelina Juliar married Gottlieb Gollmar. Five of their sons formed the well-known Gollmar Bros. Circus in 1891. Katherine Juliar married Henry Moeller, who operated a carriage and wagon shop. Moeller and his two sons, Henry Jr. and Corwin, built untold numbers of circus wagons for their cousins Gollmar and Ringling.

14

OPPOSITE PAGE is an extremely rare photo of the Parsons and Roy Circus in 1883 showing Joe Parsons doing a tight rope act. Standing at the left is Butch Parsons. Al Ringling was employed as an eight dollar a week juggler for this circus. Within a few years Al Ringling hired both the Parsons to work for him on his own circus. (Wis. Hist. Soc.)

THIS PICTURE is taken from the book, "Life Story of the Ringling Bros.", by Alf T. Ringling, published in 1901. It quaintly illustrates how the boys, in retrospect, envisioned the growth of their circus. (Wis. Hist. Soc.)

BELOW LEFT is a rare letter written by Yankee Robinson, recommending Al Ringling as an artist and gentleman. (H. H. Conley Collection)

SHOWN BELOW on the right is a page from a Springfield, Nebraska, hotel register for date of Jan. 14, 1884. When the Ringlings signed in they wanted to be sure everyone knew they were in town. This gem of early advertising was done in a variety of colors with crayons. (Mrs. Hester Ringling Sanford)

"Grand processional amazement."

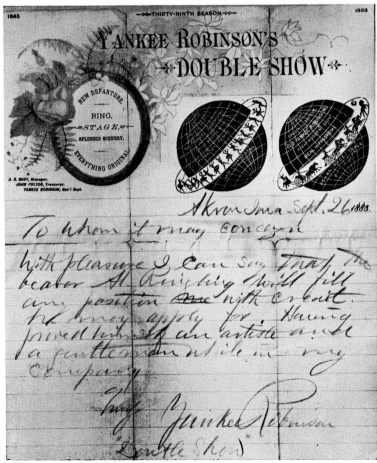

THE EIGHT RINGLINGS
(circa 1892). 1st row: Al,
Chas. and Alf. T. 2nd row:
John, Otto and Henry, 3rd
row; Ida and Gus.
(Mrs. Henry Ringling Sr.,
Collection)

The Ringlings of Baraboo

By

Alice Ringling Coerper

Baraboo is a beautiful little town with many hills, a wide swift-flowing river, a well-kept court house square, and maple shaded streets. In the nineties, and around the turn of the century, it was a delightful place in which to grow up. Those were the years when the circus had its winterquarters there and to all the Ringlings, Baraboo was home. My father was one of the seven Ringling brothers and to us the circus was not only our livelihood but a special little world.

Winterquarters were directly across the river from the Northwestern yards and on the town side. Once the animals had been unloaded, trundled across Low Bridge and tucked away securely in their barns at the end of each season, Baraboo would see nothing more of them until spring. The quarters were not open to the public and, except for those employed there, few of the townspeople had ever been inside the barns. The property was not fenced off but "KEEP OUT—NO ADMITTANCE" signs were on every door. Although winterquarters were only a few blocks from the center of town, they were never regarded as a hazard, and this confidence was indeed well deserved. Never once in all those years was there a catastrophy of any kind at winterquarters; no animals ever escaped, certain oft-repeated amusing fables to the contrary, no visitor to the barns was ever injured, for visitors had to be personally escorted and carefully guarded. There was never a fire there, even in the era of pot-bellied stoves and kerosene lanterns.

To my father and uncles the winterquarters were a business property, and no attempt had been made to make it attractive or distinctive; a stranger could have passed it by. There was no sign anywhere to identify its use or mark its entrance.

There was just a row of barns, most of them unpainted; several other buildings, one of which was the office; and another, a large three-storied brick building, was the hotel for the employees. But to us who were privileged to go there, and did whenever we had the chance, it was a fascinating place. In what dramatic contrast to the tranquil exterior of those tightly-battened barns was the pulsing activity within; the rhythmic swaying of the restless elephants, the steady beat of the practice horses round and

GUS RINGLING with his daughter, Alice, in 1899.
(Alice Ringling Coerper, Collection)

round the center pole, and the high-pitched altercation when the trick was missed, the splashing of the hippopotamus in his tank, the bounding of the panthers on their wooden floors, the roaring of the lions, the screeching of the monkeys and the squawking of the great tropical birds. These are the things I remember; these and the almost unbearable heat, and the almost unshakable smell of the wild-animal barns.

These were some of the unique components of our little world, the tangible assets of a business that was to grow apace until it outstripped all competitors; but I realize now despite the evidence of sight and sound how fragile our world was. In spite of tents and poles and calliopes and "ponderous pachyderms" ours was only a world of ideas; the ideas formulated only a few short years before in the minds of five venturesome, determined youths. The bringing together of all this heterogeneous treasure from the far corners of the earth to this obscure little farm community in the Baraboo hills was proof of the soundness of those ideas and the determination of those men. If at any time the ideas should fail, or the determination falter, how quickly would the silver wagon be emptied, the big top fall, and our world disappear.

These five men were my uncles Albert, Otto, Alfred, Charles, and John Ringling. August Jr., my father, the second oldest of the seven brothers, did not join the circus until five years after its founding. Henry, the youngest brother, waited until he finished high school.

The Ringlings were dynamic men, and handsome in appearance with their black hair and dark eyes and fair skin. Of stalwart build and dignified bearing they walked their confident way without swagger. Peaceful men, they had no quarrel with anyone; kindly men, they were quick to sympathize, and pleasantries came more readily to their lips than harsh or angry word. Their homes, for the ones who had homes, and their business were their chief interests. Their devotion to one another unmarred, in those early years, by antagonisms, jealousies, or quarrels may well have been a factor in their success.

Uncle Al. was the equestrian director, and was "Mr. Circus" if anyone ever was. A highly nervous man, sharp-eyed, quick moving, he lived for the circus and worked unceasingly to improve the show. The snap and precision that characterized the Ringling performance were his. Under his watchful eye no act ever came on late. At the first sign of a slowing down the laggards would feel the sharp staccato notes of his whistle biting at their heels. Like all the Ringlings Uncle Al. loved music, especially grand opera music. This, and his love for the theater, combined to produce those remarkable innovations to the circus, those Ziegfeldian extravaganzas "Jerusalem and the Crusades" and "The Field of the Cloth of Gold" with their Aida and Tannhauser scores.

Uncle Otto was the treasurer of the show. A quiet, methodical man, no digit was too small, no sum too large to be carefully and judiciously husbanded. Had his brothers ever bothered to look at his books they would have found them balanced to the day. He remained a bachelor all his life. Reserved and studious, and an indulgent checker player whenever little niece Alice beguiled him into a game, he was content with the companionship of a few cronies and his books. He lived at the Warren Hotel until Uncle Alfred and Aunt Della built their white mansion on the Oak Street hill and included in it a suite for him. That house is now the "original wing" of the St. Mary's Ringling Hospital.

Uncle Alfred was a natural for his job as "Superintendent of Press". He loved words and the people who wrote them. He could write literate prose and fell easily into rime, having what my children and I call the "Curse of the Pannoffs", a family failing otherwise known as "jingleitis". This gem is from an old autograph album of my father's; "And if you should happen to be in Eau Claire, or any place, or anywhere, think of something or another and write a letter to Alf. your brother". His sentimental pen is easily recognized in many of the early route books, and in that masterpiece of invention the "Life Story of the Ringling Brothers". Uncle Alfred also dabbled in photography, and used my pensive little face for a model until he found that snarling lions and hissing panthers were more challenging. He gave me a fine Kodak to encourage me in his hobby, and went on to gain considerable recognition for his innovations in wild-animal photography. A musician too, he slid easily from the trombone of earlier days to the pipe organ installed in his new home. He bought a smaller one, an old-fashioned hand-pump job for his farm, and I suspect my popularity as a guest there was due to my willingness to man the pump.

Uncle Charlie was in charge of the advertising, and being an enthusiastic showman, he took an active interest in every part of the business. An energetic man, and perhaps the sharpest member of the family, he was never known to have come out second best in any deal. He was the smallest of the brothers and very good looking, and he made up in charm what he lacked in inches. He had a ready wit and a fund of amusing stories always at his command. These he used charmingly to put at ease the difficult, and at times as a sort of smoke screen to disguise the keenness of his own discernment and to gentle the advantage which he was gaining. He was in many ways our favorite uncle, perhaps because he always played Santa Claus at the family Christmas celebrations, but probably because he was the most fun. Uncle Charlie was a fine musician. He played the violin and other stringed instruments well; he organized a stringed quartet with my sisters playing violin and viola or cello, and Aunt Edith the piano, and many a happy Sunday afternoon was spent this way. Later his own children became fine musicians.

Uncle John routed the show and made the railroad contracts. The glamour boy of the family and his mother's fair-haired child, he possessed a brilliant mind and was said to have a phenomenal memory. He took naturally to city ways and early to city living, and limited his Baraboo visits to Christmas holidays and family occasions. I recall one such visit when I was eight. Hanging around him, fascinated by his glitter I asked him how many diamonds he thought he had on, and wouldn't he like me to count them. After a thorough search, and many startings over I proudly announced a figure well in the hundreds, which included the small ones on the links of his watch chain and the monogram on his watch. But it was time wasted; he remained impressed with his diamonds; I with my ability to count. As Uncle John's horizons broadened, diamonds gave place in his affections to works of art, and both to his very beautiful wife, Mabel. After Grandma's death in 1907 he came less and less often to Baraboo.

August Jr., known as A. G., my father, managed the advance car advertising. He travelled three weeks ahead of the show in Car No. 1, which, in deference to my mother, was painted a bright "Hurley green" and named The Irish Mail. Years before, my father and his brother Al, had left their boyhood home in McGregor, Iowa, at about the same time to seek their fortunes, but their paths had led in opposite directions. By the time Al and the younger brothers were organizing their wagon show, August was well established in business in Minneapolis, happily married and awaiting the birth of his first child. Circus life had no lure for him. Five years later, with the show about to go into railroad cars, with the offer of a new department of his own to organize, and the prospect of once again living near his parents, his brothers, and his only sister, Ida, he joined the show. That fall he moved his family, including the squalling infant Alice, to Baraboo, and began a circus career which ended only with his untimely death eighteen years later.

Judged by the results, A. G. Ringling must have been the best advance advertising man of his day. In 1890, when he took over, the Ringling show was young, small and little-known. At that time and up to 1900 there were more big circuses criss-crossing America, elbowing and gouging each other at every

PHOTO OF ALICE RINGLING taken by her Uncle Alf T. in 1896.   (Alice Ringling Coerper, Collection)

turn, than at any other time before or since. It was a continuous free-for-all for the towns, the lots, the parade routes, but above all, for the billboards and the barn sides, the board fences and the store fronts, because outdoor advertising was the life blood of the circus of that era. Only the advertising brought in the customers and sold the tickets. My father was an astute man who battled with brains as well as brawn, with foresight as well as fury, with patience as well as paste; the men in his crews were carefully chosen and properly directed; instead of angry farmers and irate citizens they left behind them friends and well-wishers. In this way the Ringling advertising was protected while they went on plastering the countryside with gorgeous, gigantic lithographs in lavish abundance, for my father, like all the Ringlings, thought "big." As season followed season, and one show after another bit the dust, the name of Ringling became firmly imaged on the retina of rural America and would not be dissolved. When in 1906 Ringlings acquired Forepaugh-Sells Bros. Circus in a package deal, they turned it over to August and Henry to manage. Sadly for all of us, serious illness overtook my father during the first season out and his death in December of that year cut short a promising future.

My father was a happy man. He enjoyed a wide variety of interests, and whether he was refinishing an antique table, planting a tree, cleaning his rifle, or working out a tricky billiard shot, he sang as he worked. An intellectual man, he was well read and was always studying something. He spoke and wrote several foreign languages, but could never pronounce French to satisfy my Quebec-born mother. Scrupulously honest, he taught us to despise nothing so much as a lie. He loved his home, his family, his dogs, his birds, his books and the out-of-doors. During his last illness he said he was afraid that he would "have to miss the spring".

Uncle Henry, the biggest of the brothers, and really big, was born to be "superintendent of the front door". I'm very sure neither slippery kids, nor city slickers ever got by him. However, his gruffness was only make-believe — he was a very gentle person, quiet, agreeable, and dependable.

These were the Ringlings as I knew them when the flush of their first success still glowed in their hearts. They had in those days an understanding of children and a desire to please them. Our Christmases, with the uncles playing Santa year after year, were proof of this. But the real proof was the way they kept their circus always a children's wonderland, in colors from their penny paint box, in costumes they could recognize, with stories simple and familiar. This was, I belive, the magic sesame of their success: they had the will to pretend.

THE 1885 TROUPE of "Ringling Bros. Great Double Shows, Circus and Caravan, and Trained Animal position".
L to R back row standing: Candy Butcher, name unknown, Al Ringling, Frank Sparks, C. P. Putnam, Richard
Dialo, Alf T. Ringling, Sam Hardy, and Frank Kissel. Middle row seated: Geo. Hall, Vic Richardson, and John
Ringling. Front row on floor: Geo. LaRosa, Theo Asmus, Chas. Ringling, Dick Hunter, and Otto Ringling.

MRS. AL RINGLING was
an equestrian, as well as
a snake charmer, during
the wagon show days.

Wagon Show

By mid-April 1884 the brothers had formulated their circus plans to the extent that they released an announcement to the Baraboo *Republic*. On April 19 there appeared a news story consisting of three paragraphs announcing the organization of their circus. They had arranged for aging and retired circus owner Yankee Robinson to advise them and lend his well-known name to their enterprise. The show was named *Yankee Robinson and Ringling Bros. Great Double Shows, Circus and Caravan.* The Yankee Robinson name was used only in their first year — 1884. Never again, in all the vast and varied titles the brothers used over the years, was the name Ringling ever subordinate.

The five boys had saved their money and planned carefully for their circus, but their capital was considerably less than $1,000. As a result, they resorted to the sweat of their brows to make their money stretch. They went to the woods and cut their own poles and stakes and fashioned them with ax and draw-shave. They bought lumber and made their own jacks, stringers and seats for the bleachers. With more of their meager funds they purchased some old spring wagons, one of which they made into an advance wagon with a canvas top — covered wagon fashion. The canvas was painted red and a circus bill was pasted on each side and properly lettered. Thus, for a total cost of $17.00 they had a modest advance wagon.

On May 19, seven weeks after they arrived home from their winter theater schedule, the first Ringling Circus performance was given in Baraboo on a downtown corner lot (Broadway & 2nd Street where the Sauk County Jail is now located). The ring was nothing more than a strip of red cloth staked out to form a circle. The tent was 45 x 90 feet, with two center poles. The performance had no horses, wild animals, or dogs. It was made up of contortionists, jugglers, balancers and comedy acts interspersed with musical selections. The Ringling boys were most of the show. They played various instruments in the band, danced, performed, and led most of the acrobatic stunts and tricks. They had hired two additional musicians and three performers. The entire personnel, including performers, side show, band, crew, and owners consisted of 24 people.

Henry Moeller, who witnessed this first historic performance, remembers the tent held 600 people and all seats were filled. He said the venerable Yankee Robinson walked to the center ring with a plug hat on his gray head, which he hoped would enhance his five foot, six inch stature. What he lacked in size he made up for in the booming voice that filled the tent as he told the patrons of the fantastic feats they were about to witness, ending with, "this show is destined to become the greatest circus in the world." Yankee Robinson, to the sorrow of the Ringlings, died with his boots on in August of this first year.

Duffy Stanton, another Baraboo resident who recalled the first show, vividly remembers Al Ringling balancing a plow on his chin. Oscar Alpeter has the interesting distinction of having seen the first show by crawling under the canvas with a gang of boys. And where was Sheriff Charley Davis? He was right there holding up the canvas wall so the boys could crawl under. He figured as long as the seats were all sold, a few more boys wouldn't make much difference. After all, he reasoned, the Sheriff's office gave the Ringlings the use of the lot for nothing.

For the first six years of their existence, the Ringling Circus was a wagon or "mud" show. In circus parlance this means they used horses to pull their wagons from town to town over the dirt roads which readily became mud when it rained. There were many competitive railroad shows and dozens of other wagon shows; yet they struggled on through 114 dates and put on 228 shows that first year.

They could afford no flashy advertising, few newspaper ads, but depended on simple little hand bills. Advertisements of their competitors would have been enough to discourage most men. For example, in Baraboo, their home town, on July 1, 1884, there appeared a formidable one-third page ad in the newspaper proclaiming *Col. G. W. Hall's Big United States and Great Eastern 8 Consolidated Shows.* Later a one-half page ad in the Sept. 19 paper announced *S. H. Barret's & Co. New United Monster Railroad Shows* was coming.

Competition or not, it was a determined desire to succeed that carried the Ringling boys through their early years. Their mother had fortified them with the very sage advice that if you go into any enterprise only to make money you will fail. If, however, you go into it with a driving desire to succeed you cannot fail.

In these early wagon show days a great practical conservativeness, combined with individual exertion, was predominant in the success of their little circus. As brothers, they were a harmonious team. Each of the five gradually fell into a line of duty for which he was seemingly best fitted. It was chance that no two excelled in the same talents. Thus, did these boys develop into a perfectly organized executive body. This partnership began without any written contract or agreement and continued this way during the entire life span of all the brothers. There is no question but this cooperative spirit is the outstanding reason for their miraculous ascent in the outdoor entertainment field. There was no such thing as operating their circus by delegated authority, which ruined many another show. With five equal owners there was a Ringling on the job for every one of the vast and varied phases of circus operation.[1]

During these pioneering days the Ringling Brothers' tiny enterprise wended its way over the rutted roads with the performers jouncing on the board seats of democrat wagons. The price of admission was 25c. They had no menagerie. They owned nine wagons, but rented whatever horses they needed from farmers along the route. Everyone stopped at hotels for lodging and meals. A humble beginning indeed!

---

[1] A clear and concise description of what made the Ringlings and their circus tick is found in a brief regarding the estates of Henry and Alf T. Ringling filed before the Board of Appeals and Review in 1923 in which John M. Kelley, attorney for the Ringling Bros. made these poignant comments:—

"Ringlings began without capital, credit or business prospect. No prestige in the circus came to them either thru birth or association. They served no apprenticeship and the community in which they grew up was isolated and far removed from the atmosphere of amusement life. The Ringlings ventured in the circus at a time when the field of outdoor amusement numbered more master showmen than any other generation in history. Barnum was at the hey-day of his career. Bailey was fast approaching the Forepaugh Show and the Sells Bros. Circus. Scarcely any venture in the world offered as little prospect of reward as the circus when the Ringlings entered the field; yet there existed at that time, of which they were unaware, two important factors chiefly responsible for their success. One was the intangible assets of the firm; namely, their good bringing up; robust constitutions; striking personality; courage; high moral viewpoint; and loyalty to each other. The other helpful factor was the stage of the country's development, railroads opening up west, exhibition grounds easily had, labor and material cheap . . . Ringling Bros. achievement is an inspiration. Ringling success is a testimonial to the code of honor and honest methods that have ever prevailed in Ringling enterprises . . .A circus may fail through accident, but no circus ever came into prominence by accident. What Ringling Bros. have done is traceable to their leadership. Ringling Circus moves by reason of Ringling organization, and Ringling organization is preserved through Ringling leadership.

THIS SKETCH is taken from the book Alf. T. Ringling wrote describing the early days of the circus. The caravan is shown moving to the next show town, mostly with horses and wagons rented from farmers. (C. P. Fox Collection)

On Tuesday, May 27, 1884, the Ringlings were advertised to play Brodhead, Wisconsin. This was only the eighth town scheduled with their embryonic show. Yet to Al, having such fine memories and so many friends there, it was like a homecoming; a vindication of his boasts of years ago that, "someday I will have a circus of my own". He ran a good sized newspaper ad, which brought a fine turnout. Al must have had a feeling of pride to see a full house with so many friendly faces watching his show.

On the morning of that show day, Al stopped in to see his friend and former employer, John Laube. He purchased two lumber wagons from Laube, but wanted them equipped with iron side racks to carry tent poles. John Laube said he would have them ready that night, but the forging and fixing of the iron work took longer than anticipated. This made it necessary for Al Ringling to leave teams and men at the wagon shop with instructions to drive the wagons to Monroe, Wisconsin, their next show date, as soon as they were finished. Joe Laube, then a boy of 13, remembers well that night in his father's shop as he and his mother stood in the chilly building, holding tallow candles until two in the morning when the last bolt was secured on the pole racks.

In 1885 things began to look up. The Moeller Wagon Company of Baraboo built them a bandwagon. To dress up this first bandwagon, they wanted a large circular mirror on each side, but they quickly settled for shiny tinplate when they found out the price of the mirrors. Henry Moeller, Jr. said this vehicle was carried on the cuff, along with some other wagons, until the show was on the road and the boys had some income. They also added a museum tent in which they displayed a collection of stuffed parrots, plus a few common song birds and small animals from Central Wisconsin.

It was in this second year that the boys, in their pathetically simple, single-sheet program, spoke out in bold courageous words. The copy said that their circus would make people forget their worries and woes; that the show would exhilarate them and turn their gloom into happiness. The pitch ended with these words emblazoned in large letters across the page, *Sadness Assassinated!*

Henry Ringling, a sixth brother, joined the show in September of 1886. In this year, too, the boys were proud to point to their first menagerie made up of two cages containing a bear, hyena, monkeys and an eagle. The hyena was picked up at a bargain price because it was blind. This deficiency did not deter Alf. T. Ringling from proclaiming their hyena in true circus fashion:

"Hideous Hyena—Striata Gigantium to be seen only with the Ringling Show. The mammoth, marauding man-eating monstrosity, the prowling, grave-robbing demon of all created things, who, while the world sleeps and no hand is raised to stay his awful depredations, sneaks stealthily under cover of darkness to the cemetery and with ghoulish glee robs the tombs. His hideous, blood-curdling laughter paralyzes with terror the bravest hearts. He leaves behind him a trail of blood and the wails of the dying are music to his ears."

By 1887 the show sported five cages containing an elk, bear, two lions, a kangaroo, hyena, birds, monkeys, and deer. They now owned 60 horses, reaching the point where they no longer had to rent draft stock from farmers. Their official title was *Ringling Bros. United Monster Shows, Great Double Circus, Royal European Menagerie, Museum, Caravan and Congress of Trained Animals.*

The following year found the price of admission 50c and for children 25c. Two elephants, Babylon, and Fannie were now in the menagerie. The circus was really growing stature.

The last brother, A. G. Ringling, known as "Gus" to his family and "A. G." around the circus, joined up in 1889 as Advertising Agent.[2] Thus, all seven brothers were now with the show. In this season the circus played in 23 Wisconsin and 118 Illinois towns —no other states were booked. Their tent now had a seating capacity of 4,000.

The operation of an overland wagon show involved many interesting problems and ordeals. The boss hostler would signal the caravan off the lot and on its way around 4:00 or 5:00 a. m., depending on the distance to the next town. As the wagons moved over the road, the assistant hostler would trot his horse from one end of the wagon train to the other looking carefully for broken harness, damage to wagons, sick horses, or personnel.

The boss hostler preceded the caravan on its nightly trips. He drove what was known as the telegraph wagon. It was his duty to mark the route. At a junction in the road he would lay a branch, lath, or perhaps a rail from a snake fence across the road not to be taken by the teamsters following behind. Sometimes lime or flour was sprinkled on the road to indicate turns. This was known as railing the road." Each wagon had a kerosene lantern hanging on its tail gate. The team would automatically follow the wagon ahead, even though the teamster might be fast asleep on the jouncing wagon.

A PICTURE of the first wagon used by the advance agent. Sketch is from Alf. T. Ringling's book.
(C. P. Fox Collection)

---

[2] He was christened Charles August Theodore, but he dropped Charles and Theodore because his other brothers used these names, leaving him with just August. He then added the initial "G", which stood for nothing.

The ordeals of these nightly excursions were many — Henry Steeps, late President of Baraboo National Bank, recalled that when he was a messenger in the bank, in 1887, he read a letter that Otto Ringling had written from Markesan, Wisconsin, to Jacob Van Orden, then bank president:

"We had a torrential rain last night—slow going— our heavily loaded wagons broke through the planking of three bridges, causing endless delay—mud is deep —tempers are short, but in spite of it all, we opened the doors this afternoon on time."

Another such letter, Mr. Steeps remembers was terse and to the point,

"Horse died last night, request loan of $100.00."

William Prielipp, one-time chauffeur for Al Ringling, said that every time he drove through southern Wisconsin Al always wanted to go to Stoughton, even though it meant driving miles out of the way. Al enjoyed driving slowly through the town and past the hotel. He would then recount a terrible rainy day, May 30, 1887, when their little wagon show played Stoughton. It rained so hard and the lot was such a quagmire, no one came to see the circus. As a result, the Ringlings had no money to pay the performers' hotel bill. The personnel was instructed to quietly leave, one at a time and get out to the wagons, which were leaving for Edgerton. By the time the hotel manager realized what had happened the show was well out of town. The next day, when the Stoughton sheriff appeared on the Edgerton lot, Al was able to greet him with full payment for the hotel bill, as they had a full house that sunny afternoon. "I was glad he came," recounted Al, "as it saved me mailing the money back to the hotel."

Henry Moeller, Baraboo wagon builder, recalls another interesting incident that spotlights the frugal restraint with which the Ringlings operated their circus. The period was around 1889 and there had been much talk of dressing up the parade wagons. The Moellers were commissioned to build a number of cages. Henry Moeller had ordered two wood carved figures to adorn the corners of the lion cage. The carvings came from the Sebastian Wagon Co., New York, N. Y., who had a number of Italian woodcarvers in their employ. After they were installed on the wagon, Al Ringling was called in to put his OK on this first wagon. "Beautiful, just beautiful. Henry, let me see the bill for those carvings." It was produced, and as Al looked at the $500 price, he shook his head and commented regretfully, "Well, we can only afford one wagon like that at $250.00 for each figure! Henry, I'll tell what you do — on some of the other cages put brass tubing over the iron bars. That will dress up those dens." With that Al walked out of the shop.

ABOVE IS A NEWSPAPER AD for the infant circus as it appeared in the Brodhead (Wis.) "Independent". (C. P. Fox, Collection)

That year, 1889, proved to be their last as a mud show — the following year the Ringlings left Baraboo for their seventh annual tour as a full-fledged railroad circus. The Ringlings had decided that, to keep up with their powerful competitors, they would have to go on rails. In 1889 there were 11 such rail shows: Barnum & Bailey; The Great Wallace Show; Sells Bros. Circus; John Robinson Circus; Adam Forepaugh's Great Shows; Wm. L. Main Circus; Leman Bros. Circus; Frank A. Robbins Circus; Bob Hunting Circus; W. H. Harris Nickel Plate Shows; and Miles Orton Circus.

It was in the fall of 1889 that Adam Forepaugh, circus magnate from Philadelphia, sold the struggling Ringlings some equipment including 1 cage, 6 baggage wagons, 11 railroad cars and 3 camels. In a hand-scrawled letter dated Nov. 27 (the envelope addressed "Mr. Ringling Bros., Proprietors of Shows, Baraboo, Wis."), Forepaugh mentioned that the equipment he was selling was in fine shape, but Mrs. Henry Ringling has a distinct recollection that the camels were so badly infested with lice when they arrived that they

THE FIRST NOTICE announcing the formation of the Ringling Bros. Circus. It appeared in the **Baraboon Republic** April 19, 1884, one month before they put on their first show. (Baraboo Republic)

RELICS of the early days — top is a crude wooden money box with a removable tray. The tent was a crudely sewn handmade affair. Below: Tent poles cut from nearby woods and painted blue right over the bark. (Circus Wor.d Museum)

had to be isolated. It took all winter to get them in shape.

The Ringlings were men with a purpose. They knew what they wanted and where they were going. They were building sound foundations under their circus in those early formative days. The transition from a wagon show to a railroad circus was a mighty big step forward. The show world knew now it had to reckon with these men from Baraboo.[3]

---

[3] As a footnote to circus history, it should be mentioned that in 1891 the five Gollmar brothers of Baraboo, first cousins of the Ringlings, took their circus out on the road for the first time. Their show consisted, in the main, of the Ringling's wagon show equipment.

25

AT LEFT: A very early advertisement showing Alf T. Ringling — probably then 21 years old.
(Wis. Hist. Soc.)

BELOW—THE 1887 BAND. Chas. Ringling has been identified as second from right. The 1889 cookhouse was the Ringlings' first.
(Wis. Hist. Soc.)

LEFT is a picture of the venerable Yankee Robinson — a master showman who, in his declining days, lent his name to the Ringling enterprise.
(Walter Scholl, Collection)

ABOVE IS A LOT SCENE of 1885 showing a free attraction. Joe Parsons is seen (faintly) walking a tight rope up to the top of the tent.

(Wis. Hist. Soc.)

JOE PARSON'S SPECIALTY was tight wire acts. Shown below are his bicycle and roller skates.

(Circus World Museum)

BELOW is the 1889 cookhouse wagon — with a built-in stove.   (Circus World Museum)

ABOVE LEFT is an oil lamp used by the circus when it traveled by horsepower. The packing box was a crude affair, painted blue. At left is the money box. It was always chained to the floor of the wagon. Above is shown the trays used by candy butchers.

(Circus World Museum)

BELOW LEFT is the Ringling Bros. first letterhead. Below is one of the envelopes used by the advanced crew.

(Wis. Hist. Soc.)

THESE TWO RARE photos show the industrious Al Ringling in 1887 actually training animals. In these early formative days no job was beneath the boys if it helped to keep their circus going.

(Wis. Hist. Soc.)

FIVE OF THE SIDE SHOW acts of the wagon show days. Dialo, the strong man above. Helen Mathews with hair six feet four inches long. Below: Waino and Plutaino, 70-year old wild men of Borneo; Bertha Cunningham, a midget, and the fat man. The side show was advertised as having, also, an educated pig, headless rooster, electric lady, Indian box mystery and a magician. Strong man Dialo's favorite trick was to heat up a substance that looked like lead, until it melted. Then he poured some in his mouth, let it cool, and spit out a chunk which would be passed among people for all to handle and see.

(Circus World Museum)

TOP LEFT — Mrs. Al Ringling performed the function of snake charmer when the circus was an embryonic show. The wagons used in the early days were simple in design. Below is a lion's den. Two lovely wood carved figures adorn the front corners of the otherwise plain cage. Above is a cage containing a zebra. The wagon above was used by Butch Parsons who had the concessions. These wagons had to be of lightweight construction in order to get over the roads when they were soft and muddy.

(Wis. Hist. Society, Oliver Maxon Salisbury and C. P. Fox)

2 BIG, BRILLIANT AND BEWILDERING 2
—PERFORMANCES—

AT BARABOO,
Saturday, May 5th, '88

Stupendously Augmented, Prodigiously Enlarged.

RINGLING BROS.' Stupendous Consolidation of Seven Monster Shows, Great Triple Circus, Mammoth Museum, Colossal Caravan, Hippodromatic Carnival, Trained Animal Congress and

TWO MIGHTY MENAGERIES.

5 Champion Bareback Riders
Babylon and Sampson, the two Biggest Brutes that breathe. The Largest Elephant and the Largest Camel on Earth.
Also the Only BABY Elephant in America.
10 Acres Crowded with Exhilarating and Fascinating Sights. Armies of Attractions.
A Great Triple Circus of Champion Circus Performers.
Daring Male and Female High-air Danger Defying Sensational Artists.
Greatest Tumblers, Leapers, Gymnasts, Acrobats, Aerialists, Etc., in the World.
A Mighty Double Menagerie, containing Wild and Ferocious Beasts, Monster Serpents and Gaily Plumaged Birds.
All the Distant places of Creation Send in their Contributions to Swell our Mighty Catalogue of Wonders, Crimsoned with the Radiant Luster of the Morning Sun.
A Scene of Opulent Oriental Splendor.
A Mighty Moving Mass of Wealth, Wonders and Sweet Sounds.

A Grand Golden Street Pageant More than a Mile Long.
The Costliest of Delights, yet Costs you NOTHING.

Doors Open at 1 and 7 P. M.,

Ring Performances Commence one Hour Later

The Only Big Show Coming to Sauk County This Year
—WILL EXHIBIT AT—
Baraboo, Saturday, May 4th.
Two Performances--Afternoon and Evening.

RINGLING BROS. & VAN AMBURGH

United Monster Circus, Museum, Menagerie, Roman Hippodrome and Universal World's Exposition.

GREAT TRIPLE CIRCUS

of Champions, Finest Summersalt riders in America, Strangest Heathen Actors—the Wondrous Japanese, Marvelous Mid-air Sensations, Hundreds of Star Performers, Stupendous Assemblage of Aristocratic Horse Flesh, More Kinds of Acting Elephants than ever seen before, Giant Droves of Camels and Dromedaries, The Muster of the Nations—Spectacular Hippodrome Carnival, Babylon, the Largest; Spot, the Smallest; Fanny, the Only American born; and Jewell, the Umbrella-eared Elephants. Stupendous Double Menagerie, Startling Museum Wonders, Gabriel, the Giant Spotted Man Eater. More Clowns than any others possess. Matchless Schools of Educated Elephants, Noble Stallions, Ponies, Goats, Dogs, Donkeys, Monkeys and Savage Beasts.

RINGLING BROS. & VAN AMBURGH

Don't forget that at 10 o'clock will take place
The Free Public Holiday Parade!

The largest, longest, richest, rarest and most generously resplendent gratuitous display human resource and effort can render possible. Arabian Nights and fairy tales made real. Wild Beasts, Bands, Gorgeous Chariots, Wide-open Dens and Glorious Art and Dress in ravishing array. Something that no one can afford to miss. It is worth going 100 miles to see.

Admission to the Combined Shows 50c.   Children under 12 Years 25c.

ON THE LEFT is an 1888 newspaper ad; and on the right an 1889 ad. These were the last two years the Ringlings were a wagon show.   (Baraboo Republic)

ON RIGHT IS a news story in **"Baraboo Republic"**, April 27, 1887, describing the new show, then in its fourth season. (Baraboo Republic)

BELOW is A fascinating letter the young circus owner wrote to the bank president, Mr. Jacob Van Orden, describing business conditions in southern Illinois. (Geo. Weber Collection)

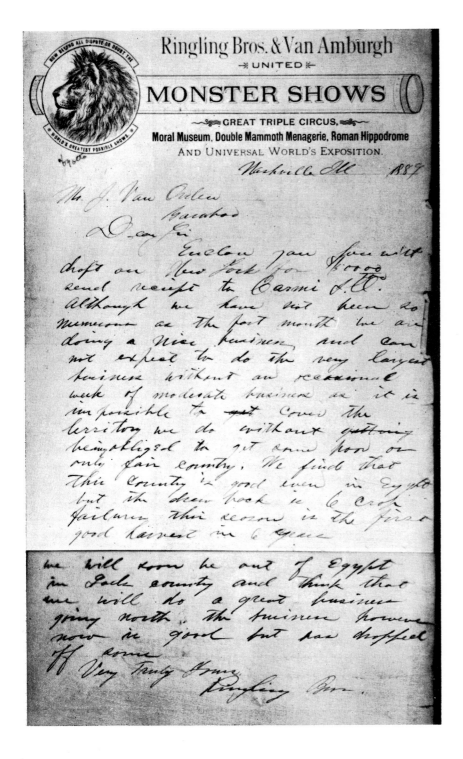

RINGLING BRO'S

Five United Monster Shows, Double Circus, Museum, Menagerie, Trained Animal Shows and Ancient Egyptian Caravan will exhibit at Baraboo May 7th.

From the fact that this institution has grown to such enormous proportions in an incredibly short space of time, it has escaped the notice of some people that right in our midst and forming a part of the business interests of Sauk County, we have one of the representative shows of America. The New York Clipper, than which there is no greater authority on matters pertaining to the amusement world, says: "In the history of the circus business the Ringling Bros. will always be recorded as the first and only real circus and menagerie to place its price of admission to the popular 25 cents standard." Baraboo, Sauk Co., and in fact the state of Wisconsin should be proud of being the home of an institution that has won such encomiums from the Metropolitan press and is already beginning to bear a national reputation as one of the squarest and most honorably conducted concerns of its kind in this country.

The Menagerie department of the Ringling Bro's. show has been increased wonderfully during the last winter. Besides purchasing the entire Menagerie of the Miles Orton show, they have steadily from time to time been making importations of wild animals from the most noted animal depots of America, until now their catalogue of zoological attractions embraces a vast number of the most curious species known to scientific research.

Their Great Double Circus embraces a coterie of star performers among whom will be found such noted riders as Joe Parsons, Mlle. La Rue; famous acrobats like the Baretta Bros., Castellos, Ortonesete; funny clowns including McCaffroty, Membardt and Gay; fearless aerialists such as Mlle. La Vanion, Mdme. Kutts, Miss Louisa Bowman and numerous male mid-air performers; noted equalibrists such as Jerome Abbey, Mlle. Luando and a score of other equally novel and wonderful components.

The Museum of Omnifarious Beings is brim full of novel curiosities interesting to the scientist as well as the public at large.

It is left to the Trained Animal Exhibit to cap the climax of this wonderful amusement mine. Every one who has seen the numerous pretty Shetland ponies owned by the Ringling Bros. have admired them, but when the marvelous education which these minute morsels of horse flesh have acquired is witnessed, all must unite in pronouncing this department a most pleasing adjunct, especially when all the other trained animals, horses, donkeys, dogs etc., are taken into consideration.

With all the dens, cages and animals which have been added during the past winter, the Ringling Bros. will have a parade of mammoth proportions. This of course is free to everybody, while the price of admission to the combined shows is only 25 cents. May 7th is the grand opening day and it is expected that Baraboo will experience a holiday such as will eclipse her greatest 4th of July celebration, for there is not a town for many miles around but will be represented by a delegation of citizens to witness the inaugural of this great amusement event.

*

Ringling Management and Philosophy

The Ringling brothers, who founded and ran the circus for the first 50 years of its existence, were men of great and humane qualities. Much has been written about them, true and not so true. It was felt that the most candid of impressions and opinions would be from those men and women who had intimately known them in their early and formative days, or had been in their employ. Comments, observations, and anecdotes of these employees and friends offer a fascinating insight on their character and make-up. For example:

Henry Moeller (circus wagon maker): "Otto Ringling always had money. His brothers always turned to him when they were short. Otto was extremely practical and efficient but not frugal. When he was a boy and worked in his father's harness shop he could cut more straps out of a side of leather than any other man."

Frank Potter (ticket seller): "Mr. Charley Ringling was very sharp. He gave the impression, as he circulated around the lot, that he was indifferent, but he saw everything that was going on."

Spot Welk (animal man): "Al Ringling always addressed his department heads as Mister. It was Mr. Denman, Mr. Soder, Mr. Alexander. He respected their positions."

Fred Terbilcox (chauffeur): "Charley Ringling and his wife loved the outdoors. Often I would drive them off to hunt or fish."

John M. Kelley (General Counsel for the Ringlings for 30 years—at one time he was a brother-in-law to Alf. T.): "Alf. T. Ringling was a great man for horses—he always rode horseback from his home to quarters. Many times he would race his son Richard, who rode a pony, down Oak Street. He took up photography in 1899 and many of the animal pictures in the circus programs and route books were his. Alf. T. was a great publicity and press man for the circus. On one occasion Al cautioned him about the embellishments in one of his press releases—Alf. T. retorted—*but Brother Al. look at the free advertising we get out of it.*"

Henry Moeller: "Al Ringling was the most determined man I ever knew."

Leonard Roser (auditor): "Soon after I started to work for the show I made out a check for $20,000 and passed it over to Henry Ringling for his signature. In a minute he handed the check back and said, *Leonard, this should be $20,000 not $50,000.* I could not believe my eyes. He had deftly changed my careless figure and increased the check. Then came a long discourse on using cleancut and unalterable figures—a lesson I never forgot.

Earl Schilling (chauffeur): "Al Ringling was strict and had a nervous temperament, but was a wonderful boss. On one occaion when I came down with malaria Al brought me into his private car where I stayed until I had my strength back."

Baraboo Daily Republic—obituary for Al Ringling, Jan. 3, 1916, written by the editor and lifelong friend: "He rarely joked—his mind was always on serious matters. He would not countenance vulgarity. Because of his trusting nature, performers always sought him for advice."

Ralph Peckham (Advance Agent): "Chas. Ringling was a stickler for neatness. Wouldn't tolerate

AL RINGLING, left, on the circus lot. Circa. 1912.
(H. H. Conley Collection)

slovenliness in any of his officials. Such things as dirty shirts, gravy stains on tie or vest, unpressed suits were taboo. I can recall one fall morning it was unusually cold and I was late and there was no warm water with which to shave. I planned to rush down to the unloading spot and take care of my duties there and then return to my car to shave before I went to the lot. No sooner did I get to the siding when I bumped into Charley Ringling. I always did wear a moustache, but I felt Charley's eyes scrutinizing my unshaven face. In his usual pleasant manner, he said, *good morning Ralph, are you growing a beard?* Yes, Mr. Charley, was my answer, and by George I did."

Jack LeClair (a clown on the show for 30 years): "Charley Ringling was a great guy and a wonderful musician. Everybody liked Mr. Charley. I can remember one time in St. Louis when, between shows, our clown band was practicing its routine. Charley walked by and stopped to listen. Then he borrowed a horn and sat down with us and joined in the session. He got a big kick out of this and so did all the boys. Henry (Buddy) North reminds me of his Uncle Charley—easy going and always with a friendly remark to the show people around the lot. On our 4th of July celebration each year we put on quite a program between shows. We had stake driving contests, singing, girls comically imitating other acts and children doing acts. Henry North was always there to hand out the cash prizes. Everybody likes Buddy North; and everybody liked Charley Ringling."

Otto Ringling, in a letter of Oct. 12, 1907, to his brothers, discloses the deep convictions the brothers had about the caliber of men they wanted around their show. He was reporting on the Barnum & Bailey Circus they had just purchased: ". . . Burke wants to stay with the show and I will turn him down . . . In my opinion, he is not in it with Snellen, or McAvoy, or even some of his assistants. He is very coarse and absolutely illiterate, gives the foulest kind of answers to his men when they come for orders and exceedingly quick tempered . . . has a tough old English sword swallower for a wife."

It was the general consensus that Al was the guiding spirit in forming, staging, and directing the show. Otto was the financial genius. He was interested in reading; loved biographies, history, and travel stories. He had a fine collection of rare books. Charles, a genial person, enjoyed and composed music. Around the circus he was a stickler for detail. He handled various phases of the circus advertising; in particular, he headed up the crew that fought the opposition.

Alf. T. leaned to literature and wrote much of the material in programs, route books and couriers in the early days; John became an expert at routing the show. These men were never inclined to be conspicuous by their actions. Rather, they were all business and extremely reticent about their personal affairs. They were always neatly and properly dressed on and off the circus lot.

The Ringling brothers had a peculiar formality, or reservedness, about them that show up in their letters. When Otto Ringling, for instance, would write to his brothers he would start the letter: "To Ringling Bros.," not "Dear Al, John, Chas. & Alf. T." Perhaps the sharp eye of efficiency caused them to use the former salutation instead of the latter. When out on tour and one of the boys wrote to their parents the letters were signed, "Ringling Bros."—one signature for all the boys. If the letter went to the bank the letter might have been signed, "Ringling Bros., per Otto R." When studying the papers and documents issued by these men there is a sense of seriousness in every thought and action. One such letter that Henry North received from one of his uncles, while at Yale, cautioned him to knuckle down to work. The letter was signed, not "your friend, Uncle John," or "Sincerely, John," but "Yours very truly, John Ringling." In analyzing the constant use of "Ringling Bros," in salutations and closings of letters, it is obvious that this gives a sense of *leveling* all the brothers to the same importance. Nowhere can there be found any indication that any one of the brothers rode roughshod over the others — all worked in unison and as a cooperative team. This feeling ran deep. The use of *Ringling Bros.* in this fashion kept all the brothers on the same rung of the ladder. This superb teamwork unquestionably had much to do with their spectacular rise in the show world.

The late Henry Steeps, President of the Baraboo National Bank, recalled that when he started working as a messenger boy in the bank around the late '90's, one of his daily tasks was to count out the money shipped in by the Ringlings. The express train arrived at 10:00 a. m., and within 15 minutes the express wagon would back up to the bank's door and unload a large canvas sack from the circus. The total was divided by five and an equal share put into the account of each brother. They never knew how much was sent in — sometimes it was $2,000, many times as high as $20,000. This cash was what was left over in the till after all the daily bills were paid.

As time went on, the Ringlings began to absorb their competition. Their first acquisition was a tiny show, W. B. Reynolds purchased to get the two elephants and a few wagons the show owned. In 1898 they leased the John Robinson show for one year. The brothers sent Henry Ringling to Cincinnati to watch over this venture.

In 1905 Jas. A. Bailey sold the Ringlings one-half interest in his Forepaugh-Sells Bros. Circus. The spring of the following year Bailey died and in June the Ringlings paid his widow $100,000 for the other half of this circus. After the acquisition of this show, the choice wagons and the best animals were shipped to Baraboo to be added to the Ringling Circus. Then the circus-owning brothers sent A. G. and Henry to Columbus, Ohio, the winterquarters, to manage the Forepaugh-Sells Bros. Circus. They were told that if they pulled this show together and managed it they could have it. A. G. and Henry did spend the winter of 1906-07 putting this circus into shape. Unfortunately, the untimely death of A. G. put a crimp in these plans. So, after the 1907 season, the Forepaugh-Sells Bros. Circus was brought to Baraboo and put on the shelf. (The Ringlings put this show out on the road during 1910 and 1911, after which this circus title never toured again.)

1907 was the year the intrepid Ringlings purchased their largest competitor—the Barnum and Bailey Circus. The purchase of this circus by the Ringlings was not a sudden and impulsive move. The final transaction occurred in the fall of the year, but probably 12 to 18 months earlier John and Otto Ringling were dickering for the show.[1]

Looking back to a year prior to the purchase of the Barnum & Bailey Circus, it is noted that the Ringlings had netted $800,000; while their adversary cleared only $100,000. This obviously poor showing frightened the Barnum & Bailey stockholders. It was apparent that Jas. A. Bailey's hand was sorely missed. Since Bailey's death in 1906, Joseph T. McCaddon, who was Mrs. Jas. A. Bailey's brother, acted as chair-

man of the Board of Directors and was a trustee of Bailey's estate. W. W. Cole was managing director of the show.

In the late fall of 1906 Henry Ringling, in Columbus, received a telegram from Mrs. Bailey in which she asked him to manage the Barnum & Bailey Circus. True to their usual practice, Henry immediately contacted his brothers and it was decided that Henry should go to Bridgeport, but this plan did not materialize. Perhaps it was their realization that the Barnum & Bailey Circus might be purchased that changed the plans.

Just after New Year's day in 1907 John Ringling was in New York preparatory to sailing on a six-week's trip to Europe in search of new acts. He visited W. W. Cole, who announced to him that the verbal agreement between the managements of the two circuses to divide the United States and rotate their tours, was off. The apportionment had been in effect since 1903. This arrangement was not a trust, but only a common sense deal not to fight each other over territories when the entire country was at their disposal. The division of territory eliminated the tremendous expense of billing wars and unnecessary free tickets. Its only purpose was to keep both shows from going into the same town on or about the same dates.

A glance at the routes indicates how the shows adhered to their gentlemen's agreement. In 1903 Barnum & Bailey played the East and Ringling Bros. played the West. In 1904 Barnum & Bailey started in New York city then moved out into the Central States. Ringling Bros. spent three weeks in Chicago, then moved East into New England, Canada, back through Wisconsin, the Dakotas and out to California and Texas. It was the same in 1905-06 — no overlapping of territory.

Cole's announcement to John Ringling that the territory deal was off was probably made in the hope that if the Barnum & Bailey show had a free hand they could better their financial record. This year was Ringling's turn in the lucrative East, and John Ringling was in no mood to knuckle under to Cole's threat. He was reported to have warned Cole he would carry Barnum & Bailey into a killing fight. This was the last thing Cole wanted. He had stockholders to account to, while the Ringlings were free to take quick and decisive action. So completely did Cole capitulate to John Ringling's counter-threat that, after Barnum & Bailey's stand in New York City, this circus jumped directly to Reading, skipping the profitable towns on the East coast. While in New York City, the Barnum & Bailey circus advertised

---

[1] The two brothers were in the east at the time and had a conference with Mr. A. A. Stewart, business agent for Mrs. James A. Bailey. After the meeting Otto wrote to his brothers in Baraboo that the price for the Barnum & Bailey show was $900,000. This included the Bailey-owned Buffalo Bill Show winterquarters, cars, horses, harness, etc. in England. It included the buildings in the Bridgeport winterquarters, 200,001 shares of Barnum & Bailey, Ltd., which would control contracts for Madison Square Garden and a long term lease for the title of Barnum & Bailey in America. Otto said Stewart wanted immediate action, or if the Ringlings wanted time they would have to deposit $10,000 for an option which would be forfeited if they failed to take up the option. The deal fell through at that time.

they would not show in Brooklyn that year. This left the eastern seaboard open for the Ringling show.

Variety magazine of Jan. 26, 1907, quoted a notice issued by the Barnum & Bailey Circus at Bridgeport — "No final arrangements would be made looking to the contracting of acts until the return of John Ringling from Europe." This suggests that the active management felt, too, that the sale was a possibility. By early summer, the sale of the Barnum & Bailey Circus to the Ringlings was fast coming to a head. Otto and John favored the purchase; while the other three brothers were against the expenditure. John, who was the youngest of the boys, argued long and hard. Finally, Charley gave in; then it was three for the purchase and two against. After listening to all the pros and cons, as was their custom, Alf. T. and Al acquiesced and the die was cast. *The Greatest Show On Earth* on July 8, 1907, became their property for $400,000, the bill of sale stipulating that the Ringlings would take over at the close of the season on or about November 1, 1907. News of the sale was withheld from the press at this time pending the acquisition of public stock in the circus.

During the summer Mrs. Bailey sent her Business Agent, Mr. A. A. Stewart, to England to pick up all the available stock in the Barnum & Bailey Show. (While in England —1898 through 1902—the Barnum & Bailey circus was incorporated under English laws and shares were sold to the public.) In order to help Stewart on his mission, McCaddon at this time emphatically denied in the press the rumors that his circus would merge with the Ringling Bros.[2] On Oct. 24, 1907, a confirmation of the sale was executed by Barnum & Bailey.

After the purchase, Al Ringling suggested that the Barnum & Bailey circus be brought to Baraboo and put on the shelf. Henry Moeller remembers Al's reason—"In the Ringling Bros. Circus we have the best circus in the world and we have the best men to run it—let's keep it that way." Al was overruled — the brothers decided to divide the U. S. into two territories and operate both shows. They did just that, and Otto went to Bridgeport to manage their new circus (he acted in this capacity until he died in 1911). Al Ring-

JOHN RINGLING and his wife, Mabel, Circa. 1918.
(Wis. Hist. Soc.)

ling then packed up and went to England for the purpose of cleaning up all the loose ends of the old Barnum & Bailey syndicate. Also, he wanted to look over the territory with the idea in mind of touring that country with the Ringling Circus. (The tour never materialized.)

Along with the purchase of the Barnum & Bailey Circus, the Ringlings acquired much equipment of the Buffalo Bill Show. In January 1909 Otto Ringling sold this Wild West equipment to Pawnee Bill for $40,000. The Ringlings were not interested in operating a wild west show and in a letter to his brothers, Otto wrote, "In my opinion this is a great deal for us, and relieves us of a lot of junk."

With the Barnum & Bailey Circus tucked under their belts, along with the Forepaugh-Sells Bros. Cir-

[2] In the McCaddon collection in the Princeton Library there is a bill of sale of the Barnum & Bailey, Limited, and all its property to A. A. Stewart. It is dated July 24, 1907. The sale price is listed at $400,000. Not enough documents have been brought to light to clarify this bill of sale paper, but it is believed, by Richard Conover, circus historian, in his book *The Affairs of James A. Bailey* that the sale of the English company's assets to Stewart was merely a paperwork affair, and very possibly transferred to Mrs. Bailey immediately thereafter

OTTO RINGLING, (with cane), and Adolph Konyot on lot of Barnum & Bailey Circus in 1911.
(Wis. Hist. Soc.)

present day—well, I must not talk big—we are the Ringling Bros. who employ and control a staff of 3,500 people and own 400 railway cars."

The circus dynasty that the five original owner-brothers had built for themselves held together. In the 23 action-packed years between their first tiny and almost pathetic circus performance and the acquisition of their giant competitor, these men had grown in stature. It is a credit to their business acumen that with each major move they ended up with a stronger hand in the show world. Their circus was fast becoming a legend.

Otto Ringling, the only bachelor among the brothers, was the first of the circus owners to succumb. At his death in 1911 his share of the big show went to the remaining brothers. In 1916, when Al died, his circus stock, too, was willed to his brothers. With the death of Alf. T. in 1919, his approximate one-third interest in the circus was left to his son Richard (who did not, however, participate in the management). Charley died in 1926 and left his approximately one-third interest in circus properties to his wife, Edith Conway. This, then, left the control of the show divided between John Ringling, Chas. Ringling's widow, and Alf. T.'s son, Richard; but John actively managed the show alone.

The hour of John Ringling's greatest triumph occurred in the fall of 1929. He was, by then, the only one of the seven brothers still living. Traditionally, the Ringling circus opened its season by showing, for the month of April in New York's Madison Square Garden, of which John Ringling was a stockholder. John, probably due to the press of a dozen other enterprises, delayed leasing the Garden for the 1930 season. When he did, he found that his most formidable competitor, the American Circus Corporation had signed a very favorable lease and was scheduled to take over the Spring opening date with their Sells-Floto Circus. News releases at that time said that Sells-Floto got the contract because they agreed to relinquish Friday nights to allow the profitable boxing shows to go on, a clause to which John Ringling had always refused to agree.

John Ringling's reaction to this news was prompt and characteristic. He simply bought the American Circus Corp.[3] for a reputed $1,700,000 and moved his Ringling Bros. Circus into the Gardens under his terms. He then truly became the Circus King of all time.

—————————

[3] The American Circus Corporation owned five active circuses, all competitors of Ringling. They were Sells-Floto, Al. G. Barnes, Sparks, Hagenbeck-Wallace, and John Robinson (in addition the corporation owned the well-known inactive titles Buffalo Bill Wild West, Yankee Robinson, and Van Amburgh).)

cus, the world now looked upon the Baraboo brothers as outstanding celebrities in the field of outdoor amusement. So it was that in January of 1908 when John Ringling went to England in search of circus talent, he grandly played the part. *Variety* magazine reported the following statement by him during an interview in London:

"You want my history. Why, I have none. I am merely John Ringling, age 39. I am one of the five brothers Ringling, sons of a Chicago merchant whose fortune was severely injured by a fire. We turned out to work, and being musical, started public concerts. These were a great success in the winter months. In the summer we worked a circus and did well. At the

By 1936, when John, the last of the incredible Ringlings died, the Ringling Bros. and Barnum & Bailey Circus had literally become an American tradition.

One season the circus was showing in Middletown, N. Y. The next stand was Danbury, Conn. and Al Ringling decided to drive to this town. He summoned his chauffeur and left Middletown for a leisurely drive with Mrs. Ringling. When they reached Danbury they checked in at a hotel. The Ringlings were given an elegant room and bath on the second floor front. The clerk rather haughtily then said, "Mr. Ringling, your chauffeur's room will be in the rear in the servants' quarters." Mr. Ringling, in great indignation, said, "No, no, I won't have that. Fred is not my son, but he is a good boy and has been with me a long time. None of that, I want him to have a room and bath next to mine." This break with New England archaism left the hotel clerk dumbfounded, but he meekly arranged for Mr. Ringling's request. This was typical of the Ringling's philosophy and treatment of their fellow men in these early days.

To delve further into the philosophy and cooperative spirit that made the Ringlings such a powerful unit in the amusement field, one has only to read the words of John Ringling in an article he wrote for *The American* magazine, Sept. 1919. This article is herewith reprinted in its entirety (with the authority of the editors) as it gives a keen insight into the thinking, planning, and operation of *The Greatest Show On Earth*.

We Divided The Job — But Stuck Together

Each brother had his part, and the others let him alone. We also discovered many interesting things about the likes and dislike of people who go to the circus.

By John Ringling
of the Ringling Brothers

Team work and strict attention to every detail of the circus business has been the key to the success of the Ringling Brothers; that, and hard work, common honesty, and a close study of what the public wants, compose all the trade secrets we have to reveal.

If there is anything in our lives or in our business that might help others, I am willing to tell it. What we know we have learned from others, and I am willing to give them back the benefit. Our education has been in the school of experience and necessity, and in the primary grades we had stern teachers. Perhaps it

is well to explain that the older brothers educated the younger. Whatever credit is due probably consists in the fact that we had common sense enough to profit by the experience of all, rather than of one.

I do not know that in the beginning we had any theories or philosophy, or even any very definite plan. We lived in a small town, and had few opportunities to study amusements; yet I cannot recall when we were not giving shows or practicing for them, trying to learn everything, from musical turns to equestrian acts. We held shows in barns, in tents, and vacant rooms. We worked hard at music, learning to play, after a fashion, upon every instrument we could acquire, as our first idea of entertainment was the concert. We had no real musical education, but "picked it up." However, love of music was inherent, and two of my brothers, Charles and Alf T., became accompished musicians in later life. We started out as a concert troupe of boys, going to neighboring towns. All five of us played in the orchestra, four playing while the other in turn ascended the stage and did some act, such as juggling, tumbling, or singing. We called it the "Classic Concert Company," but soon changed it

CHARLEY RINGLING (straw hat) and Andrew Downie, owner of Downie Bros. Circus. Circa 1920.
(Wis. Hist. Soc.)

AL RINGLING and his wife Lou. Circa 1914.

(Wis. Hist. Soc.)

to "Ringling Brothers Comedy Concert Co." Even that early we discovered that there is something in a name, and that the public's chief desire is to be amused rather than uplifted.

Our big ambition was to own a circus, with beautiful horses. We loved horses in childhood. Circus paraphernalia, however, is expensive, and we were several years in acquiring sufficient apparatus and stock to start with a road show. Meantime we were working hard, being compelled to learn not only the acts but also the business part of such an enterprise—and the business part proved the harder; it is surprising to me, in looking backward, to recall the confidence with which we tackled anything and did it. We learned that Franklin was right when he said that if you want a thing done well do it yourself. We tried hiring professional agents, and the result at first was not happy. We discovered the importance of team work, and that the hired agents would not pull together the way we brothers did. We learned that life is give and take, and that giving is really the bigger part.

In forty years, Ringling Brothers never have quarreled except that they have had some fine, old brotherly rows over matters of policy, not one of which ever left a bad feeling, because we understood that each was thinking and working for the interests of all.

One thing which we agreed upon early was that majority rules should not prevail in all cases. We never believed that any three should ever force their dictates upon two. Often, if only one held out for an idea to which the other four were opposed, we would argue and try to convince that one; but if he insisted, we agreed to try his plan. The verdict usually was: "All right. We think you're wrong, but if you insist we'll try it."

If the plan succeeded we gave him the credit, and if it failed we said nothing about it. Not all have succeeded, but some of the biggest improvements and advances we have made have been the result of trying out some idea which, at first, the majority opposed.

The first big question we encountered was that of honesty. This may sound odd, but remember that we were green country boys going into a business which at that time, was notorious. The grafter and pickpocket were parts of circus life. Many shows carried organized bands of such criminals to prey upon the people, and clashes between circus and townspeople were frequent. We determined from the first upon two policies—strict honesty, decent behavior and neatness; in fact we spent a large part of our small capital for neat uniforms. Being honest was a matter of conviction rather than of policy I doubt whether we realized the commercial worth of honesty and good reputation, but we all hated crooks and determined to keep the show clean.

We were growing, accumulating stock and equipment and enlarging our traveling territory, producing a clean, high-class one-night circus, five of us taking active part in the performances or the management. We had grown large enough for the big circuses to notice us, but we had no idea what a storm of opposition our stand for honesty would bring upon us. The grafters came to join our show, and we drove them off the lots. They started to fight us and had the aid of some of the great circuses. We were branded as "The Sunday-school Show." The big circuses attacked our routes, sent crews to harass us, and the grafters spread hand bills over towns, headed "When thieves fall out," declaring that we were opposing them because they refused to pay us a larger share of their loot.

We capitalized their opposition and discovered that it was one of the most valuable bits of advertising we ever had. We discovered that we were getting a better class of workers with the show, more loyalty from them, and better work and appearance. Also, we discovered that we were welcome to play return engagements, and that our reputation for honesty made us welcome in opposition territory, where other shows were not liked because of their grafting methods. In other words, it worked out with us just as it does in any business.

The show was growing to be a large enterprise, and while at first we were jacks-of-all trades, able to do almost anything, from leading the band to doing an equestrian act, it became necessary to specialize and divide the work. We were some time adjusting ourselves and learning which of us was best fitted for certain departments. It may seem a large problem, yet with us it was simple: each of us took over the line of work he liked best; and it succeeded, because any man does better when he likes his work.

This specialization, of course, developed us along different lines. Each assumed absolute control of his own department, and the others neither questioned nor criticized, unless asked for an opinion.

If I may be pardoned for seeming boastful, I should like to say that, in my opinion, Al was the greatest producing showman the world has ever known. He knew instinctively what the public would like or dislike, and his big success was in his ability to choose good features. In our earlier days, before we could afford to pay for the high-class attractions, we were, of course, handicapped, especially in the face of bitter and relentless opposition by the richer shows. Al clung to the idea of neatness, clean performances and fast movement. In the circus business he had the idea of speed and "pep" which George M. Cohan brought into the theatres. With a dozen rather mediocre acts, by proper staging, by "doubling," and keeping the action fast and continuous, he made the show appear better than some of those which cost twice as much to stage. He invented, brightened up, and developed some of the most successful features known to the circus.

It is a joke among the youngsters who love to try to "kid" us old fellows that, because of long experience in routing, I can put my hand out of a car window at night, feel the air, and say, "Six and a half miles from Abilene," while Al frequently was known to inquire what city we were in after the tents were up. There is truth in the joke. Each man concentrated upon his own work and "kept off" the others; consequently each man dug in and learned his own work thoroughly. My training was largely in routing, and in the old opposition days, when shows fought for territory, and when the big fellows tried to starve us out, knowledge of railroads and routes was a big help. I learned my geography that way; and Charles still insists that I am able to name the counties of any state in the United States and, if a county is named, to name the county seat, the road leading to it, and the license fee.

In what we refer to as the "opposition" days, circus life was full of thrills. It was real warfare against powerful enemies, a fight for existence on our part. After we began to grow and develop our new policy of honesty and clean shows, the big fellows fought us hard, routing their larger shows over our territory, destroying our billing, and carrying on a "campaign of frightfulness." Charles had charge of "opposition," and as a tactician he seldom was beaten.

One of their favorite means of "knocking" was to slip into our parade a "perambulator," a wagon with large signs announcing that we were a nice little show, but to wait for the big show next week. It was a constant fight to prevent the perambulator from getting into our parade, and Charles was a genius at such prevention. Once he quietly spread the word over a town that he would give a five-dollar piece for each nut off the perambulator: when it started to join our parade that perambulator fell to pieces like the one-horse shay. On another occasion some of our men greased saws, and sawed its timbers, so that at the first heavy jolt it collapsed in a heap. Another time, the opposition hid the wagon out in the country. Charles learned which road it would take, and fixed a bucket of green paint with a hose and force pump under a bridge. When the wagon started to cross it our men pumped and squirted paint until all the lettering was obliterated.

AL RINGLING—1915.
(Courtesy Mrs. Henry Ringling, Sr.)

Incidentally, such unfair fighting never profited the opposition to any great extent. In fact, it aroused sentiment in our favor. It is a question in my mind now whether it would not have been better policy to permit the perambulator to parade with us, and rely upon the sense of fair play of the American public. It is hard to see it in that light, however, when you are fighting for existence.

This experience had its effect upon us: When Ringling Brothers came to be the big show, we went to the other extreme and decided that it was best for ourselves and for the good of the entire business to encourage every circus that was clean and inclined to follow our policy of honest dealing with the public. We even aided in supplying them with acts, and in rearranging routing so that we would not conflict seriously to their detriment, and, in return, many of them have helped us by developing new acts and by lifting the standard of the business.

The psychology of the circus really is simple: Our appeal is to the elemental instincts, to the child that is in every man. What they call "the lure of the circus" is merely the great, unexpressed yearning of every human being to be young again. The circus is a drop of water from Ponce de Leon's spring. It takes people back to childhood for two hours, and makes them boys and girls again, makes them forget as nothing else will do. This fact accounts for many seemingly contradictory features of the circus. The humorists make fun of the man who borrows a small boy to take to the circus; to us in the business this is not funny. We see two things in it—the universal protest against growing old and the desire to give pleasure to others. A man or a woman enjoys the circus because the child enjoys it. Their great pleasure is in giving the child pleasure. The great pleasure of a circus man is that he gives pleasure to others.

Men and women approach a circus in the spirit of throwing away age, and becoming the child for an hour or two. You never see men dress up to go to a circus; they put on their old clothes. Many of them would pay ten dollars for the privilege of crawling under the canvas; they are coming to revive childhood memories and pleasures. The grown man is our best press agent and publicity man; the supposedly sedate head of the house is the first to see the circus posters. The first thing, when he reaches home, he tells the kiddies that the circus is coming to town; he tells them of the circuses he saw when he was a boy; how he crawled out of the bedroom window, shinned down the porch pillar, and went out to the junction to meet the circus train; how he carried water to the elephants to get in; how he crawled under the canvas one time.

That man is going to the circus, and he is going to take the kiddies—his own or someone else's, and he is going because the circus, of all forms of amusement, appeals to the elemental in man. I have been asked what things appeal to people in different parts of the

ALF T. RINGLING—1918.
(Courtesy Mrs. Hester Ringling Sanford)

CHARLEY RINGLING—1920
(Courtesy Fred Terbilcox)

country. The answer is that what appeals to the public in New York strikes just as close to the hearts of the people of Oklahoma.

Among our best patrons are the Chinese and the Indians, and they are pleased by the same things. The negro of the South enjoys the clowns; he shows the child mind most clearly. The Indians and Chinese appear stolid and do not express their emotions; but deeds of skill and horses appeal to them most. I remember one experience with Indians in Oklahoma. One of the rich chiefs reserved seats for his entire tribe, and he hired every vehicle in the town to haul them to the circus. He even got the town hearse, placed a rocking chair inside, and, sitting in the chair, led the procession, which outrivaled ours.

In recent years, I have been asked often whether the circus will be modernized, whether the universal use of the automobile will change it. It never will be changed to any great extent, because men and women will always long to be young again. There is as much chance of Mother Goose or Andersen's Fairy Tales going out of style as of the circus altering greatly. If we desired to change it, the people would not permit it.

Clowns, elephants, pretty ladies in fluffy gowns riding white horses. That is the circus!

You are not convinced? Watch a father when he breaks the news to his little son that the circus is coming. He takes him on his knee and tells the news. The boy is excited. He wants to hear all about the circus. What does his father tell him he will see?

Clowns. That is first. The elephants—g-r-e-a-t b-i-g elephants, and pretty ladies on white horses. We may bring in other attractions—the thrillers, the pomp and parades, the amazing feats of skill and daring to please others; but without clowns, elephants, and pretty ladies on white horses it would not be the circus, or the real American amusement.

The elephants, of course, are the great animal attractions. It is because they are big, and bigness appeals to the child mind; they are bigger to a child than they are to a grown person, largely, I think, because a boy three feet tall, looking up at the huge animal, sees it at an angle that makes it appear larger than it really it. Elephants excite a kind of awed admiration; tigers, the sense of smoothness, stealth; lions, the respect of majesty.

The chief interest in animals, after the elephants, is in the sea lions, which arouse amazed admiration by their seemingly human intelligence. Just what the psychology of this appeal of the sea lion to the human is I am uncertain—surprise and amazement, I believe. We know, however, that the seals are great centers of interest, and that people never grow tired of watching their tricks. Monkeys are, and always will be, the chief attractions to the children and to human beings with the child type of mind. It is much the same appeal as that of a baby.

OTTO RINGLING—1910.
(Courtesy Mrs. Henry Ringling, Sr.)

HENRY RINGLING—1917.
(Courtesy Mrs. Henry Ringling, Sr.)

JOHN RINGLING—1930
(Courtesy Mrs. Henry Ringling, Sr.)

As to horses, there exists in the human mind a love and admiration for the horse that is almost beyond comprehension. There is some psychic connection between the human and the equine animal, which is perhaps inherited. I have found but one class lacking in this love of the horse, and they are a certain people in New York; upon inquiry I learned that in their native land the horse is practically unknown. Quite recently, a returned officer of artillery in whose command were many of these people, informed me that they would as lief go into a cage of lions as into a corral filled with horses. Not knowing the horse, they fear it.

It is largely because of this universal love of horses that Ringling Brothers have opposed the idea of motorizing the circus. Looking further, we know that, within a short time, the horse will be almost as much of a curiosity to the public as the giraffe was a generation ago. Do you realize how few of the new generation ever have seen a four- or six-horse team? Our circus horses, which of course are selected with the greatest care, are almost as much of an attraction, either in a city or in the country, as are the rare animals collected from all over the world to form the educational feature of the shows.

Besides that, we do not believe that people want to see machinery in motion when they come to a circus.

They want the "human interest." If they love machinery, they will go to a mechanical exhibit. They want to see big, sweaty, brawny men performing feats, whether of strength or of skill and daring; the crowds which watch the erection of the big "top" would be disappointed if the poles and canvas were to be lifted by machinery; they gather to watch and admire the skill and strength of men.

People come to a circus in a mood different from that in which they approach any other amusement, possibly excepting baseball; circus crowds are proverbially the best-natured in the world, for men, and women who come to a circus leave all care and worry at home. They are kids again—excited, good-natured, seeking a chance to laugh either at the show or at each other. All the jostling, the rough handling, the pushing, the jamming, and discomforts are part of the day's fun. They are kids again, and no kid objects to being jostled or jammed in a crowd. They will scramble at the ticket wagon, fight to reach the entrance, laugh at torn clothes and wilted collars. If the doorkeeper grabs a man and shoves him down the right passage, he does not get mad. At a theatre he would want to fight; but at a circus he grins. It is because he is playing boy again for a few hours.

In the performance you will discover, if you analyze the acts, that in practically everything the circus man is playing to this child-interest in grown people. We understand that men and women are there to forget care, and therefore strive to avoid anything that might tend to suggest anything unpleasant or bring back any sorrowful memories. No act that might suggest accident or injury is permitted.

You may recall that for years the circuses strove to secure the most exciting "thrillers." It was said that the nearer a man or woman came to breaking his or her neck the higher the salary. Now you may observe that, to a great extent, the dangerous and seemingly dangerous acts have been cut out. This is because we discovered that at the climax of such acts four out of five of the woman and children turned away their faces and refused to look.

Showmen, whether performers or employees, are a clan apart from all others. We believe they are broader, more liberal, and freer than the average American, and we know that they are intensely American. This is partly due to the rough outdoor life, the hard work, and the absence of temptations to a softer life. Partly, too, it is due to the broadening effect of meeting and seeing hundreds of thousands of people, and unconsciously studying life in many localities. Morally, circus people are perhaps the cleanest class in the world, probably for the same reasons. The life they lead brings them into close, almost family, relations, the boys marry young, and one generation trains the next in the acts.

One thing which perhaps would surprise the outsider is the entire absence of any false pride. Their pride in their work is remarkable; but there are no false ideas. This may be partly the results of the old training, when everyone "doubled in brass." They learned to help one another, to do any work that was necessary. The highest paid artist feels not the slightest hesitation about helping with the canvas, or doing any other work, if it is for the good of the show. In a way, a circus becomes a sort of commune, each member trying to help the others. I have seen a man, ballet master of the Metropolitan Opera in winter, but with us in summer, jump into a mudhole and put his shoulder to the wheel of a mired wagon. Ernie Clark, who perhaps is the greatest aerialist ever developed, head of a family of remarkable performers, holds hoops for the equestrians to leap through. Our highest-paid publicity men do not hesitate to seize stickers or paste pots and work as bill posters, if an emergency demands such work.

Part of this is the result of tradition and training; but we feel, also, that much of it is loyalty to the organization and to us. Our men and women are extremely loyal, and this is probably due to the fact that we have kept close to them and are sincerely interested in them and their welfare. In fact, I think that a great bulk of all labor troubles could be eliminated if employers kept in closer contact with their workers. Employers should have an interest in those associated with them, and when workers feel that the boss really likes them, misunderstandings are avoided.

The respect of the trouper for women is almost beyond belief. It is much of the same spirit that is seen in the Western outdoor man, and probably is the result of knowing so few women intimately. If you were to take the finest lady in the land onto a circus lot and introduce her, say to a boss hostler in rough clothes, and perhaps dirty, he would greet her with a deference and dignity that would impress her because of its realness.

May I be pardoned for speaking thus of our people. But I feel justified in doing so, because I admire them and know what they are.

The business end of a circus is, of course, vital. The expenses are extremely heavy, especially in these days of high cost. Every detail must be carefully watched; minutes count in huge sums, and efficiency is at a premium in every department. I have heard it remarked that there is a great leakage and extravagance.

One expert declared that we waste thousands of dollars on telegrams alone. The truth is that what he calls leakage is not wastage. We have a habit of sending long telegrams running into hundreds of words. It is expensive, but not waste. We send such telegrams to save time and delays. Our business is in constant motion. But beyond saving time, our object is to avoid mistakes. The average person who sends a telegram counts pennies. He takes the risk of not making clear his meaning. We send letters by wire, and if we avoid one such mistake a year it pays.

Another point we long ago settled upon is that, whenever one of the Ringlings employs a person, none of the others will discharge him for any reason. The one who hired him is entirely responsible, and must deal with the situation himself. The acceptance of such complete responsibility has been a good thing for each of us, causing us to exercise more care than perhaps we would have done otherwise; and it certainly has avoided any chances of clashes of authority.

Further than that, we never permit personal likes or dislikes to enter into business relations with our employees. I am conscious that we have violated this in permitting personal *likes* to control our moves sometimes, but *dislikes* do not count. If a man is efficient, is valuable to the organization, and considered the best person available for a certain position, he holds the job.

I have spoken elsewhere of our policy of honest dealing with the public, and perhaps some may criticize the statements, and argue that we are not strictly honest in our advertising, especially on bill boards. Such a charge would be unwarranted. We insist upon honesty, and never have—nor ever shall—advertise any attraction that is not shown. But, you may charge, the bill boards exaggerate. That is true, and there is a very simple reason for this: The public likes and demands such exaggeration and the flamboyant language of the posters fills this demand.

The language of the circus poster is unique. Originally it was the result of opposition shows striving to outdo one another in startling announcements. Charles, who is the greatest scholar in the family, and an authority on words, created a new vocabulary and the style caught public fancy. We understand now, although we did not at the time, that we had struck upon the child-appeal in another form . All children, and all primitive minds, love big words, and love exaggeration. The boy who sees four dogs in the back yard invariably says there are a thousand dogs out there. When he offers to bet, he always wants to bet a hundred million billion dollars. He is not striving to deceive, but to express bigness in his own way.

The circus posters do the same thing: there is no effort to deceive the public—but to express the hugeness of everything in figures that carry the idea. If we have fifty elephants, and say a hundred, it pleases rather than offends. On circus day, everybody wants to think and talk in big figures, because on circus day we are boys and girls again, and we want to believe that there are a hundred million trillion elephants in the parade, and a billion funny clowns, and whole bushels and bushels of beautiful ladies on white horses.

(Reprinted from American Magazine Sept. 1919)

The personal respect the Ringling men had for each other was most remarkable—no one who knew them can ever remember their quarrelling. Never did a brother try to outdo the other, or ride rough-shod over him. In running their circus business, Mrs. Henry Ringling said they had many arguments wherein the discussion became heated. Occasionally, one brother would flare up in order to put his point across, but after thrashing out the problem and a decision was made, the boys always parted good friends.

An eye witness to one of these stiff debates was Henry Moeller. One winter day he was doing some iron work on a tiger cage when he received a call from Charley Ringling asking him to come over to the circus office immediately. Henry, who was a first cousin to the circus owners, did not bother to change, but went over with his leather apron and work clothes, assuming they had some urgent repair job for him. Upon arrival he was ushered into a room in which sat Alf. T., Charley, Al and Otto Ringling. Al explained to Henry that with John Ringling in Europe, they needed a man to take his place on a decision that had to be made. He was told to approach the problem with an open mind, offer any suggestions or ideas he had and then vote as if he owned 1/5 of the circus.

Moeller recounted, "There was plenty of table pounding and stiff arguing. The discussion see-sawed back and forth for over an hour. It was just like a court trial. After the vote was taken the decision was final. The boys all immediately became engrossed in other problems and I went back to the wagon shop." When asked what was the point at issue on this occasion. Henry said, "Well, I am not so thinkable any more, but I recall it had something to do with putting the Forepaugh Show back on the road."

ABOVE, Mrs. Charles Ringling, who, after her husband's death, controlled almost half of the circus stock. In 1943 her son, Robert (below) became President of the circus and remained in this position thru 1944 and 1945. (Robert died in 1950 and Mrs. Ringling in 1953). (RB&BB)

SEASON 1919

RINGLING BROS AND BARNUM & BAILEY COMBINED SHOWS

WINTER QUARTERS BRIDGEPORT CONN

GENERAL OFFICES No. 221 INSTITUTE PLACE, CHICAGO, ILL.

OFFICIAL TOUR

Date	Town	State	R. R.	Miles	Date	Town	State	R. R.	Miles
Mar. 29					Aug. 26	Mankato (Afternoon only)	Minnesota	C. St. P. M. & O. R. R.	94
Apr. 26	New York	New York	N. Y. N. H. & H. R. Rs.	55	" 27	Sioux Falls	South Dakota		153
Wk Apr. 28	Brooklyn		Bush Terminal		" 28	Sioux City	Iowa	C. M. & St. P. R. R.	91
Wk May 5	Philadelphia	Pennsylvania	Bush Terminal and P. R. R.	90	" 29	Omaha	Nebraska	C. & N. W. R. R.	100
SUNDAY					" 30	Lincoln		C. B. & Q. R. R.	55
May 12	Washington	Dist. Col.	P. R. R.	137	SUNDAY				
" 13					Sept. 1	Kansas City	Missouri	C. B. & Q. R. R.	210
" 14	Baltimore	Maryland		40	" 2	St. Joseph		C. R. I. & P. R. R.	64
" 15					" 3	Topeka	Kansas		90
" 16	Wilmington	Delaware		70	" 4	Junction City		U. P. R. R.	72
" 17	Camden	New Jersey		30	" 5	Concordia			71
SUNDAY					" 6	Salina		A. T. & S. F. R. R.	77
May 19	Newark	New Jersey	P. R. R.	92	SUNDAY				
" 20	Easton	Pennsylvania	P. R. R. and C. R. R. of N. J.	70	Sept. 8	Denver	Colorado	U. P. R. R.	454
" 21	Wilkes-Barre		C. R. R. of N. J.	101	" 9	Colorado Springs		C. & S. R. R.	74
" 22	Scranton			20	" 10	Pueblo			45
" 23	Binghamton	New York	D. L. & W. R. R.	57	" 11	Garden City (Afternoon only)	Kansas	A. T. & S. F. R. R.	215
" 24	Elmira			57	" 12	Wichita			230
SUNDAY					" 13	Enid	Oklahoma	C. R. I. & P. R. R.	98
May 26	East Liberty	Pennsylvania	P. R. R.	345	SUNDAY				
" 27					Sept. 15	Oklahoma City	Oklahoma	C. R. I. & P. R. R.	87
" 28	Allegheny			7	" 16	Okmulgee		Frisco	136
" 29	Youngstown	Ohio		65	" 17	Tulsa			45
" 30	Cleveland		P. R. R. and N. Y. C. R. R.	92	" 18	Coffeyville	Kansas	A. T. & S. F. R. R.	117
" 31					" 19	Joplin	Missouri	M. K. & T. R. R.	84
SUNDAY					" 20	Springfield		Frisco	93
June 2	Buffalo	New York	N. Y. C. R. R.	182	SUNDAY				
" 3	Rochester			68	Sept. 22	Ft. Smith	Arkansas	Frisco	178
" 4	Syracuse			81	" 23	Muskogee	Oklahoma	Mo. Pac. and Frisco	77
" 5	Utica			90	" 24	Ada		Frisco	119
" 6	Schenectady			78	" 25	Ardmore		G.C.&S.F.andA.T.&S.F.R.R.	90
" 7	Albany			17	" 26	Chickasha			110
SUNDAY					" 27	Lawton		C. R. I. & P. R. R.	54
Wk June 9	Boston	Massachusetts	B. & A. R. R.	200	SUNDAY				
SUNDAY					Sept. 29	Fort Worth	Texas	C. R. I. & P. R. R.	154
June 16	Lowell	Massachusetts	B. & A. and B. & M. R. Rs.	27	" 30	Dallas		Texas & Pacific R. R.	32
" 17	Fitchburg		B. & M. R. R.	30	Oct. 1	Hillsboro		M. K. & T. R. R.	66
" 18	Worcester		N. Y. N. H. & H. R. R.	26	" 2	Temple (Afternoon only)			68
" 19	Providence	Rhode Island		35	" 3	Houston		G. C. & S. F. R. R.	215
" 20	Fall River	Massachusetts		57	" 4	Beaumont		Gulf Coast Lines	89
" 21	New Bedford			14	SUNDAY				
SUNDAY					Oct. 6	San Antonio	Texas	Ft. W. & D. C. R. R.	115
June 23	Springfield	Massachusetts	N. Y. N. H. & H. R. R.	158	" 7	Austin		M. K. & T. R. R.	83
" 24	Hartford	Connecticut		26	" 8	Waco			110
" 25	Waterbury			31	" 9	Corsicana		St. L. S. W. R. R.	55
" 26	New Haven			28	" 10	McKinney		H. & C. T. R. R.	57
" 27	Bridgeport			17	" 11	Greenville		M. K. & T. R. R.	32
" 28	Stamford			23	SUNDAY				
SUNDAY					Oct. 13	Paris	Texas	Texas Midland R. R.	52
June 30	Paterson	New Jersey	N.Y.N.H.&H.,C.N.E. and Erie	159	" 14	Terrell			84
July 1	Jersey City		Erie R. R.	17	" 15	Marshall		T. & P. R. R.	116
" 2	Trenton		P. R. R.	50	" 16	Shreveport	Louisiana		42
" 3	Reading	Pennsylvania	P. R. R. and P. & R. R. R.	74	" 17	Texarkana	Arkansas	K. C. S. R. R.	73
" 4	Harrisburg		P. & R R. R.	54	" 18	Little Rock		Mo. Pac. R. R.	145
" 5	York		P. R. R.	27	SUNDAY				
SUNDAY					Oct. 20	Memphis	Tennessee	C. R. I. & P. R. R.	133
July 7	Altoona	Pennsylvania	P. R. R.	159	" 21	Jackson (Afternoon only)		N. C. & St. L. R. R.	85
" 8	Johnstown			37	" 22	Nashville			153
" 9	Greensburg			46	" 23	Chattanooga			151
" 10	Sharon			100	" 24	Knoxville		Sou. R. R.	111
" 11	Erie			76	" 25	Asheville	North Carolina		129
" 12	Jamestown	New York	N. Y. C. R. R.	80	SUNDAY				
SUNDAY					Oct. 27	Richmond	Virginia	Sou. R. R.	379
July 14	Akron	Ohio	Erie R. R.	183	" 28	Newport News		C. & O. R. R.	75
" 15	Canton		Erie and P. R. Rs.	47	" 29	Petersburg		C. & O. and S. A. L. R. Rs.	97
" 16	Mansfield		P. R. R.	74	" 30	Norfolk		N. & W. R. R.	81
" 17	Zanesville		B. & O. R. R.	87	" 31	Rocky Mount	North Carolina	N.&W.-N and P.Bt.-A.C.L.	116
" 18	Wheeling	West Virginia		85	Nov. 1	Raleigh		A. C. L. and Sou. R. Rs.	69
" 19	Parkersburg			95	SUNDAY				
SUNDAY					Nov. 3	Charlotte	North Carolina	S. A. L. R. R.	173
July 21	Charleston	West Virginia	B. & O. and K. & M. R. Rs.	134	" 4	Greenville	South Carolina	Sou. R. R.	107
" 22	Huntington		C & O R. R.	51	" 5	Spartanburg			32
" 23	Chillicothe	Ohio	C. & O. and N. & W. R. Rs.	95	" 6	Columbia			94
" 24	Columbus		N. & W. R. R.	51	" 7	Augusta	Georgia	Georgia R. R.	83
" 25	Dayton		C.C.C. & St. L. R. R.	69	" 8	Athens			116
" 26	Lima		B. & O. R. R.	71	SUNDAY				
SUNDAY					Nov. 10	Atlanta	Georgia	S. A. L. and Sou. R. Rs.	73
July 28	Detroit	Michigan	B. & O. and M. C. R. Rs.	129	" 11	Anniston	Alabama	Sou. R. R.	104
" 29					" 12	Birmingham			63
" 30	Pontiac		G. T. R. R.	29	" 13	Montgomery		L. & N. R. R.	97
" 31	Flint		P. M. R. R.	58	" 14	Columbus	Georgia	C. of G. R. R.	95
Aug. 1	Saginaw		M. C. R. R.	33	" 15	Albany			99
" 2	Lansing			62	SUNDAY				
SUNDAY					Nov. 17	Tampa	Florida	A. C. L. R. R.	413
Aug. 4	Toledo	Ohio	P. M. R. R.	120	" 18	Orlando (Afternoon only)			92
" 5	Ft. Wayne	Indiana	Wabash R. R.	94	" 19	Jacksonville			147
" 6	Jackson	Michigan	N. Y. C. R. R.	100	" 20	Waycross	Georgia		75
" 7	Battle Creek		M. C. R. R.	45	" 21	Savannah			97
" 8	South Bend	Indiana	G. T. R. R.	75	END OF SEASON				
Aug. 9-17	Chicago (Grant Park)	Illinois	N. Y. C. R. R.	86	HOME RUN				
Aug. 18	Indianapolis	Indiana	N.C.Y.and C.C.C.&St.L.R.Rs	186	Savannah to Acca Jct			A. C. L. R. R.	513
" 19	Terre Haute		C.C.C. & St. L. R. R.	72	Acca Jct. to Potomac Yard			R. F. & P. R. R.	110
" 20	Watseka (Afternoon only)	Illinois	C. & E. I. R. R.	100	Potomac Yard to Belvidere			P. R. R.	256
" 21	Milwaukee	Wisconsin	C.&E.I.Belt-C.M.&St.P.R.Rs	168	Belvidere to Maybrook			L. & H. R. R.	71
" 22	Rockford	Illinois	C. M. & St. P. R. R.	99	Maybrook to Bridgeport			N Y N. H. & H. R. R.	106
" 23	Madison	Wisconsin		82					
SUNDAY									
Aug. 25	Minneapolis	Minnesota	C. M. & St. P. R. R.	290					

AT END OF each year the circus usually issues an "official tour" sheet showing all towns played for that season. Here is sheet for 1919, the first year the Ringlings added the Barnum & Bailey title to their own name. Amazing statistics the circus has accumulated over the years are many. Ringlings have played in every one the 48 states, and many Canadian provinces. Over 1,800 different cities have seen the show, which has given over 31,000 performances. The Ringlings have scheduled Chicago more than any other city, followed by Milwaukee, Detroit, and Boston. The great show trains, in traveling 12 to 17,000 miles per season, have racked up an incredible total of close to a million miles.

(Wis. Hist. Soc.)

ONE OF THE trucks used for the "arena" circus tour in 1957 and 1958. (Fred Pfening, Jr.)

THE 1957 tentless circus at Pomona, California. (RB&BB)

AT THE END of each season the circus issues a route book in which appears an entire list of the show's personnel and their jobs; the program; entire season'sroute; statistics of the big show's size and equipment; photos and stories. In the early days, the tour was written in form of a diary—each episode of the day was dutifully listed. This is one of the more fascinating forms of printed circus history. The page below is from the 1894 route book. (Fred Terbilcox Collection)

BENEATH WHITE TENTS. 147

LANSING, Iowa. **Thursday, June 28th.**

B. C. R. & N. and C. M. & St. P. Rys., 76 miles. Hotel Dudley. Weather fine. Afternoon house packed. Night house big. An interesting exhibition of wrestling is given by Mike Rooney and Woody Gillette. The two young gladiators make the match more interesting to themselves by a five-dollar bet, while many on the outside stake numerous amounts on the result. Mr. Gillette was the winner.

PRAIRIE DU CHIEN, Wis. **Friday, June 29th.**

C. M. & St. P. Ry., 31 miles. Hotels City and Germania. Weather pleasant but hot. Afternoon house packed. Night house big. The ferries running between here and McGregor carried thousands of people over from Iowa to see the World's Greatest Shows.

RICHLAND CENTER, Wis. **Saturday, June 30th.**

C. M & St. P. Ry., 70 miles. Hotels Central and Merchants. Weather very hot. Afternoon house overflowing. Night house big. A running stream at the back of lot offered inducements that few of the male population of our great circus city could withstand and many took a dip into its liquid depths. During the leaps here, Mr. Wm. Leondor hurt his knee by the bursting of one of the smaller blood vessels in that member. Matt and Wm. Marshall were visited by their parents and by the wife of Wm. M. This is the home of Dick Booth, one of the corps of cornets in '91.

DARLINGTON, Wis. **Monday, July 2d.**

C. M. & St. P. Ry., 138 miles. Weather cool and pleasant. Fine lot on Fair Ground. Afternoon house big; night house big. The home of Albert and Frank Parsons, and the lemonade, always good, is to-day superexcellent. It is quite a novelty to see a horny-handed son of toil or other acquaintance of the Parsons say, "Frank, gimme some lemonade." "Here's your change, Bill," says Frank, and so the conversation continues all day long and at night the Messrs. Parsons know they have more friends than they ever thought they had.

DELEVAN, Wis. **Tuesday, July 3d.**

C. M. & St. P. Ry., 103 miles. Hotel Park. Weather hot. Afternoon house good. Night house fair. Mrs. Shafer, wife of our Teutonic character impersonator, visits.

OCONOMOWOC, Wis. **Wednesday, July 4th.**

C. M. & St. P. Ry., 62 miles. Hotels Casper and Jones. The biggest day of the year, bigger than St. Patrick, Die Wacht am Rhine, Garibaldi, and a thousand others all put together, is ushered in with the brightest of bright summer weather. Red, white and blue everywhere. Countless flags decorate big-top, menagerie, museum, horse tents, cooking tents, and everybody with the show wears the national colors. Even the horses, ponies and donkeys have red, white and blue ribbons braided into their manes and tails.

> "What constitutes a State?
>   Not high-raised battlements or labored mound,
> Thick wall or moated gate;
>   Not cities proud with spires and turrets crowned;
> Not bays and broad-arm'd ports,
>   Where, laughing at the storm, rich navies ride;
> Not starr'd and spangled courts,
>   Where low-brow'd baseness wafts perfume to Pride.
> No:—*men*, high-minded *men*,
>   With powers as far above dull brutes endued,
> In forest, brake, or den,
>   As beasts excel cold rocks and brambles rude;
>   *   *   *   *
> These constitute a State."

These and the small boys with the fire-cracker and the jolly Fourth "constitute a state," and often two states, if we count the state of intoxication which often prevails along with the patriotism on this great day. But it was not so at "Cooney." There was simply pure, unalloyed patriotism and the circus. There was a grand dinner at the cook house given to the employees of the show. Space forbids publishing the full bill of fare. It was a grand affair, however, and highly enjoyed by all, who voted Mr. Haley the prince of landlords. Many resorters from the hotels and cottages on the lake visited the show to-day. Among others, Mr. E. Kohl, who has one of the most beautiful summer residences on the pretty lake for which Oconomowoc is noted.

Orrin Hollis was to-day kicked by his horse, and rushed into the dressing-room exclaiming that the kick had landed just over the heart, but was assured that the heart was on the other side. Mrs. Fred. Madison was a visitor. Spencer Alexander left for home on account of sickness. P. M. Rice, tuba player, closed and Mont Billman took his place. Band marched from hotel to lot first time this season.

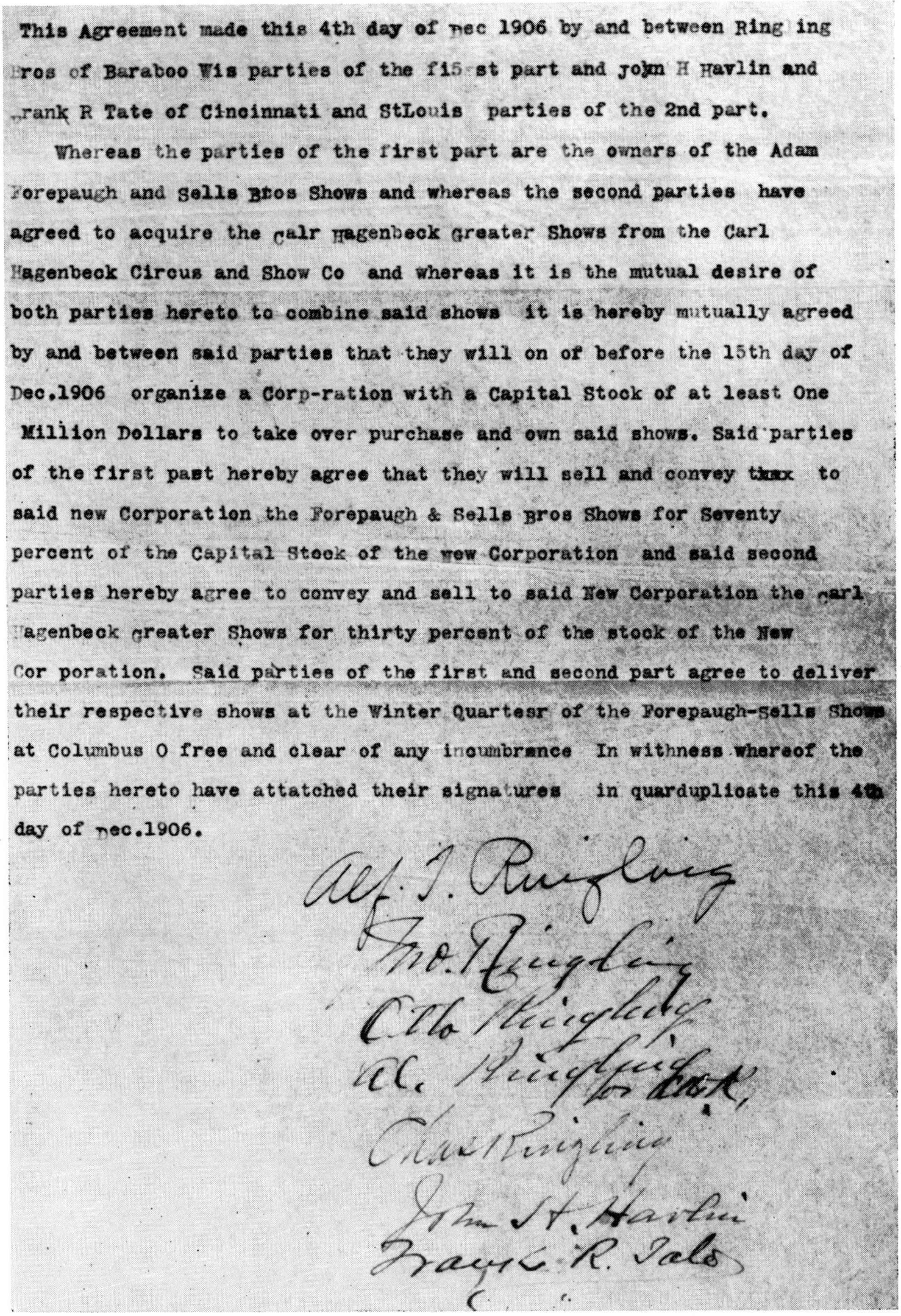

This Agreement made this 4th day of Dec 1906 by and between Ring ing Bros of Baraboo Wis parties of the first part and John H Havlin and Frank R Tate of Cincinnati and StLouis parties of the 2nd part.

Whereas the parties of the first part are the owners of the Adam Forepaugh and Sells Bros Shows and whereas the second parties have agreed to acquire the Calr Hagenbeck Greater Shows from the Carl Hagenbeck Circus and Show Co and whereas it is the mutual desire of both parties hereto to combine said shows it is hereby mutually agreed by and between said parties that they will on or before the 15th day of Dec.1906 organize a Corp-ration with a Capital Stock of at least One Million Dollars to take over purchase and own said shows. Said parties of the first past hereby agree that they will sell and convey thax to said new Corporation the Forepaugh & Sells Bros Shows for Seventy percent of the Capital Stock of the new Corporation and said second parties hereby agree to convey and sell to said New Corporation the Carl Hagenbeck Greater Shows for thirty percent of the stock of the New Cor poration. Said parties of the first and second part agree to deliver their respective shows at the Winter Quartesr of the Forepaugh-Sells Shows at Columbus O free and clear of any incumbrance In withness whereof the parties hereto have attatched their signatures in quarduplicate this 4th day of Dec.1906.

[handwritten signatures]
Alf. T. Ringling
Jno. Ringling
Otto Ringling
Al. Ringling
Chas Ringling
John H. Havlin
Frank R. Tate

THIS IS THE ORIGINAL CONTRACT by which the Ringlings, in 1906, sought to acquire interest in the Carl Hagenbeck circus. This deal fell through because Havlin and Tate were unable to get clear title to the Hagenbeck name. The following year circus owner Ben Wallace of Peru, Indiana, purchased the Hagenbeck Show and called it the Hagenbeck-Wallace Circus. He was sued for using the Hagenbeck name, but the judge ruled that if he bought the circus he bought the name.   (Walter Scholl Collection)

Cincinnati Ohio April 1st 1911.

Mr John M Kelly,
Baraboo Wis.,
    Dear Mr Kelly:
                I was greatly shocked to learn, this morn-
ing, of Otto Ringling's death and commend your prompt action in
postponing the Cincinnati meeting. The circus fraternity has lost
a splendid man and it will be a hard matter to fill his place . I
have always been a warm admirer of Mr Ringling's business methods
and his ability as an organizer and as the financial head of the
three circuses.

                        Very Truly Yours,

                            John G Robinson

RICHARD T. RINGLING, was the son of Alf. T. He became imbued with the idea of running a circus of his own. In 1917 he put on the road a truck show and called it "R. T. Richard's Supreme Show of the World", letterhead above. The show folded in three years' time.
(Circus World Museum)

LEFT—Letter from John Robinson at time of Otto Ringling's death praised Otto's business methods. (Mr. Kelley was personal lawyer for the Ringlings).

IN 1899, while their great adversary was in Europe, the Ringlings appropriated the Barnum & Bailey subtitle, "The Greatest Show On Earth".
(Sauk Co. Hist. Soc.)

BELOW—1906—Attention to detail had much to do with the Ringlings' success. There were enough Ringlings to watch all phases of the great circus.
(Circus World Museum)

Tragedies

Oftentimes the loosely used cliche, *the show must go on* sounds limp and hollow. Where it could be most poignantly used, on a circus lot after a windstorm, fire, or heavy rain, the phrase is never heard—it is taken for granted by the entire personnel of the show. When the circus is stricken with a heartbreaking tragedy of any description, a wretched and lonely feeling pervades the unit. The circus finds itself among strangers and hundreds of miles from home. When the big show comes to grief, no matter what the cause, it must endure these rough times as part of the game—the immediate problem then becomes *get the show on the road.*

For the Ringling Bros., the first real tragedy struck early in 1888, their fifth season. They had increased the size of the show and the price of a ticket from 25c to 50c. That spring proved to be wet and rainy and not conducive to large crowds. For weeks on end business had been bad and, in addition, they missed many afternoon stands because deep mud enroute slowed them up. This then was their plight when in desperation they wrote to the Baraboo bank asking for a loan of $1000 to carry them through. Actually, the situation was so serious that conceivably the circus would have folded then and there had the loan been denied. In substance the letter read:—

"We want to cut the size of our show and ship excess wagons and equipment back to Baraboo. We will drop the admission back to 25c. Also, we need to get some additional handbills printed—please loan us the $1,000 to do these things."

The letter went on,

"The mud and clay is awful. To get our wagons off some lots and to get thru the morass on some roads, we are forced to rent farmers' teams. We are paying them anything they ask just to help us out of the mud. We are pulling our wagons apart—we have lost over half of our dates."

Again the letter pleaded,

"We are willing to give you any collateral you ask for, we will sign over the show if you will send on the $1,000. We do not see how we pulled thru as well as we did so far—things were so tough."

The letter, written on hotel stationery was signed, *Ringling Bros.* One can only imagine the frightfulness of this ordeal, where only their combined courage carried them through. They got the loan and finished out their season.

The second tragedy to strike the circus was a train wreck on May 17, 1892—the only serious train wreck incidentally, the Ringlings ever had. The route book called it *Black Tuesday* and reported:

"The show was enroute to Washington, Kansas, when an appalling crash awoke us. Pouring out into the night our men perceived a chaos of wrecked cars, some crushed to utter kindling wood; others hurled headlong into a lake of mad waters, whose undermining power had wrecked a trestle and our train. The lake was full of dead and drowning horses. With humane bravery our men plunged into the waters to pull the necks of the horses out of the water. Robert O'Donnell was found in a mass of bloodstained wreckage with a splintered piece of scantling driven clear thru his head. His brains were strewn in every direction." The route book story went on—"26 magnificent draft horses were floating dead in the river. Other horses had ripped bellies, or broken legs, and had to be killed. Two crowded sleepers just escaped destruction. Four seriously injured men were sent to a Kansas City hospital. The wives of the various Ringlings showed great womanly kindness in their constant ministrations to the stricken. 40 head of horses were lost in all; which were replaced immediately by purchasing stock locally and ordering a carload from Chicago."

THE SHREDDED BAGGAGE HORSE TENT, after a severe hailstorm—circa 1925.
(Irvine Heatherington Collection)

The show missed only its Washington stand and went on to play Concordia, Kansas, the following day.

Windstorms are unpredictable monsters. Boss canvasmen are adept at reading the warnings in the sky and are always ready to put in an extra stake line to guy down the big top, or to move in a barricade of wagons to break the wind's force. Sometimes, if there is time, the tents are lowered. There have been blowdowns in Niagara Falls, Ellsworth, Kansas, and Crookston, Minnesota. In 1945, in Dallas, a severe wind took down the horse top and other small tents, but the big top withstood the storm. After a 20-minute delay the storm passed and the show went on.

With its vested responsibility toward all patrons, the management must ever be alert to anticipate trouble. Such was the case in Sterling, Ill. on a hot August day in 1912. Al Ringling was standing in front of the main entrance just before the doors were opened to let in the milling crowd. At this moment a barn burst into flames a quarter of a mile away. Al immediately issued orders not to open the doors until the fire was extinguished. At the height of the fire the wind shifted and burning bits of shingles began to blow in the direction of the big top. Some of the debris landed on the tent, which caught fire and it burned to the ground. Due only to Al Ringling's quick and cautious decision, not a person or animal was injured.

In Cleveland, on August 4, 1942, just before noon a circus worker, who had been fired for laziness, deliberately set fire to a pile of straw near the animal tent, "To get even" he told police. The flames flashed through the straw, up the canvas, and within a matter of minutes the menagerie tent was a horrible bedlam of animals writhing in agony, or madly dashing about. Sixty-five beasts were either burned to death, or mercifully shot. The list included four elephants, 12 zebras, 13 camels, four lions, several tigers, leopards, monkeys, pumas, and other miscellaneous specimens. The loss to circus property in those few disastrous minutes was $200,000 and was not covered by insurance.

Big John Sabo, boss animal man, who had been with the circus since 1915, said, "I would rather lose my right arm than to see something like this happen." Visibly affected he cried, "I like them all like babies. I felt like bawling when I found out that Maggie and Mabel (the brindled Gnus) had died."

It was then that the circus veterinarian, Dr. J. Y. Henderson proved his worth. He moved in fast. The elephant men were given special preparations and told to paint the burnt areas of the animals' bodies.

Camels, zebras, and caged animals were sprayed with a soothing preparation. No people were hurt, no horses lost, but the afternoon show was cancelled. The evening performance went on without mishap.

When a tragic accident strikes the circus animals, it is a mournful event in a special way. Such a calamitous happening occurred in 1941 while the circus was in Atlanta. Eleven of the show's elephants died of arsenic poisoning. It was a $110,000 financial loss to the circus, but more than that, to see these magnificent troupers fall, one by one over a period of two or three days was a sickening and heart rending sight to all the show personnel. First Lizzie; then Alice; Puqua (the African); Clara; and Peggy;—troupers all. The poison could have come from sprayed grass they had eaten, but regardless of the whys and wherefores, tragedy is stark and sudden on the circus when it does come.

The 1938 labor strike was a costly tragedy to everyone concerned. Since April of that year in New York, the circus management and the union had been trying to negotiate a contract. The end came in Scranton, Pa. in late June. With business way below normal, John Ringling North, Circus President, announced a 25% cut in wages for everyone as the only means of keeping the show on the road.[1]

The Scranton lot was a sea of mud and water. The Mayor ordered the circus out of town. North agreed to pay full wages to a skeleton crew to take the show back to Sarasota. On the afternoon of June 27, a crew of 205 men began to tear down, but the union called off the crew again until additional demands were met. Finally, after five days of haggling, the equipment was loaded onto the railroad cars and the bedraggled circus went back to winterquarters. When this happened, the nation's press found it hard to believe that the

[1]The *New York Herald Tribune* summed up the problem:— "Often in conflicts of this kind one can point to the reactionary attitude of the employer as at least equally to blame, with the stubborness of the workers for the impasse. But in this case we find Mr. North laying all his cards on the table in an effort to save the circus thru frank negotiation. At the wage scale originally set, the circus could not continue without courting bankruptcy. The depression had cut its gate far below the figure calculated. To permit it to go on, he proposed a 25% reduction without discrimination, and for justification offered to open his books to the scrutiny of the union. The union wasn't interested, so instead of five more months of steady employment, both performers and roustabouts are about to become jobless and the American public—all the kids from 5-80 years of age—is to be cheated of a traditional entertainment."

young, and young in heart, would not see the show that year.

The *Christian Science Monitor* in an editorial, described the feeling of consternation that swept over the U.S.

"Can it be possible that the circus *The Greatest Show On Earth,* of course, has turned back to winter quarters because of a disagreement over little things like profit and wages? The news taxes credulity. Whoever heard of a circus in winterquarters in the summer? Say it isn't so. The circus can't turn its back like that on the boys of America. Congress has gone home, but couldn't a special session be called? Or the League of Nations? The mirth of the nation is at stake. Human rights of million of boys, their fathers, grandfathers, and uncles are in jeopardy. They might get along without bread, but not without the circus."

At this time the Ringling-owned Al. G. Barnes-Sells-Floto circus was playing in the Dakotas. Not bothered with labor troubles in the agricultural Midwest, John North decided to augment this circus with outstanding features of his Ringling Circus, in order to give employment to key performers and personnel whom he had under contract. The overnight, mid-season transition of the Al. G. Barnes-Sells Floto Circus from a 30-car to 50-car show made circus history. The smoothness and dispatch with which this manuever took place is a credit to the men who ran these outfits. Here is an eyewitness account of how this intricate wedding took place. Mike Tshudy, who was boss hostler for the Barnes Floto combine, related:

"On July 9 our show was in Jamestown, N. D. The next day, Sunday, July 10, when we arrived in Redfield, N. D. we found the RB&BB big top, seats and all, set up along with their cookhouse. 20 Ringling cars had arrived from Sarasota. Also included was extra Ringling light plants, part of the sideshow; four Caterpillar tractors, 5 trucks, Gargantua, and his 26-foot cage; some ring stock, Frank Buck, Terrell Jacobs and his cats, the Concellos, and other acts. The Barnes wagons were all parked on one side of the lot and any equipment that was needed was taken over and added to the new show. Monday, July 11, we gave our first show of the new combine at Redfield. That night everything of the Barnes Circus that was left over and was not needed was loaded onto the flats and shipped back to quarters at Peru, Indiana. The transition was very smooth—no confusion and in the matter of a day we became a 50-car show moving in two sections instead of a 30-car one-section show." This new show was billed as "Al G. Barnes-Sells Floto Circus" presenting Ringling Bros. and Barnum & Bailey stupendous new features."

The worst tragedy in the annals of the Ringling Circus occurred during the afternoon show on July 6, 1944, at Hartford, Connecticut. With nearly 7,000 people enjoying the performance, the big tent suddenly became a holocaust. As fire leaped up the side walls and raced across the top of the canvas, Merle Evans swung his band into *Stars and Stripes Forever*—the circus disaster tune. The sound of this tune moved all employees into high gear—all horses and elephants were immediately led off the lot. The lions and tigers, who had just finished their act, were quickly shuttled into their cages and tractors pulled them out of danger.

People stampeded toward the exit through which they had entered the big tent, forgetting, in their panic, that every foot of its circumference was loose canvas and an exit to safety. Circus employees begged people to go out the opposite end of the tent, still not on fire. The band continued to play—three minutes had elapsed since the first flicker of fire was seen; the poles, with their guy ropes burned, began to fall—then suddenly the fire was over—six minutes had elapsed. But the agony lingered for hundreds of families. 168 men, women and children lost their lives—hundreds more were badly injured.

The agony lingered, too, for the circus management. The feeling of responsibility to the victims was uppermost in their minds. In addition, the circus lost its big tent, poles, and seats. Rigging for many performers and acts was destroyed. Five of the top circus employees were arrested on charges of manslaughter (and subsequently served sentences and were ultimately pardoned by the State of Connecticut). After all the smoke and confusion was cleared away the Ringling Bros. Circus found itself saddled with over four million dollars in damage claims.

In the aftermath of this appalling calamity, the Ringling management displayed again the attitude and integrity that made their circus such an outstanding institution. They did not contest their indirect responsibility in the catastrophe; instead, they and the Hartford city officials set up a special court to hear and judge all claims. No contest, the circus said—we will pay the damages. In the annals of U.S. business and industry, there has never been such a display of moral obligation. Instead of folding the show, the management dragged the charred ruins back to Sarasota, where everyone pitched in to rehabilitate the circus.

After the fire, Mrs. Charley Ringling, grand trouper that she was, offered advice that was reminiscent of her husband and his brothers. She insisted the circus go back on the road immediately; not fold up and wait until next year. She counselled that if the show did not

go out now, it would never go out again. The big show did go back on the road.

Back at winterquarters everyone went to work—miracles of speed and ingenuity were performed. Everyone was paid full wages and within four weeks' time the circus was back in business, although without a tent, opening in the Rubber Bowl Stadium on Aug. 4th at Akron, Ohio. The rest of the season was played in the open, in coliseums, and stadiums. All rigging was hung from two lines of poles (10 in each line) and proved successful.

The following spring at the corporation board meeting, a resolution was passed to wit: that the directors enforce and adopt the sentiment expressed in an editorial appearing in the *Hartford Times* on April 9, 1945, as follows:

"They (the five circus officials who were sentenced for involuntary manslaughter) are in a sense the victims of circumstances and they may be sure they will be so regarded. No stigma will attach to their names as a result of their sentences."[2]

TOP: In 1941 at Atlanta the Ringling herd was grazing along the RR tracks where they had just unloaded. A poison sprayed on the grass killed 11 of the elephants.   (Time, Inc.))

THE MENAGERIE FIRE of 1942 in Cleveland, Ohio, leveled the tent causing the death of many animals and injury to countless others. Shown above is a singed camel standing in mute agony.   Below is a pitifully burned elephant—its hide burned to a crisp.
(Cleveland Press)

In 1954, ten years later, all newspapers carried a story that the Ringlings had paid off the last of over 600 claims that resulted from the fire. All of the circus profits for these ten years had been set aside to pay these claims.

Circus people felt particularly sad about the Hartford fire, as it was the first time that any tragedy to the circus had caused the loss of life to a patron. It didn't help their feelings any when on June 30, 1950, the news services carried the story that a pyromaniac had admitted to deliberately setting this fire, as he had many others in numerous states. An agonizing end, indeed, to a harrowing chapter in the Ringling story.

<hr />

[2] An important footnote to this fire story is the fact that the circus had tried unsuccessfully to obtain the necessary quantity of a new canvas flameproofing compound that was developed for the Armed Services. It was at that time pointed out by the Army that no civilian concern was allowed the use of the compound. However, Ringling Bros. Circus was granted the necessary priority to obtain their requirements in 1945 (the year following the fire) and all their canvases from then on have been so treated.

TRAGEDY TO WORKMEN AND HORSES is a muddy show lot. The endurance of man and beast is sorely tested.
Above is a 1938 lot—a dreary sight indeed. (Caterpillar Tractor Co.)

RIGHT—Niagara Falls, N. Y. muddy lot in 1917. Hitched to the heavy wagon is an eight-horse team of blacks. Hitched to the rings on the side of the wagon are two teams of grays—one a six, the other an eight. (These are called hook rope teams). The boss hostler in center (white shirt) encourages teams.
(Steve Albasing)

55

RINGLING BROS. AND BARNUM & BAILEY
COMBINED

□ THE WORLD'S LARGEST □
AMUSEMENT INSTITUTION

GENERAL OFFICES   WINTER QUARTERS
NO. 221 INSTITUTE PLACE   BRIDGEPORT, CONN.
CHICAGO, ILL.

                                    Bridgeport, Conn.,
                                    February 9, 1924.

Mr. Henry Moeller,
Baraboo, Wis.

Dear Mr. Moeller:-

          This will acknowledge your favor of
the 7th inst. with bill of lading attached and we thank you
for your trouble and the promptness of the shipment.

          Regarding the fire; it was quite a serious
thing. The building in which we had our paint shop, blacksmith
shop and Alfonso's shop was completely destroyed. This was a
two story brick structure and one of the largest we had. Besides
the shops there was a very large storage room on the first floor
and you know how circus equipment accumulates in storage and this
was no exception. Everything in this store room was lost and
our two automobiles, several cages, including three giraffe
wagons the "hip" den and the "rhino" cage and the red ticket
wagon. The ring curb wagon, two candy wagons and numerous
other pieces of equipment that we need for the opening, were lost.

          Regardless of this loss we are in excellent
shape have engaged a new building that was already equipped
for a blacksmith shop and another large building for our
paint shop so that we can go on with the repairs we have to
make. We have arranged with two large concerns in Brooklyn
and one of the large body building concerns in Bridgeport
to handle most of the new work so the show will not be delayed
a minute.

          Thanking you for your interest and with
kindest personal regards, I am,

                              Sincerely yours,

                              F. J. Wassell

     P. S. We lost most of our grand stand chairs and
a great part of our reserved seat plank and that is why we
wanted the stock we had in Baraboo shipped to Bridgeport.

LEFT — A letter written in 1924 describing the fire at Bridgeport winterquarters. Henry Moeller was in charge of the Ringling-owned, but abandoned, winterquarters in Baraboo, Wisconsin.
(Circus World Museum)

BELOW — In midseason 1938 tragedy struck the circus in the form of a strike. The show folded and returned to winterquarters. Some equipment and acts were then sent to augment the Ringling owned Al. G. Barnes & Sells-Floto Circus.
(C. P. Fox)

Start Every Day Right

The Hartford Courant

Weather Forecast
Fair, Continued Warm
Further Details on Page 13
Sun rises 5:33 a. m., sets 8:29 p. m.

ESTABLISHED 1764, VOL. (Daily Edition) CVIII   HARTFORD 1, CONN., FRIDAY MORNING, JULY 7, 1944.—22 PAGES   XXX   Member of the Associated Press   4c PER COPY

139 Die, More Than 225 Hurt In Circus Fire
Five Arrested On Manslaughter Charges
U.S. Troops Menace Heights Above La Haye

Closing Ring About Nazis' Anchor Point

Storm To Forest's Edge, Probably Still Hold Railroad Station In Northern Outskirts

Foe's Rear Areas Mauled From Air

Chartres, Argentan, Cerences Pummeled By Allied Planes; 3 Towns Liberated

Supreme Headquarters Allied Expeditionary Force, France, June 7...

U.S. Troops Go Ashore On Manim

Island Flanking Japs' Noemfoor Airdrome Is Captured Without Resistance

BY ASSOCIATED PRESS.

Advanced Allied Headquarters, New Guinea, Friday, July 7.—United States troops have occupied Manim...

Job Ceilings Lifted For Disaster Work

Employment ceilings for all persons needed to assist in work connected with the circus fire have been lifted, William G. Ennis, WMC Area Director announced Thursday.

Undertakers, cemeteries and morgue attendants may employ all hands declared, saying that the WMC office is terminating help. Anyone who needs assistance is asked to contact the WMC office.

Speaking for Mr. Ennis Assistant Director Arthur A. Nielsen said Thursday night that the WMC officials had received many calls asking permission to hire extra workers. The temporary lifting of employment ceilings applies only to those concerns aiding in relief work, he commented.

Flames Of Death Sweep Across Big Top Filled With Circus Crowd

While panic-stricken thousands fought their way from the blazing big top Thursday afternoon, a young amateur photographer caught this graphic picture of flames eating their way across the enormous canvas in a few all too brief moments. (c) Spencer Torell.

Panic And Blaze Trap Hundred

Relatives Seek Their Dead at State Armory; Hospitals Crowded; Cages Block Exit for Many as Flames Sweep Over Big Top in 10 Minutes; Many Ordered Back, Charge; Wide Inquiry Started, Inquest Set for Tuesday

One hundred and thirty-nine persons were killed and upwards of 225 injured within 10 minutes Thursday afternoon when fire, apparently starting from a carelessly discarded cigarette, swept through the big tent of the Ringling Brothers and Barnum and Bailey's Circus at the Barbour Street show grounds in the worst civilian disaster in Connecticut's history.

Thursday night, as the death list grew, every hospital in Hartford was crowded with the injured. The big State Armory on Broad Street was turned into a morgue. There the bodies of men, women and children, most of them burned beyond recognition, lay on canvas Army cots, covered with blankets.

As investigations into responsibility for the disaster were pressed by police officials, Prosecutor S. Burr Leikind of the Police Court announced the arrests, on charges of manslaughter, of four circus officials, Mr. Leikind said.

Known Dead

THE HARTFORD FIRE—Photo showing the big tent in flames—the press throughout the nation headlined the horrible tragedy. Aerial view of the big top after fire had leveled it.   (Hartford Courant)

Confesses He Set Circus Blaze That Killed 168

Columbus, Ohio—(AP)—Robert Dale Segee, 21, Circleville, Ohio, has signed statements admitting he set the Ringling Brothers circus fire in Hartford, Conn., that killed 168 persons and injured 412 others in 1944. Harry J. Callan, Ohio fire marshal, made the disclosure Friday.

Callan said that Segee also admitted setting between 25 and 30 major fires in Portland, Me., between 1939 and 1946, other fires in New Hampshire and Ohio, and that he is personally responsible for the slaying of four persons.

Callan said that all of Segee's statements had been carefully checked by his investigators since Segee was taken into custody last May 17 on the farm of a relative near East St. Louis, Ill.

A Pickaway county (Ohio) grand jury Friday indicted Segee on two charges of arson, stemming from fires in Circleville, Ohio.

Prepared Statement

Callan's prepared statement about the Hartford fire said:

"Segee was employed by the Ringling Brothers and Barnum & Bailey circus from June 30 to July 13, 1944. He joined the circus on June 30 at Portland, Me., and the day he joined the circus there was a fire on tent ropes that was extinguished without loss.

"The circus moved from Portland, Me., to Providence, R. I., and while there another small fire occurred on the tent flap, which again was extinguished without loss.

On July 6, 1944, at Hartford, Conn., the major fire occurred, which took the lives of 168 people. "A thorough and comprehensive investigation of the facts concerning Segee has disclosed, according to his own admission, that he is responsible for that and other major fires, places and dates of which were given."

Tells of Girl's Slaying

Callan said Segee said his first slaying was a 9 year old girl, beaten to death with a stone during a fit of anger. He identified the victim as Barbara Driscoll, 9, slain on a river bank at Portsmouth, N. H., Sept. 5, 1938.

Other victims, identified by Callan were:

A watchman who caught Segee setting a fire in a warehouse in Portland, Me., Mar. 16, 1943; a 12 year old boy, strangled to death on the beach at Cape Cottage, Me., in 1943 "to the best of his (Segee's) recollection," and a Japanese boy, killed in Japan in 1949 while Segee was in United States army of occupation.

The last three victims listed by Callan were not identified by name, but the fire marshal said all three were actual slayings as shown by his and army investigations.

ABOVE—The Akron Rubber Bowl Stadium, August 4. Less than a month after the great fire the circus had rehabilitated itself and finished out the season in ball parks and stadiums without its tent. (Wis. Hist. Soc.)

LEFT—This story was carried over the Associated Press wires on June 30, 1950. (Milwaukee Journal)

FAR RIGHT—All circuses jealously guard their ownership of titles. In 1938 the Ringling owned Al G. Barnes circus was combined with Sells-Floto Circus to keep both titles active. It did not mean a show twice as big as before. This lithograph has an added interest, as it had imprinted on it the title, "John Robinson Circus". 1938 was the year a labor strike caused the Ringling Circus to go back to winterquarters in midsummer. The main features of the Ringling Circus were sent to augment Barnes Sells-Floto. This litho shows how this fact was advertised. (C. P. Fox Collection)

Advertising

ADVERTISING is the heart of the circus. Designed to sell tickets, it pumps the blood of life into the great show. The Ringlings quickly became masters in the art of selling their wares to the public. They had to because their show was born when there were 50 or more big shows on the road, each offering stiff competition.

The Golden Age of circus advertising was from 1880 to 1910. Posters of today do not compare with the beautiful and colorful lithographs of that era, but for a very good reason. In the old days posters were made up for leisurely reading. Today, they are designed for fast moving traffic, hence, detail and handsome artwork have been, in the main, scrapped.

In 1907, just after the Ringlings had purchased the Barnum & Bailey Circus, they sent Ralph Peckham, their General Agent, to the Bridgeport winterquarters to investigate the situation in regard to billposters for the coming season. On December 15, the Ringlings wrote to Peckham as follows: . . .

"we will order from here (Baraboo) all contracts for contracting agents; in fact, everything for the advance of the Barnum Show, but we want your list of the brushes and handles—we will know what to order in that line. Concerning the paste cans, you must supply those. We have been using barrels with our show. They are cheaper and better.

. . . if any of the Ringling billposters write you, consult us concerning them before signing, as we had a considerable number of bad ones we let out for crooked tickets, etc., especially a Boston bunch, that we will not want to get on the cars of either show, as they are no good and will only cause trouble. In corresponding with your men, get them to give age, weight and height, as we do not want any fat men, they being no good for wagon routes—too big a load—other objections obvious; ditto, long skinny ones. This is for your information."

This letter is a typical example of the attention the Ringlings paid to detail in the operation of their circuses.

The privilege of hanging posters in stores, pasting on barns, or tacking on buildings is paid for by giving the property owner free tickets to the circus. A pair of tickets is the minimum, but the quantity of passes depends on the number of the posters put up. Passes are also given to the press, police, city officials, railroads, or anyone else (and hundreds show up), whom the circus feels can help them. The pass problem is one that haunts the circus at all times. In 1930 it became so serious that John Ringling wrote to Zack Terrell, who managed the Ringling owned Sells-Floto Circus:

"I want to call to your mind the plan you and I had when you were in Sarasota, of cutting the complimentary tickets down to something like a sane basis before we spoiled Chicago thereafter for the show business. We should hold the tickets down to the absolute minimum and not turn everybody loose with a pocketful of complimentaries in Chicago."

The Ringlings disseminated most of their advertising from an advance railroad car, which quietly and without any ballyhoo slipped into town, coupled to the rear of a passenger train. The circus owned its advance car and they wanted it to move from city to city in a passenger train, which it usually did. Occasionally, it was dispatched in a fast freight. After being spotted on a siding in the depot area, the crew inconspicuously spread out over the city, each man with his *hod* of paper. These innocent-looking bundles were soon to blazon out the news that the circus was coming to town. Overnight, it seemed, the city was plastered from one end to the other with colorful, gaudy posters, all dated with the day the circus would arrive—about two weeks hence.

In years past the Ringlings had two or three Advance Cars preceeding the circus. In 1892 they had four, all christened with fighting names, which was the tempo of the day:—

No. 1 Cannon Ball—A. G. Ringling, Mgr.
No. 2 Thunder Bird—Charles Ellis, Mgr.
No. 3 Battle Bolt—Tom Dailey, Mgr.
No. 4 War Eagle—Charles Walters, Mgr.

These were baggage cars, or coaches, converted to this special use. They were fitted out with bunks for the crew, storage space for posters, an office for the car manager, and a large boiler used to produce steam for cooking the paste. The circus, never one to miss a bet, advertised the show on the side of these cars. They were generally red, silver, or white, with large lettering trimmed in gold. Often colorful pictures of ferocious-looking animals adorned the sides of the car. By the 1940's the Ringlings had cut down to one Advance Car, but supplemented it with crews of men with station wagons. These crews covered all of the outlying areas and cities as far as 50 miles from the show town. In 1955 the railroad Advance Car was discontinued altogether.

In recent years the crews of the Advance Cars stayed in each town for as many days as the show was billed. Each man was given an important street to post and he started out with his hod of 120 posters and date sheets. He figured these were good for about 30 locations, unless he struck a big empty store with lots of window space. This kind of a display was called a *hit* and was a credit to the billposter if he could secure it. Eddie Jackson, a veteran of many years on the Ringling Advance, had a quiet and gentlemanly approach when he entered a store with an eye to hanging circus paper. "Can I give you two free tickets to Ringling Bros. and Barnum & Bailey for the privilege of putting some posters in your window?" Then with a twinkle in his eye, he addded, "we only have a *little* show, but I think you will enjoy it." Eddie was rarely turned down.

Circus advertising paper is measured in sheets. A sheet is 28" x 42". Posters range in size from half sheets to 24 sheets. The ordinary billboard takes a 16-sheet poster with an additional eight sheets for the date. Lithographs are profusely used. For years they have been considered the backbone of circus advertising. Frederick "Babe" Boudinot, a 40-year veteran of the Ringling Advance, said that in 1949 over 5,000,000 lithographs, handbills, and cards were used. To put these on sheds, fences, and buildings required 3,000 barrels of pastemaking flour, and 14,000 pounds of tacks. In 1915 it was estimated Ringlings used 10,000 lithos a day. The stand in Topeka, Kansas, in 1892, probably made some kind of a record, as 24,000 sheets were used.

By 1892 the Ringling boys were beginning to feel their oats as showmen. Were they not starting with their ninth season? Didn't they now have a 28-car railroad show? Such self-assurance called for a new title to advertise their circus. In 1887 they called their show *Ringling Bros. Big United Monster Show, Great Double Circus Royal European Menagerie, Museum, Caravan and Congress of Trained Wild Animals*. This title was not all encompassing, so in 1889 they used the sub-title, *World's Greatest Possible Show*. By 1891 they were using *Ringling Bros. World's Greatest Railroad Shows, Real Roman Hippodrome, 3-Ring Circus and Elevated Stages, Millionaire Menagerie, Museum and Aquarium and Spectacular Tournament, Production of Caesar's Triumphal Entry into Rome*. Probably, *The Greatest Show On Earth* sub title used by their giant competitor, Barnum and Bailey, rankled them; so it was that in 1892, the Ringling Bros. Circus became known as *The World's Greatest Show*.

With their new title the Ringlings felt that they had gathered the necessary prestige to challenge the Barnum & Bailey outfit in one of its strongholds. Milwaukee was picked as the site—and what a fight it was! In advertisements in the Milwaukee papers, James A. Bailey strained hard to scorn and ridicule the Ringling boys, but his vituperative attack made it obvious he knew he was in a tough fight. Barnum & Bailey billposters moved in and either tore down Ringling paper, or covered it over with their own—they plastered Milwaukee with "Wait for the Big Show." In one Barnum & Bailey ad during this fight these bitter words appeared:—

"Like a big boy who puts on his first pair of long pants and exclaims *I am a bigger man than my father,* so did this show crawl out of the mud of a wagon show career less than two years ago, buy some second-hand stuff that had been discarded as unfit for further use by the Barnum & Bailey and Forepaugh Shows, paint it up and emblazon their names where those of these great showmen had been, and then with arrogant assumption and under false colors, try to deceive their neighbors by announcing the *World's Greatest Shows* and copying almost verbatim the advertisements of the Barnum & Bailey greatest show on earth. Mr. James A. Bailey, the manager of the latter great exhibition, seeing deception and misrepresentation posted all over the dead walls of the city, stepped in and told the facts, and the indignant truth is now terrifying these conscience-stricken deceivers like forked lightning out of a tropical sky playing around a piratical craft."

It was a bitter battle, but Milwaukee didn't wait—they gave the Ringlings two straw houses, which, in circus parlance, means a full house.

The entire Ringling troupe developed a great feeling of confidence and almost smugness toward their huge adversary, James A. Bailey and his Barnum & Bailey Circus. Evidence of this attitude can be found in a poem that appeared in their 1895 route book:

HOW DO YOU LIKE US, JAMES?
(Lines to His Royal Highness, the "King of the Earth")

It's many a day, since last we met,
Guess you remember it, Jim,
In good old Dutch Milwaukee,
When you weren't in the swim,
We were not quite as big then,
But everybody knows
We wouldn't have been so mean
If you hadn't trampled on our toes.
Well, that little affair was settled.
And we recovered all our claims;
It was a kind of stunner,
How do you like us, James?

We never met you since that time,
Though we tried to pretty hard;
Perhaps you felt offended,
And didn't want to play in our yard.
But when we struck Chicago,
And packed 'em to the door,
Guess it made you feel uneasy;
Thought you'd tackle us no more.
So you met us in St. Louis,
And called us naughty names.
And we didn't do a thing to you.
How do you like us, James?

You had eyes on several towns,
In old Indiana State.
But we got in ahead of you
And told them all to "wait."
You wouldn't heed our warning, Jim,
Or mind what we would say;
Had the "Hoosiers" all their way.
And the five little boys from Baraboo
They came to see us, old and young,
And all did loudly claim—
That there was a bigger than the biggest;
How do you like us, James?

You couldn't fight us with the sword,
So you tried it with the pen,
And enlisted your newspaper friends
To roast us now and then.
But all is fair in war, Jim,
And when the war does come—
If you run short of powder,
Darn it, we'll lend you some.
If you get lonesome this winter, Jim,
And are fond of playing games,
Why, we'll give you two on checkers;
How do you like us, James?

In 1889, in a bold stroke, to needle their competitor, the sub-title, *Greatest Show On Earth* was appropriated and appeared on Ringling's route book. The great Barnum & Bailey aggregation had gone to Europe. Before he left, James A. Bailey fitted out his other circus, Forepaugh-Sells Bros. into the size and style of a show he felt sure would keep the upstart boys from Baraboo under control. The European tour was a fatal mistake. The Ringlings moved into the East anyway and captured the Barnum & Bailey territory, to never again relinquish domination of the American Circus scene.

The billing wars between the circuses increased in ferocity as the years rolled by. Rival brigades would cover and recover each other's paper. Fist fights between the advance crews of rival shows were common. If an advance man, calling at the express office to pick up his lithograph shipment, noticed a shipment for another show he would pose as the agent for the rival circus and ask that the posters be reshipped to a town miles away. Then he would send his assistant to the office to get his own paper.

Every yearly route book that reported such battles always ended the entry by claiming victory. Examples of this can be seen in the terse comments in the 1890 route book—
"opposition with the Wallace Show at Independence, Decorah, Muscatine, and Perry, Iowa. *Ringling Brothers absolutely victorious.*"

Or, in the 1891 route book—

"opposition with the Forepaugh Show at Rockford, Ill., Clinton, Iowa, Milwaukee, Oshkosh, and La Crosse, Wisconsin. Very creditable to Ringling Bros."

The billing wars got into such a heated state of affairs that in 1910 a truce was called. In Chicago's Palmer House the Showmen's Association was formed, with every circus owner of any importance there. One of the declarations of this historic conference was a promise not to "over bill any rival's paper."

Either the showmen could not control their advance agents or didn't care to, however, for the Secretary of the Showmen's Association, John M. Kelley (attorney for the Ringlings) began to receive distressing reports and complaints of covering over paper by rival shows. Within 60 days the situation was out of hand.

As the years went by, the viciousness seemed to disappear, although the competitive spirit remained. Now, in this quiet era of circus advertising, it is not uncommon to see lithographs from two different shows in the same store window, or on the same barn. There might be a few, "Wait" signs if two circuses are scheduled for the same town—mild tactics, mild, indeed.

Very early in their circus career, the Ringlings started to use their portraits on lithographs and couriers. Their pictures on their advertising, they reasoned, would instill confidence in their show. Their first such poster was made before John, Charles and Alf T. had grown mustaches. This was in the days when the circus was still a wagon show, traveling from town to town by horse power.

In 1911, Otto Ringling died—the first of the five circus owners to go. The practice of using their portraits was discontinued out of respect for him. It was not until 1933, their Golden Jubilee year, that a new poster appeared bearing their portraits. John Ringling was the only one of the brothers still living. In 1936 another portrait poster was printed on which appeared the faces of Bailey and Barnum, as well as the Ringlings.

In all their years, the Ringlings were never censured by press or public for their advertising or performance. No lithos, or ads, ever appeared that were not of a clean and wholesome nature. They never resorted to any promotional gags of an undignified or dubious nature. The feeling that this circus has engendered throughout America is best expressed by Mr. Herbert Hoover, former President of the United States—

"I have, for many years, admired the Ringling family for the high level of decency and unique entertainment at which they have held *The Greatest Show On Earth*."

CHARLE SMITH AND ROBERT DECKMAN are two old-timers. Their lithographs are pasted fast and square. (C. P. Fox)

BELOW—Eddie Jackson, a trouper of many years, posting a cafe window. (C. P. Fox)

TOP PHOTO is 1895 Car No. 2. Below it is illustrated an 86-foot long car that was added to the show in 1948. It has showers, washrooms, and berths for crew; also workbenches for folding lithos, and a large steam boiler for making paste (photos below right)).

(Wis. Hist. Soc. and C. P. Fox)

BELOW LEFT is the silver painted advance car moving to the next town in a fast passenger train. Circa. 1948.

(C. P. Fox)

Opening of the Biggest of all Big Shows!

FOR THE SEASON OF 1892.

Ringling Brother's World's Greatest Shows!

WILL POSITIVELY EXHIBIT IN

BARABOO, SATURDAY, April 30.

The Largest, Greatest and Most Complete Exhibition on Earth. The Superb of Years of Persistent Effort.

Re-Enforced by Untiring Enterprise and Unlimited Capital.

CÆSARS TRIUMPHAL ENTRY INTO ROME

Employing in its representation, hundreds of men, women and children, and delineating with remarkable fidelity, the life and people of the Roman empire when the mistress of the world, set high upon her seven hills, was at the Pinnacle of her glory.

A Princely Fortune Spent in Regal Wardrobe.

Roman Warriors in Glittering Armor, Actors Courting the Dramatic Muse; Senators, Patricians, Censors, Gladiators, Wrestlers, Jugglers, Charioteers, Dancers, Artisans, Musicians, Citizens, Slaves, Prisoners of War.

REAL ROMAN HIPPODROME!

3-Ring Circus, Elevated Stages, Mighty Millionaire Menagerie, Royal Aquarium, Mammoth Museum of Marvels, Far-Famed Horse Fair and Equine Congress, Embracing 350 of the Finest Blooded Horses in the World, together with the greatest Aggregation of

EUROPEAN AERIALISTS, GYMNASTS, ACROBATS, RIDERS and Arenic Specialists of Every Description, Ever Exhibited in this or any other country, Sumptuous and Unparalleled Production of the Resplendent Spectacle.

GLITTING GOLDEN CHARIOTS, MASSIVE TABLEAU CARS AND PRANCING WAR HORSES.

All Combining to form the most imposing picture of Classic Splendor Ever Conceived in the mind of man.

MORE HIGH-SALARIED PERFORMERS,

More Features, More People, More Animals, More and Bigger Elephants, and More New and hitherto unthought of Novelties than any two other shows. All Exhibited under the Largest tent Ever Constructed,

REED SISTERS! | VERNON BROS.,

Europe's Premier Equestriennes, secured at the Enormous salary of $800 per week. | Absolute Kings of the Air The highest salaried aerialists in the World.

MIKADO'S TROUPE OF ROYAL JAPANESE EQUILIBRISTS

Prince Chablean, the Percheron Beauty, sired in Normandy, weighing 1800 pounds, and the proud possessor of a mane full 9 feet in length; the Largest Living Hippopotamus, two mighty herds of Ponderous Performing and dancing Elephants

TREMENDOUS REVIVAL OF THE CIRCUS MAXIMUS!

Terrific Gladiatorial Combats, Absorbing Trials of Strength and Endurance. Grand Gala Day Sports and Spectacles.

A Page of Classic History set before the Modern World!

Jockey Races, with Ladies and Gentleman Riders; novel Elephant and Camel Races; child-delighting Pony Races with Monkey Riders, Laughable Donkey Races with Clown Drivers.

FREE DAILY PAGEANT OF SURPASSING SPLENDOR!

MAMMOTH Highway Locomotive Hercules! | MOSCOW'S Far Famed Cathedral Bells!

A Marvelous Mechanical Invention, moving through the streets with the ease of a Passenger Engine, and drawing one of the sections of the Colossal Parade. | A Reproduction of the Famous Chimes of the Kremlin Tower, the Music of which can be heard in melodious cadence a dozen miles away.

The Procession leaves the show grounds promptly at ten o'clock on the morning of exhibition. It is worth coming a hundred miles to see. It is over a mile in length. Ten of the thirty dens of performing wild beasts are exhibited free and open upon the streets; ten kinds of music make the air merry with sweet melody; long caravals of elephants and desert-born dromedaries bring the life of the orient to the doors of the occident; scores of sun bright chariots reflect the prismatic colors of the rainbow; hundreds of gaily caparisoned horses delight the eye. No postponement on account of weather. The procession moves, rain or shine.

TWO COMPLETE PERFORMANCES DAILY. AFTERNOON AT 2 NIGHT AT 8

DOORS OPEN ONE HOUR EARLIER.

ONE TICKET AT THE USUAL PRICE ADMITS TO ALL THE COMBINED SHOWS.

CHILDREN UNDER 12 YEARS HALF PRICE.

Special Excursion Rates on all Railroads.

$5,000 = $5,000

CHALLENGE

..They Must Come into the Open or take to the Woods.

Throwing Innuendoes From Ambush will no Longer be Tolerated -- They Must Now "Fish or Cut Bait."

RINGLING BROS.

ARE DETERMINED TO FORCE THEM INTO THE OPEN FOR A FAIR FIGHT AND NO FAVORS. IT MAY BE HARD ON PRETENDERS, BUT IT IS JUSTICE. TRUTH AND CANDOR DEMAND THAT THE INSTITUTION SEEKING TO RAISE ITSELF IN PUBLIC ESTIMATION BY CLAIMING TO BE A COMBINATION OF TWO SHOWS AND A RIVAL OF THE RINGLING BROTHERS, MUST BE EXPOSED.

The preposterous buffoonery of a pretended challenge of $1,000 that it is the largest show coming to Texas this year is now answered by the Ringling Brothers in terms unmistakable, backed by facts and made indisputable by the deposit of a $5,000 Forfeit. This means business. They cannot now escape. It is not a contest of words, but a question of cold facts. Not a controversy between empty titles and high-sounding phrases, but figures that cannot lie. Not a combination of names, but of resources. These points must be settled and settled right.

They claim to be "more than double the size of any other show coming to Texas this year," that they have two big menageries, two big circuses, two big hippodromes, two biggest parades and the old time worn dodge of claiming a multi-millionaire confederation of two colossal, consolidated, grand, greatest, glimmering, glittering, glammering aggregated aggregations.

Now what do sensible people gather from this bluff and bluster? Positively nothing.

Now what does the $5,000 deposited by Ringling Brothers mean to sensible people? Everything!

Ringling Brothers, having determined to ascertain the truth or falsity of the statements made by the pretended double show, and to forever settle the question of supremacy, caused to be made and attested under oath on this date, Thursday, September 17th, 1896, an exact inventory of the circus property of the alleged combine of two shows, and also that of Ringling Brothers' World's Greatest Shows, and having ascertained the absolute facts regarding the size of the several shows coming to Texas this year, the Ringling Brothers have this day deposited in the City National Bank, of Dallas, Texas, the sum of $5,000, as attested by this receipt:

> ### Office of City National Bank.
> **DALLAS, TEX., Sept. 17th, 1896.**
> This is to certify that RINGLING BROTHERS have this day deposited with this bank Five Thousand Dollars (5,000.00) in Cash.
> (Signed) E. O. TENISON, Cashier.

DALLAS, TEXAS, SEPTEMBER 17, 1896.

The above sum of $5,000 will be donated by Ringling Bros. to any charitable institution in the state of Texas, provided that the Ringling Bros., have not on this date more Horses, Cars and Cages of Animals than any other show, or alleged combination of two shows, coming to Texas this year, provided that any other show, or alleged combination of two shows, shall make a deposit of $5,000, the same to be donated to any charitable institution in the state of Texas, provided THEY have on this date less Horses, Cars and Cages of Animals than the Ringling Bros.; said $5,000 to be deposited with the above bank and receipted for under exactly the same conditions as set forth in this document, and to be deposited and publicly announced at least three days prior to Ringling Bros.' date in Dallas in order that the public may have time to know the result of the contest before the date of either show.

[SIGNED] RINGLING BROTHERS.

This Test Must and Shall be Open and Above Board, Let the Lightning Strike Where It Will.

Now, as the Ringling Brothers clearly demonstrate, by their $5,000 Challenge, that they have more cars, more cages, more horses, ponies, elephants and camels, more circus performers in rings, aerial spaces and stages than any other show coming to Texas this year, how can a combination of two shows be carried on a less number of cars than the Ringling Bros., require to carry what is only claimed to be one show?

How can two Menageries be housed in a less number of cages than are required by the Ringling Brothers for what is only advertised as one menagerie?

How can two Shows be conveyed from the cars to the ground and back by a less number of horses than the Ringling Brothers require to haul what is advertised as one show?

How can two circus performances be given by a less number of performers than are engaged in presenting what the Ringling Brothers advertise as one circus?

By what sort of magic or hocus-pocus are these things done?

A TIMELY CAUTION TO THE PUBLIC.

Beware of false announcements in regard to Ringling Brothers' date. An effort will be made by means of an ambiguously worded circular to deceive you into the belief that Ringling Brothers' World's Greatest Shows will not exhibit in Fort Worth on their advertised date. Do not believe any such false and misleading announcements RINGLING BROTHERS NEVER CHANGE THEIR ROUTE OR DATE. DESPITE ALL STATEMENTS TO THE CONTRARY, THE GRANDEST, THE BEST, THE MOST POPULAR AND BEYOND ALL COMPARISON THE BIGGEST OF ALL BIG SHOWS WILL EXHIBIT IN

THIS 1892 AD featured the mammoth highway locomotive "Hercules". It was a huge steam engine built by J. I. Case Co.
(H. H. Conley, Collection)

AN 1896 "RAT" SHEET issued during a red hot fight with the Forepaugh-Sells Bros. Circus in Texas. When two circuses moved into the same territory at the same time the billing wars resulting became vicious and uncompromising, as attested by this flyer.
(H. H. Conley Collection)

ABOVE is a "hit" which in circus parlance means a "big splash of advertising". This shed at Baraboo is 40 miles from the show town of Madison, Wisconsin.

(C. P. Fox)

RIGHT is a biller report for 1923 showing 7,578 sheets had been posted in two days in Detroit.

(Wis. Hist. Soc.)

BELOW ON LEFT is an 1896 poster with an amazing modern flair; a poster specially printed for San Francisco's Chinatown residents; and on right a fine "hit" of cloth banners tacked to the frame building.

(Wis. Hist. Soc. and C. P. Fox)

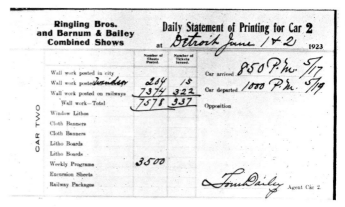

Ringling Bros. and Barnum & Bailey Combined Shows	Daily Statement of Printing for Car **2** at Detroit June 1 & 2, 1923		
		Number of Sheets Posted.	Number of Tickets Issued.
Wall work posted in city			
Wall work posted *Junction*		204	15
Wall work posted on railways		7374	322
Wall work—Total		7578	337
Window Lithos			
Cloth Banners			
Cloth Banners			
Litho Boards			
Litho Boards			
Weekly Programs		3500	
Excursion Sheets			
Railway Packages			

Car arrived 850 P.m. 5/17
Car departed 1000 P.m. 5/19
Opposition

Tom Daily Agent Car 2.

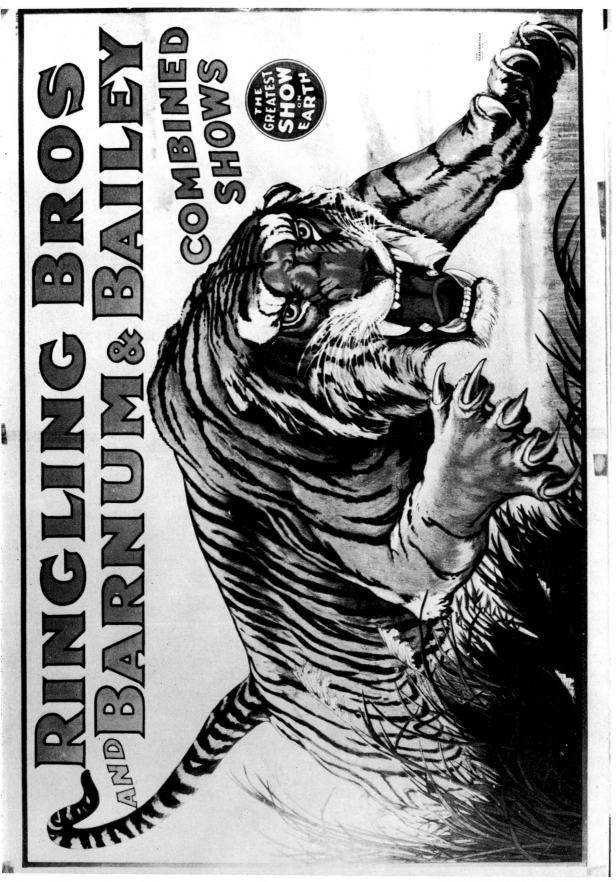

ONE OF THE MOST FAMOUS CIRCUS POSTERS of all time. The Strobridge Lithograph Co. paid the great animal artist, Charles Livingston Bull, $1,500 to paint this sensational tiger—Circa 1915.　　(C. P. Fox Col.)

AN 1892 ADVERTISEMENT from the "Milwaukee Sentinel" of the Barnum & Bailey Circus that was trying to get people to wait for their show. No holds were barred in these vicious billing wars.
(Milwaukee Public Library)

PORTRAIT POSTERS were used to instill public confidence in the show. Above is the 1905 litho. The practice was discontinued in 1911 when Otto Ringling died. It was not resumed until 1933. (Strobridge Litho Co.)

LEFT: these banners in South Bend said "Wait", meaning people should not waste their money on the smaller Cole Bros. Circus coming earlier in July of 1949. (Otto Scheiman)

ABOVE: A 1945 billing stand. As compared to the rough billing wars of earlier days, this was almost a gentlemanly procedure where the Arthur Bros. Circus was not overposted. (C. P. Fox)

RIGHT is a 1936 version with P. T. Barnum & James A. Bailey added.

CIRCUS LETTERHEADS over the years have been flashy and fascinating. Below 1894 era minces no words in proclaiming the size and scope of the circus. Left is an exciting one from 1892 done in gold and black. (George Weber Collection)

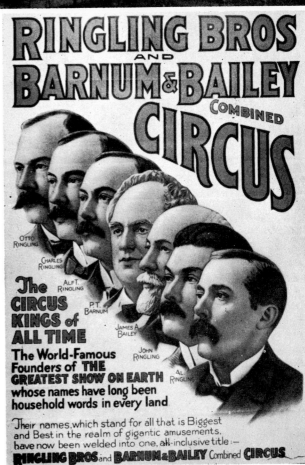

THE

Only Big Show

Coming to Waterford this year.

Next Wednesday, Sept. 23d,

RINGLING BROTHERS'

Great -:- Double -:- Show

AND MUSEUM OF LIVING WONDERS !

The Largest and Best 25 Cent Show on Earth, Containing all of the Prominent Features of the Amusement World.

50 New and Startling Features 50

3 —GREAT -:- CLOWNS— 3

3 HOURS OF SOLID FUN ! 3

Amoor the Largest Baboon Living.

The Largest Snakes ever placed on exhibition.

DON'T FAIL TO SEE

THE GRAND FREE FLIGHT TO THE CLOUDS

Which takes place every day at 1 P. M. Don't fail to see this marvelous trip. Remember, this is Free to all. Also remember the Ringling Bros. always fulfill every promise made. So be sure and look for this great Free Show, and remember the Street Parade takes place, rain or shine.

FUN FOR THE LITTLE FOLKS

HEAR OUR SUPERB ORCHESTRA

Wait for it ! Watch for it !

Don't fail to witness it. Why? Because it fills its bills to the letter, and gives better satisfaction than any other tent show on wheels and the price of

ADMISSION IS ONLY 25 CENTS !

Remember, Two Performances each day at 1 and 7 P. M.

NEWSPAPER advertisements were always an important means of publicizing the circus. The Ringlings learned early how to do it. Here is an 1885 ad. The largest snake mentioned, exhibited by Mrs. Al Ringling and the "Grand Free Flight to the Clouds" are both illustrated in the Wagon Show Chapter.

C. P. Fox Collection)

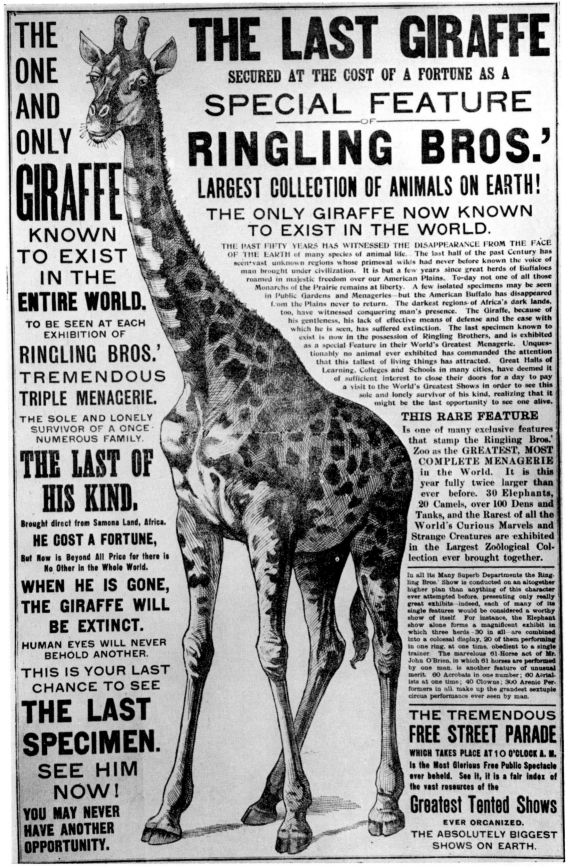

THE ONE AND ONLY GIRAFFE

KNOWN TO EXIST IN THE ENTIRE WORLD.

TO BE SEEN AT EACH EXHIBITION OF

RINGLING BROS.' TREMENDOUS TRIPLE MENAGERIE.

THE SOLE AND LONELY SURVIVOR OF A ONCE NUMEROUS FAMILY.

THE LAST OF HIS KIND.

Brought direct from Samona Land, Africa.

HE COST A FORTUNE,

But Now is Beyond All Price for there is No Other in the Whole World.

WHEN HE IS GONE, THE GIRAFFE WILL BE EXTINCT.

HUMAN EYES WILL NEVER BEHOLD ANOTHER.

THIS IS YOUR LAST CHANCE TO SEE

THE LAST SPECIMEN.

SEE HIM NOW!

YOU MAY NEVER HAVE ANOTHER OPPORTUNITY.

THE LAST GIRAFFE

SECURED AT THE COST OF A FORTUNE AS A

SPECIAL FEATURE

OF

RINGLING BROS.'

LARGEST COLLECTION OF ANIMALS ON EARTH!

THE ONLY GIRAFFE NOW KNOWN TO EXIST IN THE WORLD.

THE PAST FIFTY YEARS HAS WITNESSED THE DISAPPEARANCE FROM THE FACE OF THE EARTH of many species of animal life. The last half of the past Century has seen vast unknown regions whose primeval wilds had never before known the voice of man brought under civilization. It is but a few years since great herds of Buffaloes roamed in majestic freedom over our American Plains. To-day not one of all those Monarchs of the Prairie remains at liberty. A few isolated specimens may be seen in Public Gardens and Menageries—but the American Buffalo has disappeared from the Plains never to return. The darkest regions of Africa's dark lands, too, have witnessed conquering man's presence. The Giraffe, because of his gentleness, his lack of effective means of defense and the ease with which he is seen, has suffered extinction. The last specimen known to exist is now in the possession of Ringling Brothers, and is exhibited as a special Feature in their World's Greatest Menagerie. Unquestionably no animal ever exhibited has commanded the attention that this tallest of living things has attracted. Great Halls of Learning, Colleges and Schools in many cities, have deemed it of sufficient interest to close their doors for a day to pay a visit to the World's Greatest Shows in order to see this sole and lonely survivor of his kind, realizing that it might be the last opportunity to see one alive.

THIS RARE FEATURE

Is one of many exclusive features that stamp the Ringling Bros.' Zoo as the GREATEST, MOST COMPLETE MENAGERIE in the World. It is this year fully twice larger than ever before. 30 Elephants, 20 Camels, over 100 Dens and Tanks, and the Rarest of all the World's Curious Marvels and Strange Creatures are exhibited in the Largest Zoölogical Collection ever brought together.

In all its Many Superb Departments the Ringling Bros.' Show is conducted on an altogether higher plan than anything of this character ever attempted before, presenting only really great exhibits—indeed, each of many of its single features would be considered a worthy show of itself. For instance, the Elephant show alone forms a magnificent exhibit in which three herds—30 in all—are combined into a colossal display, 20 of them performing in one ring, at one time, obedient to a single trainer. The marvelous 61-Horse act of Mr. John O'Brien, in which 61 horses are performed by one man, is another feature of unusual merit. 60 Acrobats in one number; 60 Aerialists at one time; 40 Clowns; 300 Arenic Performers in all, make up the grandest sextuple circus performance ever seen by man.

THE TREMENDOUS FREE STREET PARADE

WHICH TAKES PLACE AT 10 O'CLOCK A. M. Is the Most Glorious Free Public Spectacle ever beheld. See it, it is a fair index of the vast resources of the

Greatest Tented Shows

EVER ORGANIZED. THE ABSOLUTELY BIGGEST SHOWS ON EARTH.

SURELY THE PRESS AGENT had tongue in his cheek when he wrote this giraffe copy in 1895. It is symbolic of the claims in the war of words between the big circuses. (Wis. Hist. Soc.)

THE GREATEST SHOW ON EARTH

THE TRAINS MORE THAN ONE AND ONE THIRD MILES LONG LOADED WITH TEN THOUSAND WONDERS FROM EVERY LAND

LITHOGRAPH ABOVE of the 1920 era did much to excite the imagination and bring people to the ticket wagons.
(C. P. Fox Collection)

BELOW—LOADING the trains at Sarasota winterquarters. Two polers guide wagons up the runs. When the Ringling Circus traveled by rail, 30 or more railroads were traversed in this yearly operation, covering 12,000 to 17,000 miles. For the rental of their locomotives, train crews, and use of their tracks, Ringling Bros. paid the railroads over one-half million dollars annually, in recent years. In a typical move from Chicago to Milwaukee—90 miles—the circus was charged $2,500.
(Caterpillar Tractor Co.)

Circus Trains

In the spring of 1890, on May 3rd, the *Ringling Bros. World's Greatest Shows* played Baraboo, their home town. That night the circus was loaded onto 16 railroad cars (plus two advertising cars) and entrained for Dodgeville, Wisconsin. This move was their first by rail and inaugurated for the Ringlings, a great advance over the plodding wagon show of their first six years.

From that year forward the number of railroad cars increased year by year, as the circus increased in size, until the climax—108 double-length cars of the 1947 season, the largest railroad circus in the history of any circus in the world.

And so the Ringlings quickly grew up. They now had a big railroad circus that could stand up to any competition in the country. The circus moved by rail, so it could cover more territory, play the larger cities, and put out a bigger and better show. The circus owns all its own railroad cars which are of four types.

The advance cars preceded the circus and their crews handled all the advertising. The circus train proper is made up of stock cars that carry elephants, horses, zebras, camels, etc.; flat cars that carry all the wagons, trucks, tractors, and lastly, the coaches for the personnel. The cars are all extra long—70 to 72 feet—for convenience in loading. For example, a 72-foot car will usually take four wagons; while a standard railroad flat would only hold two wagons. Then, too, rail rates are based on car miles; the rates being the same for long cars as for short ones.

The movement of the Ringling Circus over the rails of America meant a tremendous business to the railroads. In 1949, for example, the Great Show moved its 267 wagons, cages, trucks, tractors, dozens of elephants, hundreds of horses, and 1,450 employees on four trains. Section one, when fully loaded, weighed 1,350 tons; Section two, 2,100 tons; Section three, 1,950 tons, and Section four, 1,450 tons. This was a total of 6,850 tons of circus hauled on 89 double length cars, the equivalent of a 178-car freight train. The thought that taxes credulity is that this gigantic load of equipment was moved, not just into one city, but into 100 cities all across the continent—and at each

BEFORE THE ERA of trucks and tractors, horses pulled the wagons across the flat cars. When a wagon reached the runs a stout rope was hooked to a heavy ring on rear of wagon. This rope was then encircled around snubbers, shown above, and as a wagon rolled down the ramps a man slowly released the rope. He controlled the speed of the massive wagons as they rolled down to the ground level.

(Atwell—Milw. Jour.-Wis. Hist. Soc.

BIKES AND BOYS, cars and kids of all ages help to add to the excitement of watching the circus trains unload in the early morning of show day.
(Credit Caterpillar Tractor Co.)

stand was unloaded, tents put up, and two complete performances given; then the tents taken down and everything loaded back on the railroad cars.

In any given season (in circus language the word *season* is used instead of *year*) there were always a number of interesting statistics involving a railroad circus. In 1946, for instance, the circus travelled 12,443 rail miles. There were 218 exhibition days in 107 cities. The show visited 25 states. The longest run was 394 miles from New Orleans to Memphis. The shortest run was 10 miles from one side of Detroit to the other. To make the 10-mile jump the circus was loaded onto the trains just as for the 394-mile move.

As with every phase of the Ringling Circus, the loading and unloading of the trains was done with meticulous planning and carried out with precise efficiency. It was not chance that loaded the wagons on half the cars with poles to caboose and the other half with poles to engine on a given night. The twenty-four hour man wired very specific instructions back to the trainmaster as to how to load the trains so the wagons and trucks would all be faced properly for efficient unloading the next morning.

When the first section rolled into town, it was spotted for unloading. The razorbacks pulled the ramps from under the end wagon and set them in place. These ramps are called *runs* and thus the spot where the trains were unloaded, to all circus people, were known as *the runs.* Other men were removing the wedge-shaped blocks from under the wheels of the wagons and unhooking safety chains. Still others were putting steel plates over the gaps between cars so the wagons could be pulled from one car to another until they reached the runs. In years gone by, horses, or sometimes elephants, pulled the wagons across the flat cars. When they reached the runs a snubbing rope was fastened to a ring on the back of the wagon to ease it down the ramp slowly. In recent years trucks, or tractors, did this job.

Loading of the trains was the reverse of unloading. It was not haphazard, as each railroad car was just so long and would take only a certain combination of wagons. Wagons can vary in length from a 12-foot stake driver to the 40-foot wagon that carried the 62-foot big top poles.

Most of the circus trains personnel cars had showers and hot water; all had porters who made up the beds and kept the cars immaculate. One car had very short berths for the large array of midgets, and, of course, there was a special berth for the fat lady and one for the tall man. One car, for single girls, had a car mother to look after the girls; another was for family groups; still another for single men. The working crew had their own cars with a bunk for every man, no matter how lowly his task on the show. The coaches were all numbered, but were also named for either states or cities. As one walked down the line of red trimmed silver coaches the names—Atlanta, Evanston, St. Louis, San Antonio, Los Angeles, Wisconsin, New York, Connecticut, etc., were seen.

In the early days of the circus, when Mrs. Al Ringling still traveled with the show, she took a very personal and deep interest in all employees. Every morning before she went to the lot she would methodically walk through all the coaches to see if there were some employee lying sick in his bunk. If so, she would arrange for a doctor to come in and see to it that the man got the proper care. In 1936 the show added the *Florence Nightingale* to the train. This was hospital car No. 99 and added great comfort to the circus people, but was kept in the show train only one year, although 1949 brought another innovation—a laundry car that was equipped to do dry cleaning.

Of course, the circus owners had their own private cars. In 1921 both Charles and John Ringling had cars connected to the circus train. These cars had a cook, valet, and secretary who stayed with the car whether either of the Ringlings were with the circus or not. These men, with their vast enterprises, left the show frequently, sometimes for a day, a week, or even a month, but whenever they appeared on the lot their cars were waiting for them. John Ringling's car was the *Jomar.* The name was derived by taking the first two letters of his name and combining them with the first two letters of his wife Mabel's name and adding the "R" for Ringling. This was one of the largest and most richly appointed private cars ever built—its reputed cost, $100,000. It contained a living room in natural wood furnishings, a row of staterooms, full sized bathroom, show, dining room, kitchen, and quarters for the chef and butler.

And, thus, with speed, dispatch, comfort and elegance did the *Greatest Show On Earth* move across America by rail.

ABOVE IS A VIEW of the second section in the mid '40's, as it rolled through the countryside in the early morning. Below is the "Flying Squadron", as the first section is called, as it stopped briefly at 2 A. M. enroute to the next show town.

(C. P. Fox)

ABOVE IS A 1905 TRAIN about to leave Baraboo in the Spring. Note lead bars, side poles, eveners and other paraphernalia hanging on the side of the heavily loaded wagons. (Leonard Roser)

BELOW—BY THE 1950's all the wagons were equipped with pneumatic tires. Seen here is the unloading at Madison, Wis. Equipment moves down ramps called "runs." (C. P. Fox)

ABOVE is the massive pole wagon with its 65-foot long load. It moves slowly over the flat cars for its next show in Milwaukee. Below—in the late 30's and early 40's the circus used its elephants to do much of the work formerly done by horses. Note man at pole of wagon guiding it over the flats. Note also the steel plates forming a bridge from one car to another.

(C. P. Fox)

HORSES, ELEPHANTS, CAMELS, and zebras are hauled in special stock cars. Shown above and below left is the unloading process.

(C. P. Fox)

BELOW—IN 1947 Ringlings purchased 25 surplus hospital cars from the U. S. Government and rebuilt them into comfortable living quarters for the crew and performers.

(C. P. Fox)

BELOW RIGHT—LOADING is the reverse of unloading. Here in this 1916 view a team pulls a tarpaulin covered parade wagon up onto the flat cars.

(Steve Albasing)

Street Parade

One of the most glorious and delightful aspects of the circus is now gone forever. In its heyday the parades purpose was to advertise the shows presence in town and stir up excitement, interest, and enthusiasm in the people. And this it did—for no other advertising medium ever devised so played upon the three key senses of man. For the eye there were the gigantic gold leafed bandwagons pulled by 10-horse teams; scores of beautifully appointed ladies riding on sleek well-groomed horses; colorful zebras; clowns riding donkey carts; haughty camels, and plodding elephants bedecked in gorgeous red velvet robes covered with sparkling spangles; glorious wood-carved tableaus representing far away countries; open cages and dens of wild animals, colorful birds and reptiles from all over the world. For the ear there were many bands high up on wagons and playing stirring circus music; there were bell wagons, organs, and the shrieking. puffing, blowing steam calliope. Then there were special sounds that could only be heard in a circus parade . . . the deep-throated knock of the heavy wheels caused by the slight lateral motion of the wheel when it hit the axle housing; the soft shuffling sound as dozens of elephants slid their sandpaper-like feet on the pavement; the clopping of 40 shod hooves as a ten-horse hitch passed by; the rattle of chains on the eveners; the sudden roar of a tiger or lion. Then, too, the parade imparted to the nose very special odors that added a thrilling touch of reality to the whole spectacular pageant — a fantastic array of wild animals, each with its own peculiar jungle scent drifting out from the cage; the individual exotic aroma of the camels, not quite like a horse; and the dense, penetrating odor of the elephants.

So, as the parade passed, the hordes of people lining the main street on the morning of show day were properly put into a holiday frame of mind. It was the kind of advertising that reached right into a persons heart and created a yearning to see the show.

As the Ringling Circus grew, so did the street parade, as it was generally understood in those days that the size and scope of any good show could be determined by the size and scope of its parade. The 1912 street procession was typical of these pageants—herewith is the exact parade order for that season which was seen by hundreds of thousands of people in 145 cities in 26 states from Wisconsin to Mississippi, and from New York to Oklahoma. In addition, in this year Ringling's played 11 cities in Quebec and Ontario.

RINGLING BROS. PARADE ORDER SEASON 1912

Buggy	2 horses
John Agee, Parade Marshall	
4 Lady Buglers (Mounted)	4 "
2 Men Buglers (Mounted)	2 "
6 Ladies (Mounted)	6 "
6 Men (Mounted)	6 "
Bandwagon No. 1	10 "
15 men in band	
Cage No. 51	4 "
" No. 52	4 "
" No. 38	4 "
" No. 46	4 "
" No. 45	4 "
" No. 40	4 "
Cinderella Nursery Float	8 Ponies
Forepaugh Tableaux Wagon No. 4	8 Horses
Ticket Sellers Band 8 Mouth pieces	
1 Bass Drum	
1 Snare Drum	
Round Mirror Tableaux Wagon No. 30	4 Horses
8 Ladies Riding on wagon	
with fantastic uniforms	(Covered)
Zebra Float—2 persons in float	4 Zebras
Egypt float—2 camel men drivers	16 Camels
2 camel men assistants	
Queen on float	
Santa Claus Nursery Float	8 Ponies
Cage No. 41	4 Horses
Cage No. 37	4 Horses
Cage No. 49	4 Horses
Roman Chariot	4 Horses
Roman Chariot	4 Horses
Forepaugh Tableaux Wagon	6 Horses
8 Ballet girls - Fantastic costumes	
Lion Tableaux Wagon	6 Horses
12 piece side show band	
Forepaugh Rhino Den No. 27	8 Horses
Cage No. 20—5 Japanese riding on same	4 Horses
Cage No. 63	6 Horses
Hippopotamus Den No. 42	8 Horses
Old Woman in Shoe Nursery Float	8 Ponies
18 Mounted Women	18 Horses
Forepaugh Tableaux Wagon No. 3	6 Horses
Clown Band - 9 Pieces	
Tableaux Wagon No. 5	6 Horses
5 ladies riding on same	
Persia Float Queen riding in float	4 Horses
	(Covered)
Russia Tableaux - 4 girls riding same	8 Horses
United States Tableaux	8 Horses

Goddess of Liberty and 10 girls riding on same
Spanish Float - Queen and 2 pages riding same .... 8 Ponies
Cage No. 66 .... 4 Horses
Cage No. 43 .... 4 Horses
Cage No. 44 .... 6 Horses
German Tableaux Wagon .... 8 Horses
    Band out of concert band
    10 mouth pieces and 2 drums
27 Mounted Men .... 27 Horses
Open Den No. 35 .... 4 Horses
Open Den No. 50 .... 6 Horses
Open Den No. 36 .... 6 Horses
Open Den No. 47 .... 6 Horses
Open Den No. 65 .... 6 Horses
Open Den No. 76 .... 4 Horses
Open Den No. 71 .... 4 Horses
Open Den No. 29 .... 6 Horses
28 Elephants—Elephant Men Attendants
Tableaux Wagon No. 4 .... 6 Horses
    5 elephant hunters riding same
Great Britain Tableaux Wagon .... 8 Horses
    10 ballet girls riding same
Calliope—Mr. Gifford, Player .... 8 Horses

Officers of Parade

R. Diller	Denny Curtis
John Dudley	Geo. Law
Jack Foley	Frank Doyle
Geo. Denman	

Some of the more splendid parade wagons had beautiful allegorical wood carvings mounted on them. These carvings were fastened to platforms which, in turn, could be lowered down into the body of the wagon when not in the parade. Such wagons were cumbersome and highly impractical for they could not be used to haul any circus paraphernalia as the carvings took up the cavernous interior. They were parade pieces only. Typical of this style of vehicle was the gigantic "St. George & the Dragon" Wagon. It was over 11 feet high (not counting St. George), and approximately 20 feet long. Its name was derived from the glorious life-size carvings that were built onto a platform on top of the wagon. These carvings showed St. George on his white charger running his spear into a writhing dragon. The carvings were so enormous that in many towns it was necessary to have men with long poles riding the wagon to raise overhead trolley wires and telephone lines.

The Ringlings purchased the St. George Wagon from Adam Forepaugh in 1890. When they received it they had the carvings removed and the top of the wagon fitted out with seats for musicians. This then became their No. 1 Bandwagon in the parade. The huge interior of the wagon, no longer needed for St. George, was put to good use hauling elephant trappings. St. George, his horse and dragon were relegated to a cart and became a float in the parade pulled by zebras, donkeys, or in some years, ponies.

Henry Moeller of the Moeller Wagon Company in Baraboo, Wisconsin, said that when the Ringlings were beginning to "feel their oats" they ordered three of

these elevator-type parade wagons. The platform rode up and down on four corner posts or tracks and was pulled up by means of a hand winch. Henry admitted, with a sharp twinkle in his eye, that "all three wagons weren't worth a tinker's dam and at the end of the season Charley Ringling ordered me to rebuild them into regular baggage wagons." Moeller pointed out that "if the wagons were setting level the elevator worked all right, but if one wheel was down in soft ground, or if the wagon was spotted on a slope, everything was thrown out of whack and then they had a *helluva time* to operate the mechanism. Plenty of cussing went on, I guess."

All the beautiful woodcarving on the sides of the parade wagons was gold leafed, never painted. The gold leaf was truly gold, rolled out to a tissue-thin sheet. It was sold in small books, three and a half inches square, with 25 sheets to the book. Around the turn of the century a book cost approximately 75 cents. There were special tools for applying this delicate leaf, among them a *gold knife,* a *tip,* and a *cushion.* George W. Langdon, who worked for the Moeller Bros, Wagon Company in Baraboo, found the job of applying the leaf to the Ringling wagons so tedious that he invented a small device to do the job. He called it a gilding machine.

Each of the carved gold-leafed wagons had a canvas cover lined with *hush cloth.* This was kept on the wagon at all times, except when out in parade, to protect the beautiful vehicle from the elements.

The calliope, or steam piano, always brought up the rear of any circus parade. The calliope (pronounced by all circus people as cal-e-ope to rhyme with canteloupe, Webster notwithstanding) is made up of a series of various toned whistles mounted in two parallel rows on pipes through which steam passes. When a valve below the whistle is released, steam shoots through it to give the calliope its brazen voice. A series of wires run from the release valves to a keyboard.

Thus, when the operator played a tune on the keys, he was releasing steam under different whistles. The music resulting was shrill and blaring, but even more stirring than the skirl of bagpipes, and it carried for a mile or two—against the wind.

The Ringlings had a large 32-whistle steam calliope. A huge upright coal-burning boiler to generate the steam was tended by a fireman all through the parade. They also had an air calliope which operated on the same principle as the steam unit but was a much smaller instrument. It was mounted in a cute little wagon, usually pulled by ponies. A compressor, powered by a gasoline motor, provided the air to play the instrument.

A wonderful anecdote about Al Ringling and the importance he attached to the steam calliope is told by his former chauffeur, Earl Schilling. During the season of 1913, while touring the south, the boiler flues in the calliope burned out. To Al a circus parade without a steam calliope was a catastrophe of great magnitude and he showed his disgust when he looked impatiently at the silent instrument.

Schilling, who prided himself on being able to fix any piece of machinery, told Al he could re-flue the boiler. Al nervously stomped his cane and said, "You can? Earl, get anything you want—spare no expense, but get that boiler fixed." With that Earl went over to the calliope to size up the situation. From the nameplate on the boiler he got the address of the manufacturer in Louisville. He sent a telegram ordering a new set of flues and special tools to enable him to do the job. When the flues arrived by express it took Schilling two days to finish the job. Then he ordered the boiler fired up. When it had a good head of steam and black smoke pouring from the stack, he told the calliope player to send the strains of *Beautiful Ohio* out across the showgrounds. Earl related that at about the third toot of the whistle, the door of the white ticket wagon flew open and Al, with his coat tails flying, came across the lot. He was all smiles. "That music, that black smoke, wonderful—wonderful," said Al. Then he told Earl to send the Louisville boiler company an extra $100 to cover the loan of their tools. "If they are good enough to loan us the tools, we want to pay for their use—it's worth it," Al commented. When Earl got his next pay check there was an extra $200 with a note saying, "for fixing the calliope."

The Ringling Circus paraded until 1920, at which time it succumbed to progress. As early as 10 years before there had been much agitation among showmen to discontinue the street parade. Ben Wallace considered it an absolute waste of time and money and a useless and unnecessary drain on men, animals, and equipment. He so wrote to the Ringling brothers, trying to get them to agree to discontinue the parade. He would if they would, Wallace said—but his campaign was premature. The Barnum & Bailey circus had eliminated their parade one year, but quickly reinstated it the next season when business fell off and the hue and cry of the public demanded it.

By the twenties, however, the Ringlings had no choice, as traffic problems in downtown areas were becoming critical and a slow-moving parade didn't help the situation. Cities were paving streets with asphalt and the heavy, steel-tired wagons rutted the pavement on hot summer days; thus, parade license fees went up as complications increased. Then, too, with cities fast growing populations, show grounds convenient to the center of town were disappearing in a welter of houses, forcing the circus to use lots in the outlying districts.

Thus, the parade route became so long (10 miles in some instances) that it was impractical to get the parade downtown and back in time for the afternoon performance. Today, these free and fabulous parades of the Ringling Circus are but a glorious memory.

Modern progress, alas, has brought nothing to equal those magnificent pageants of the past.

GLORIOUSLY WOOD CARVED side panels from an animal den. Made in about 1870 for Sells Bros. Circus, they were subsequently on the Forepaugh-Sells Bros. Circus when the Ringlings bought this circus and shipped it to Baraboo.

(C. P. Fox)

TOP LEFT—typical, highly decorated, but comparatively small, bandwagon of 1890 era.

(Circus World Museum)

TOP RIGHT—"United States" bandwagon built in 1903 by Bode Co. of Cincinnati, along with the "Russia" wagon, above left, and "Great Britain" wagon, above right. (Circus Hall of Fame)

THE SNAKE DEN had glass sides and a lady snake charmer sat inside during parade. Note serpentine theme is carried out on wood carving decorations. (Bob Parkinson Col.)

THE "TWO HEMISPHERE" BANDWAGON is one of the largest ever built—27 feet long. (Ed Hillhouse Col.)

ABOVE is an eight-horse hitch pulling in parade the beautiful gold and white wood carved "Great Britain" band-wagon. Note the four lines in each hand of the driver leading down to each of the red-plumed Percherons
(Harry Simpson Collection)

THE PARADE was once described thusly: — "Triumphal march and pageant, a mighty millionaire's eye-feast, a dazzling river of silver and gold, a processional amazement walling all the highways with humanity—a mile of gleam, gold, glint and glistening glamor". A study of the faces of the children in this classic photo (taken by Harry Atwell) seems to prove the above description was surely true. Some can't take their eyes off the wagon that just rolled by; others are already looking at the next in line.
(Atwell-Milw. Jour.-Wis. Hist. Soc.)

SHOWN ABOVE is one of the dozens of parade features, the beautifully robed camels and dromedaries and below, of course, a full complement of gorgeously costumed ladies, on sleek, well-groomed horses.

(Harry Simpson and Wis. Hist. Soc.)

LEFT—rather than paint decorative designs on wagon
sides, the circus, in the parade era, resorted to beautiful
wood carved scrolls, figures of children, animals, etc.,
as shown. These wood carvings were generally covered
with gold leaf.   (C. P. Fox)

A MOUNTED BAND

Originality, progress and continual advancement are the watchwords of the Messrs. Ringling Brothers. What other shows have done for years they want nothing to do with. Old-fashioned street parades, with a coterie of unshaven circus attaches arrayed in weather-beaten uniforms of divers hues, such as everyone expects to see in a circus parade, are conspicuously absent in their pageant. There is not a wide-mouthed clown driving a diminutive donkey in their parade. There are not a dozen women, arrayed in faded silk habits of once brilliant hues, riding thick-necked work-horses. There are not any of the score or more of antiquated features, old as the hills and tiresome to the eyes of everyone, in the spectacular street carnival afforded by the Ringling Brothers' World's Great Shows. There is, however, a series of absolute innovations, beginning at the very head of the great parade and covering everything in it, over its mile and three-quarters of length.

And, to start with—just to mention one feature that speaks volumes for itself—the circus band, comprising forty musicians, will be found mounted upon matched white horses, full caparisoned in the richest of habiliments. The members of the band are uniformed in the full dress of United States artillerymen. Their accoutrements are all correct, even to the waving red plumes on their helmets. And, best of all, this band is not merely for display but it is a musical organization of the very highest order of merit.

Prof. Ganweiler, formerly band director in the Second United States Cavalry, which has the only mounted band in this country except the one now with the Ringling Brothers' Shows, is a director of a lifetime experience, and accredited with being one of the best arrangers and leaders in the country, as well as a cornet virtuoso ranking with the very best. He has also perfected his mounted band, that even though they ride horses that cannot be supposed to walk in step, much less keep time, their music is so perfectly rendered that a marching body of troops would be able to keep perfect measure with it.

It is an odd and brilliant spectacle. Leading the band, come two orderlies, each bearing guidons, all correct and according to military demands. Following these are a group of military, wearing the latest uniform of the Kaiser's Body Guard, of Prussia. After them come members of the band playing lively airs and latest popular marches, their horses in columns of twos or fours and every man and horse in correct military position. The bass drummer was the only member of the band who had any difficulty. The heavy thud of his drumstick upon the drum, which is almost over the horse's head, made the animal restless, but as the days went on he got more and more used to it, and by the time the summer was half spent a cannon wouldn't startle him.

There was not a little fun at Tattersall's in Chicago last April when the mounted band began rehearsals. They stood the horns all right, but at the first thump of the big brass drum, the horse jumped out from under his rider like a shot. It is said that the drummer hit the ground in perfect time with the measure of the music, but it cannot now be proven. The mounted band, however, is a reality and a most satisfactory feature of a parade that has created a positive sensation in every city in which it has been seen.

GEORGE GANWEILER, MUSICAL DIRECTOR.

THE MOUNTED BAND rode bareback. The saddle blankets were red velvet with gold ribbing sewn on for flash.

(Bob Parkinson Col.)

THE "BELL WAGON" is one of the most unique and beautiful parade wagons ever built. Tunes on its nine huge bronze bells were played by pulling spring-primed levers that had wires connected to the various clappers. (See photo below). The bells were cast in Milwaukee by the Campbell Foundries in 1892. The Milwaukee Ornamental Woodcarving Co. fashioned the glorious carvings and the Moeller Bros. of Baraboo built the wagon. (C. P. Fox)

THE LONG LINE of ponderous pachyderms, shuffling down the main street was in itself a sight to draw thousands of townspeople to the parade. Elephants were taught to "tail-trunk" to keep them in a straight line; also, to keep their curious trunks out of trouble. (See left).

(Atwell-Milw. Jour.-Wis. Hist. Soc. and C. P. Fox)

THE SHRIEKING, blaring, wonderful and glorious sounding steam calliope brought up the rear of all parades. The "steam piano" could be heard for miles. That was its mission—to attract attention.

(G. Herbert Whitney)

Canvas City

Alf. T. Ringling very aptly described the big top as the main circus tent is called:—"In the principle of its construction every large tent is what is called a round top; and if it is oblong when erected, sections which are known as middle pieces have been laced in between the two half circles composing the round top." The 1892 top could thus be described as a 180 foot round top with four 50-foot middle sections or 380 feet long.

The big top has varied in size from year to year. As a result, the seating capacity also changed. In the Ringling's first year the tent was 45 feet wide and 90 feet long. In 1955 the tent had grown to 206 feet by 386 feet. While conditions and sizes of the tent varied from year to year, the big top generally seated 8,000 to 10,000 people.

In 1893, their tenth season, the total canvas used lined up like this:

Big Top - 180' x 430'
Menagerie Top - 90' x 330'   Dining Tents - 70' x 140'
Dressing Room Tent   Wardrobe Tent -
            70' x 100'   40' round
Side Show Tent -   Harness & Repair Tent -
            90' x 130'   40' round
7 Horse Tents -   Blacksmith Shop Tent -
      Each 40' x 70'   40' round

Before erecting the big tents, three important factors had to be considered in deciding on the lot to be rented. Namely, size, substance, and the location of the lot. This decision was made as a result of careful preliminary planning.

Size — the big show needed 10 acres of land to fit comfortably, but could be squeezed onto a smaller lot in an emergency. It wasn't only the area of ground the tents would cover that had to be considered; there must be room for the movement of trucks, tractors, spotting of dozens of vehicles, movement of horses, elephants and performers. Then, too, was the ground level? The circus couldn't put on a show on a hillside.

Substance — the contract agent next considered the condition of the lot. If it was sandy, would the tent stakes hold? If it had some soft spots, would the trucks and wagons bog down? If it was a filled-in dump,

were there pieces of glass, scrap metal and wire that would endanger the show's personnel and stock? While the lot looked fine and firm today, what would its condition be after a sudden cloudburst? These questions had to be answered in a favorable way for the circus before the lot would be rented.

Location — the third factor was as important as the first two. Was it too many miles from the rail sidings where the show was to unload? Was water readily available? Were surrounding streets too congested and narrow to allow access to the gigantic circus equipment? Was there adequate parking space for patrons? Was the lot convenient to bus and street car lines?

It wasn't the easiest of tasks to find a 10-acre lot that would meet all these specifications. Many American cities were by-passed because of the lack of proper show grounds. To forestall such catastrophes, some cities today are purchasing a vacant lot and setting it aside as a circus ground. LaCrosse, Wisconsin, did just this in 1955. When Ringlings played there in early August of that year, the city fathers dedicated the lot.

Otto Ringling realized that the lot problem would one day be a serious one. He, alone of the five brothers wanted to purchase a vacant lot in each of the major Ringling show towns, so the circus would always be assured of a place to set up. Henry Ringling North said his Uncle Otto's thought was that as time passed all circus lots would gradually be swallowed up by the ever growing communities, which is precisely what happened. Had the big show followed Otto's suggestion, it is interesting to speculate on the value of such holdings in this day and age.

The day before the circus arrived in town the 24-hour man checked over the lot. It was his duty to tend to all final details. He would wire back to the boss canvasman on the show "good lot—firm." This meant the lot was dry and would hold stakes. If the lot had a pothole or two, at vulnerable spots in relation to the tent layout, he arranged for a few loads of cinders to be hauled in. The 24-hour man arranged with the police department for the route the circus trucks and wagons would take from unloading point to lot. This route was mapped out to avoid congested areas, steep hills, and streets with questionable bridges. Nothing was left to chance.

On circus day, the Flying Squadron (the first section) arrived in town early. The boss canvasman and his crew proceeded to the show grounds immediately upon arrival to lay out the lot. This consisted of locating every pole, stake, and piece of canvas. The center poles (62 feet long) were located first — they were t h e spine of the big tent. Iron pins tied with white ribbons were driven into the ground at the exact spots where the poles would stand. Then, with tape measure, a line was marked off at right angles to the line of center poles. The ends of these lines were equal distances from the center poles. This, then, became the stake line and blue-tagged iron pegs marked out the locations for the stake driving crew. Iron pegs with red ribbons marked the spots where the main pole guy wires were staked out.

In years past, one of the most intriguing sights in watching the circus tents being erected was the sledge gangs driving stakes. This operation was described in the 1895 route book:

"Sledge gangs work with the precision of automations, one sledge stroke following that of the next by a fraction of a second, all the sledges constantly swinging and yet it seldom happens that one is caught by its successor. A remarkable performance, when it is considered that the strokes come with a rapidity that sounds like a stick scraped along a picket fence. In a very short space of time a forest of iron bound stakes rear their heads in every direction."

This method of driving stakes eventually gave way completely to mechanical drivers. The removal of stakes from the ground is done by a hydraulically operated beam on the rear of a tractor. The beam, to which a chain is fastened, is lowered over the stake. The chain is looped around the stake and the beam is then raised, pulling the stake from the ground. This operation is faster than the old two-wheeled, hand-operated stake pullers.

Once the five-foot-long stakes were driven, approximately three feet in the ground, and the main poles were up and guyed out, the crew laid the quarter poles on the ground in their correct locations. The quarter poles encircled the center poles in two lines. Some 20 poles 47 feet long formed an inner circle and 34 poles 37 feet long fromed an outer circle. The hippodrome track was outlined between the two rows of quarter poles. The sidewall poles were then spotted. More than 100 of them, each 17 feet long, held up the outer edge of the canvas.

The tent, in the form of huge bales of canvas, was unloaded from trucks and the canvas sections laid on the ground, unrolled, and laced together into one gigantic piece. The sidewall poles were thrust into sockets around the edge of the canvas and pushed into a vertical position. The big tent then resembled a huge saucer. By winch power on a jeep, the canvas was slowly raised or pulled up the main poles. When the canvas reached approximately the halfway point, the quarter poles were partly positioned; were permanently positioned after the huge canvas reached the top of the main poles.

BELOW are "bull stakes" and "bull rope". These stakes, located at each end of the tent, are anchors for the main poles. Right is view of tent stakes. Note iron band around top to keep stake from splitting.
(C. P. Fox)

JIMMY WHALEN was Ringling's boss canvasman for over 25 years. See photo above of Whalen at work laying out the lot in Fort Collins, Colo—1916.
(Steve Albasing)

"Heave it—weave it—shake it—take it—break it—make it. Move along." Such was the chant of the gang boss who directed the tightening of the guy ropes around the tent. He chanted in a rhythm timed to coordinate a concerted pull on the rope by 12 or 15 husky crew members. With each pull on the rope a bit of slack was taken up. On the last intonation, *"make it,"* the half hitch on the stake was shoved down on the stake as far as it would go. When this crew had encircled the tent and taken up the slack on some 600 guy ropes the boss canvasman knew his big top was secure.

Ringlings used 60 to 70 miles of rope on the great show when it was under canvas. There was tent rope for raising and holding the tents, bolt rope for edging canvas, general purpose rope for tackle, yacht manila, or hemp ropes where softness and extreme smoothness were required for trapeze use, etc. In the tent itself, 75,000 yards of canvas was used, with the big top being replaced every year. The roof was a strong blue twill, while the sidewalls were a tightly woven white drill. The canvas was the finest available and was all made flame-resistant by a special process approved by the National Board of Fire Underwriters. When dry, the big top weighed 20 tons, but after a few days of rain it weighed three and one-half times as much, which added tremendously to the complications of moving the big show.

The Ringlings have tried many innovations with their tents. In 1939 they started using the blue canvas top. This enabled them to more effectively use spot lights and other lighting arrangements, as the blue canvas darkened the interior during the afternoon performance. It was also this year that the first serious consideration was given to air conditioning the big

top. The show carried three flat cars of special wagons and a crew of 50 men to handle this equipment. These wagons were spotted around the big top at intervals. From each came huge canvas ducts that were laid on top of the tent, the ends opening directly above the patrons. Through these ducts blew cool air which came from ice-filled compartments in the special wagons. It was advertised that the tent was kept 20 per cent cooler, but the innovation lasted only a few years, as the expense far outweighed the results.

BELOW is the letter Otto Ringling wrote to Whalen hiring him away from another show. (Wis. Hist. Soc.)

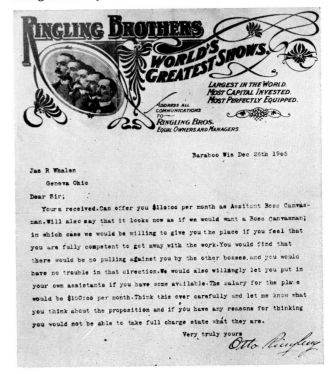

EIGHT MEN around this stake, each with a heavy sledge hammer, make quick work of driving it into the ground. The sledges whack the stake with the precision and rapidity of a boy running a stick along a picket fence. (Atwell-Milw. Jour. Wis. Hist. Soc.)

AT LEFT is a mechanical stake driver that outmoded the fascinating scene above. Below is old-time method of pulling stakes now done hydraulically.

(C. P. Fox and Wis. Hist. Soc.)

RINGLING BROS. AND BARNUM & BAILEY
COMBINED
THE WORLD'S LARGEST AMUSEMENT INSTITUTION

GENERAL OFFICES
10 221 INSTITUTE PLACE
CHICAGO, ILL.

WINTER QUARTERS
BRIDGEPORT, CONN.

SARASOTA, FLORIDA, Jan. 1, 1924.

Cousin Henry:

   I have your long letter of December 22d.
Very glad to get it. I let Fred Warrell worry along
about his canvas loader for this season. I remember too
our stake-driver troubles, and that it took about nine years
to perfect a stake-driver. If it takes nine years to
perfect this canvas loader, I will not be standing on the
lot to see it work. So let's forget it and go fishing.

   We are opening up a bank here--The Ringling
Trust and Savings Bank-- on Saturday. Expect to lend a
lot of money and lose a little; if we make some we will
be happy.

   I am sorry you couldn't find the little
pictures of the Ringling brothers that we were talking
about. Please don't send those you have; keep them, and if
ever I want them I will come up some night and take them away
from you.

   Glad to know the auto truck is all in order.
Maybe we can use it for a fishing trip some time next summer.
Also glad to hear you have had fine weather.

   Hope your health will keep good and that you will
not work any more than is good for you.

   With regards, I am

    Yours truly,

     Chas Ringling

Mr. Henry Moeller,
Baraboo, Wisconsin.

THE LOT has been laid out. The stake drivers are banging away—top left. Top right, the poles have been pulled erect and guyed out. The canvas bales have been unrolled and laced together. The side wall poles are being pushed up into position. 2nd row left—the canvas is being slowly pulled up the main poles. The quarter poles are pulled into position. 2nd row right—taut and firm the tent is up ready to accept the seats, rings, and props. (C. P. Fox)

ON RIGHT is a letter Chas. Ringling wrote to Henry Moeller in regard to a mechanical stake driver. It sheds interesting light on Mr. Ringling's philosophy.
        (Wis. Hist. Soc.)

BELOW—purchase order for a season's canvas requirements. A new big top was used each year.
(Wellington Sears Co.)

THE TENT is up, the flags are flying, the show is on.
(RB&BB)

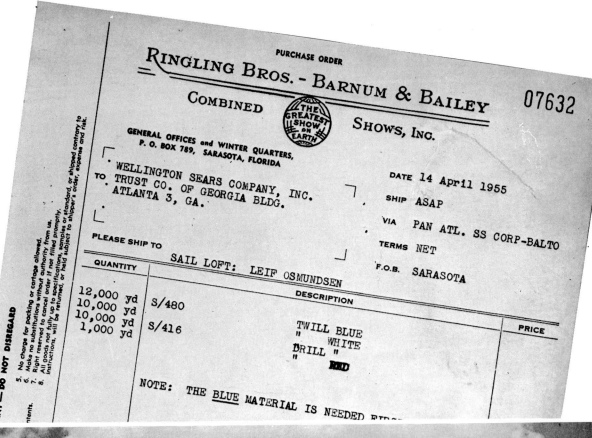

PURCHASE ORDER

RINGLING BROS. - BARNUM & BAILEY

COMBINED SHOWS, INC.

07632

GENERAL OFFICES and WINTER QUARTERS,
P. O. BOX 789, SARASOTA, FLORIDA

TO
WELLINGTON SEARS COMPANY, INC.
TRUST CO. OF GEORGIA BLDG.
ATLANTA 3, GA.

DATE 14 April 1955

SHIP ASAP

VIA PAN ATL. SS CORP-BALTO

TERMS NET

F.O.B. SARASOTA

PLEASE SHIP TO
SAIL LOFT: LEIF OSMUNDSEN

QUANTITY		DESCRIPTION	PRICE
12,000 yd	S/480		
10,000 yd		TWILL BLUE	
10,000 yd		" WHITE	
1,000 yd	S/416	DRILL "	
		" RED	

NOTE: THE BLUE MATERIAL IS NEEDED FIRST

(vertical text, left margin)
'ANT — DO NOT DISREGARD
5. No charge for packing or cartage allowed.
6. Make no substitutions without authority from us.
7. Right reserved to cancel order if not filled promptly.
8. All goods not fully up to specification, samples or standard, or shipped contrary to instructions, will be returned, or held subject to shipper's order, expense and risk.

BEFORE THE DAYS of tractor power, the first pole up received an assist from dozens of men—above. Horses or elephants supplied the power to raise pole. (Atwell-Milw. Jour. Wis. Hist. Soc.)

"HEAVE IT—weave it—shake it—take it—break it—make it. Move along". Such is the chant of the boss man who directs the tightening of guy ropes around the tent.—(below right.) (C. P. Fox)

BELOW LEFT—Interior view of partially raised tent. The quarter poles will be finally set in place after canvas reaches the top of main poles. (G. Herbert Whitney)

ABOVE is photo of Ringling lot in 1890 at Whitewater, Wis., the first year as a railroad show. Note only three main poles and one row of quarter poles.

(Oliver Maxon Salisbury.)

OPPOSITE PAGE—Ringling's immense, sprawling circus lot. From left is the sideshow tent with its banner-line facing the crowds. Next is the menagerie tent, then the main tent. To its right are dressing room tents and a tent for performing horses. At right is the cookhouse.

(RB&BB)

BELOW—Tent filled to capacity—the hippodrome track is seen between the two rows of quarter poles. The circus had a six-pole top in this era—the 1940's.

(RB&BB)

Circus People

"Hey, Humpy," called a man standing in the door of the horse barn at winterquarters. At that exact moment Al Ringling emerged from the elephant barn next door. He heard the salutation and turned red with anger. Mr. Al was extremely sensitive about his slightly rounded shoulders, and the thought of being addressed as "humpy" was too much to bear. He strode up to the guilty man and furiously exclaimed, "Did you call me that? Did you call me Humpy?" excitedly stomping his cane.

"Oh, no, Mr. Al, I wouldn't do that. I was calling the camel man—everybody calls him humpy." With that explanation the incident passed as Mr. Al well knew that it was a rare circus man who was not called by a nickname; and most camel men were *big humpy, little humpy, big-nose humpy,* or some other such descriptive name.

Nicknames were hung on a man as a result of some incident, physical defect, nationality, or perhaps, another circus he had worked for. Steve Albasing, who came to the Ringlings from 101 Wild West Ranch, for example, was forever after known as "101 Heck". These names were never resented and once given, always stuck. Peanut Nose Bob; Step and a half; Deafy Denman; Broken Jaw Smitty; Smiley; Goofy John; Paddlefoot Dick—all related to physical peculiarities. The circus owner was referred to as The Governor; the legal adjuster as The Patch. All harness makers were Waxy. There were countless Blackies; Whiteys; Shortys; Frenchies; Baldys; Reds—each with another descriptive name to identify them; such as Rattlesnake Red; Baraboo Red; Pony Red; or Low-down Red. Although the reasons for some of these names are lost, they will go on and on as one of the fascinating aspects of circus lore. Among other particularly choice names are Side Wall Fatty, Quack Quack, Silk Sock Shorty, Buggy Stump, Stud Horse Slim, Pie Car, Haywire Gaffe, Pinwheel, Apples Welch, and Kid Glove Kingston.

The most priceless nickname of all was reserved for a huge, hulking individual with a broken nose and a few missing teeth. Some circus wit, with the ability to perceive the ludicrous, dubbed him Precious.

The Ringlings over the years established their show

as *the* circus to work for. Judging from the number of years most of the key men were on the show, it is obvious that there was a pride of association with the Big One, as the Ringling show is known. This loyalty, plus the deep knowledge of circus problems, learned by moving the tented giant under any and all conditions, has pulled the circus through some of its most trying times.[1] These and dozens of others are and were the backbone of the circus. They advertised it, moved it into town, put it up, supervised the performance, and then took it down—rain or shine—mud or sand—cold or intense heat, the show went on as scheduled.

Mrs. Henry Ringling, Sr. related:

"I recall my husband discussing various workman and the problems of getting good loyal and steady men. If a bum came on the show for a job, he was scrutinized carefully and if the decision was made to give him a job, he was given so much to do that he had no time to get into trouble. This early trial period was followed by giving the man added responsibility until his capacity was reached. The Ringlings then decided they had a good man for the ultimate job that the workman in question had earned for himself." Mrs. Ringling further stated that, "it was always the policy to give their men three good square meals a day as they always felt fine after a good meal. I can recall many conversations between the Ringling brothers and always a man's character was brought up, as they tried hard to make something out of every man. They themselves always worked hard, never had time for play or relaxation; thus, expected the same from their men. I don't ever recall any of the Ringlings ever laying off a man because he got too old to travel. These old timers were always put on odd jobs at winterquarters."

---

[1] Here are a few veteran Ringling men, past and present:—Bill Yeske, wagon maker; Jim Whalen, canvasman; Dave Blanchfield, truck supt.; Geo. Denman, elephant boss; Dexter Fellows and Bev Kelley, press; John M. Kelley, General Counsel; Fred Bradna, equestrian director; Pat Valdo, performance director; Herbert Duval, legal adjuster; Merle Evans, bandmaster; Capt. Bill Curtis, boss canvasman; Babe Boudinot, advance; Frank Braden, press; George Werner, boss canvasman; George Blood, Supt. cookhouse; John Snellen, canvas; Spencer Alexander, Supt. Baggage stock; Leonard Aylesworth, canvas.

Al Ringling had such a deep appreciation for loyalty that in his will he remembered five old reliable hands. He bequeathed a sum of money to seven nieces and nephews; his share of the Ringling Circus, Forepaugh-Sells Bros. Circus and the Barnum & Bailey Circus to his brothers Alf. T., Chas., John, and Henry. But the will also bequeathed the sum of $5,000 to James R. Whalen, boss canvasman; $5,000 to Chas. Rooney, boss hostler; $5,000 to John Agee, equestrian director; $10,000 to Tom Buckley, circus treasurer; $3,000 to Chas. Smith, boss animal man.

The workmen always referred to the Ringlings respectfully as "Mr. Charley," or "Mr. Otto." In return the brothers had a reputation of never being crude or gruff in the issuance of orders to their men. Al Ringling's diplomacy in handling men (except when he thought he was called "Humpy") is well illustrated with the following story. The time was around 1913. The show had a Buick used in the spec, but also used by one of the superintendents for emergency errands. Mr. Al was being driven downtown in his own car this particular day when he suddenly spotted the circus's Buick in front of a saloon. He drove around the block, came back and parked next to the Buick. Even though Al was not a drinking man he went into the saloon where three familiar voices came loudly from the back room. Al stepped up to the bar and ordered a drink for everyone in the place, including the three in the back room.

When the bartender returned he said the boys wanted to know who bought them the drink. Mr. Al said, "Tell them it was their boss," and he headed for the door to go out. The barkeep was a bit bewildered and said, "Oh, no sir, those boys back there are circus men," and to which Al replied, "Yes, I know." The tavern keeper's jaw dropped as he said, "Are you Mr. Ringling" "Yes," said Al, "now go and give the boys the answer to their question," and with that left the saloon. The spec Buick was never used for that purpose again.

Wages on the Ringling circus are paid as in any industry—according to a man's ability and responsibility; thus, his value to the show. In recent years, the bosses of various departments such as canvas, trucks and cookhouse might get as high as $500, or $600 per month. Bosses of the less important departments would receive $300 to $450 per month. From these top figures, the wages range downward to $35 and $50 per week, for truck and tractor drivers.

In addition to these general wages, all workmen get three square meals a day, plus sleeping quarters and the protection of workmen's compensation. Star performers may get as high as $500 per week, but they really must be outstanding to command this wage.

ABOVE—Three great stars of 1900 season
(Library of Congress)

BELOW—Bird Millman (1920); one of the all-time great tight wire artists. (Wis. Hist. Soc.)

SHOWN HERE are a representative few from the army of R i n g l i n g e m p l o y e e s who have served many years with the Big One (as the Ringling Circus is known to all show people). Top row — David Blanchfield, Supt. of trucks; Leonard Aylesworth, Supt. of Canvas; John Sabo, Supt. of Menagerie; second row— F r a n k B r a d e n, Press Agent; Al Butler, General Agent; George B l o o d, Supt. of Dining Dept. Third row: Willie Carr, 24-hour man; G e o r g e Smith, General Manager. (Robt. Good & RB&BB)

IN THE 1901 ROUTE BOOK there appeared the following caption for the pictures shown below:
"There are 40 women with Ringling Bros. Circus. Each is mistress of the art which gives distinction to physical culture. An outdoor life pleasantly spent under sunny skies among flowers and trees, even though the cause to work, gives them an advantage of health, which tends to make a moral, as well as a physical type. The grace of form and coloring of beauty which go hand in hand with correct training are to be found in the well-bred circus woman in their finest expression. Indulgence of the table and postponed hours of sleep are not for her. The laws of health are sensitively adhered to by the woman who achieves success in this work. An artist of agility or equilibrium must have a steady nerve and head, as well as strong and supple muscles. Hygienic living is essential. That she should be admired for physical grace and beauty as well as athletic skill and daring is, therefore, simple reading, and but the plain logic of natural laws. A life nurtured under such wholesome influences for bodily well being cannot fail to benefit in its higher nature. No better illustration of this fact could be presented than the portraits here given of some of those who gave lustre and importance to the performance of Ringling Bros. Circus the season just closed. Anyone who reads, even as he runs, must discern in these facial types not only beauty of feature, but something of sweetness of nature which lent so much to the harmony and personal pride that distinguished the circle of performers with Ringling Bros. during 1901."

Madam Bonnie

Miss Julia Lowanda

Mlle. Regine

Miss Nettle Carroll

Miss Theol

Madam O'Brien

Miss Ida Niaco

Miss Pearl Forepaugh

Miss Stella Lovenberg

Miss Grace Jenks

Madam Feeley

Ringling Bros Circus - Season 1890

ABOVE is a group of performers, season 1890.
(Wis. Hist. Soc.)

AT LEFT is Lil Kerslake with his trained pigs. He was one of Ringling's most productive clowns.
(W. H. Woodcock Collection)

RIGHT—May Wirth, great Australian bareback rider —circa 1916. (Steve Albasing.)

From this figure, the scale drops down to a minimum of $50.00 per week, paid the ballet girls. A few outstanding big name clowns may get as high as $250 per week, but most range from $75 to $175. The production clowns, those with fancy props, gags and acts are, of course, the better paid. The musicians average $100 per week. Performers, too, get meals and accommodations, which may range from an upper berth to a stateroom. With space on circus Pullmans at a premium, the struggle for better accommodations can only be determined by the importance of the act to the circus.

The performers (called Spangle Pratts by the workmen) are responsible for the show that is put on within the big top, and to the general public this *is* the circus. So much has been written about these stars, who vie with the heavens in quantity and brilliance, that this phase of the great Ringling circus will, admittedly, be glossed over. However, here are some interesting aspects of the daily life of the people who inhabited the canvas city.

The star performers in years gone by used baggage wagons as dressing rooms; while everyone else used the dressing room tent. This tent was divided into two sections—one for the men; the other for the ladies. With the advent of the large mechanically folding seat wagons, the dressing rooms were all located under the seats of the big top. Each performer, or group, was assigned to a specific wagon, or the large area between the wagons. The dressing room tent was used for the spec costumes. The wardrobe wagons were drawn directly into this tent. With space at a premium, each performer was allotted, at the beginning of the season, a specific number of trunks for his props, rigging or costumes.

The question of who was the greatest of all circus stars always brings forth deep discussions. Old-time circus men like Fred Bradna and Merle Evans said, without hesitation, that it was Lillian Leitzel, the aerialist; others argue for May Wirth, the Australian bareback rider; or Clyde Beatty and Alfred Court with their wild animal acts. Maybe the bareback troupes like Cristianis or the Hanneford family are the greatest. Still others prefer the Wallendas, high wire specialists; or tight-wire artists like Bird Millman, Nio Niatto, or Con Colleano; or Flying Trapeze artist Alfredo Condona. The question is academic—to the children watching the circus, *every* performer, year after year is great, astounding and stupendous.

Lizzie Rooney was the star bareback rider of the Ringling show at the turn of the century. While recalling her years under the canvas, she always referred to the *ladies* of the circus, never the *girls*. "On the Ringling show they were very strict. Women were

not allowed on the show unless they were ladies. After breaking the rules for a second time, no further warning was given. The girl just found her trunk left on the lot and she was through," said Lizzie.

ABOVE—Lizzie Rooney, dainty and talented bareback rider of the early 1900's.   (Wis. Hist. Soc.)

BELOW—Mabel Stark, one of the greatest female animal trainers, who specialized in training tigers— 1938.   (C. P. Fox.)

TYPICAL SCENE on circus lot any day of any season—filling the performers' pails with fresh water.
(Atwell-Milw. Jour., Wis. Hist. Soc.)

LOU JACOBS, a veteran Ringling clown, chats with the author's children, Barbara and Peter. Lou is known as a producing clown because of the many sensational gags he perpetrates. Even though the children watch him make up his face they are not sure Lou is the same man when he again talks to them.

"Let's go to the circus," he says, and off they go.

(C. P. Fox)

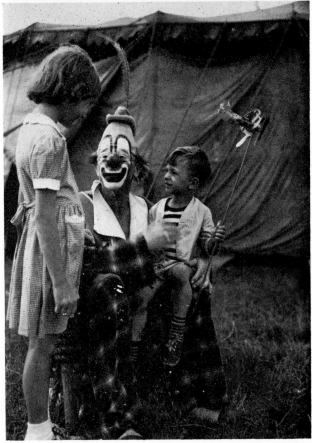

(Credit C. P. Fox)

Circus Day

Circus ticket sellers, in the early days, on occasions had problems that called for more than the usual amount of tact and diplomacy. Such was the experience of Alf. T. Ringling in 1895. Said he:

"A Paducah judge and two attorneys had made up their minds to 'shake down' our show and it may be said (lack a day) that they were successful in their purpose. Mr. Vogt (circus treasurer) and myself were selling tickets for the night show when at about 8:30 we were shocked to find staring us in the face two large Colts in the hands of a couple of constables who politely (?), though firmly, requested us to accompany them to the local bastile. They had us foul, there being no way of escape out of the ticket wagon we silently, though sadly, did the constable's bidding and wended our way towards the prison place, accompanied by a bodyguard of 7 tried and true guardians of the peace and commonwealth of "old Kentuck." We found the judge to be a man very fond of referring continually to the law and made up our minds that whatever the charge, we were apt to get the full limit.

"We were charged with aiding, abetting, giving an exhibition without a license. Of course, we had our license in the ticket wagon, but to prove it to these people it would have been necessary for us to stay there and produce the paper at a trial the judge proposed to hold the next week. They would not give us an immediate hearing and wanted a bond of $500 each. It was the impossibility of our staying over to fight for our rights, and so, after a deal of parleying, we compromised the matter by paying over to our legal friends one hundred and fifty samolions. After shaking us down in shameful manner we were politely invited to step over to a neighboring barroom and take a drink. Need it be said, we refused."

George Ade once said of the Ringling Bros.:

"They found the business in the hands of vagabonds and put it into the hands of gentlemen. They started with nothing whatsoever in a little town up in Wisconsin and became the circus kings of the world by adopting and observing the simple rule that it is better to be straight than to be crooked."

As a matter of fact, their competition was so incensed at the respectability of the Ringling Circus that they sarcastically referred to it as the *ting-a-ling* show.

Until the Ringlings came along, circus men traditionally used every means to separate the town suckers from their money. They ran crooked gambling joints in connection with their shows and short-changed patrons at ticket wagons. Some circuses carried a staff of pickpockets to rob the patrons outright; others sold the privilege of working their showgrounds to dips, sneak thieves, gamblers, three card monte men, or shell workers. Circus fixers bribed public officials to wink at these depredations. High pressure tactics were used to sell reserved tickets and concert tickets.

The Ringling brothers changed all this. They took every precaution to keep their showgrounds free of thieves. Jiggs Block, the giraffe keeper, recalls that when the circus detective caught a pickpocket on the showgrounds he was handcuffed to a tent pole where all patrons could see him—a neat little sign proclaiming his crime. If a ticket seller was caught short-changing a customer he was fired on the spot.

In 1895 the Ringlings took their 12-year old circus to St. Louis for a six-day stand. After the third or fourth day the newspapers began to loudly acclaim the circus. The St. Louis *Globe Democrat,* for example, editorialized the show in these words:

"10's of thousands of men, women, and children, who have patronized the wonderful circus of the Ringling Bros. may well wonder whether capital or enterprise could possibly gather together in one gigantic show such a grand aggregation of up-to-date attractions. No such realization of the circus has before visited St. Louis. The circus of the past was but a drop in the bucket compared to the Ringling Bros. today. But it is not merely the gigantic scale, superlative quantity of acts, completeness of menagerie, and peerless appointments of the circus that draws it close to the people. Its greatest merit lies in the fact that from beginning to end it is an absolute clean show. Vulgarity, coarseness, offensiveness of any kind to the eye or ear are conspicuously absent. Their attendants are polite and there is an utter lack of off-hand brutality and toughness, often inseparable from travelling shows."

And so their reputation grew, and as it did and the years went by, their policy paid off handsomely in huge crowds wherever they played. The biggest income each year for Ringlings has been at Madison Square Garden in New York City, where they play for five to six weeks every Spring. In 1948, for example, 924,000 people saw the big show during its 33-day stand there. This lucrative Garden stand has, on occasion, brought in some fabulous daily grosses; as in 1954 when there were three days that exceeded $70,000.

On tour, between two and three million people see this circus each year. In 1950, one of the best years, 3,179,000 people saw the show. During the ten-year period—1946 through 1955—the circus averaged a five and a half million dollar yearly gross. Their best single day ever, under canvas, occurred in 1946 at Philadelphia. The tent, that year, had a seating capacity of 11,000. The circus grossed $43,000 from the two performances, plus another $10,000 from the side show.

Circus ticket sellers have minds that function like lightning, plus nimble fingers that deftly make correct change while the surging crowd pushes a constant stream of money in front of them. They develop an uncanny ability to handle the important character who wants the best seats in the house for an already packed show about to begin in 10 minutes. They have the patience of Job when, after explaining the difference in grandstand and reserved seats, a lady with a retinue of 10 children can't make up her mind which she wants, or changes her mind after she has purchased the tickets. They must handle with utmost tact the patron who appears at the night show with passes for the afternoon performance. Then too, they must have the wisdom of Solomon when a scraggly haired, dirty-faced moppet bursts into tears when he is told the few nickels he put on the counter are not enough to pay for a ticket. But they love their work.

One ticket seller, commenting on his profession, put it this way. "There is a certain fascination connected with this job. To witness the mighty rush for tickets of admission and to help gather in a goodly harvest of the shiny shekels of the realm is quite irresistable."

The circus is something most parents can't wait to take their children to—and so it was in 1913. With the circus in Bakersfield, California, Charley Ringling decided to have his chauffeur, Fred Terbilcox, drive him to Los Angeles, their next show date. Approximately 20 miles outside of Los Angeles they came upon an old, decrepit Model T Ford, stopped on the side of the highway.

"We could see six poorly dressed kids standing around the car and a man trying to mend a tire," said Fred as he recalled the incident.

"Mr. Charley told me to stop the car and see if we could be of any help. The man told us that this was his second flat tire and he had run out of patches. He went on to say that he just had to get to Los Angeles, as he had promised to take his kids to the circus. Mr. Ringling told me to give the man enough patches, not only to fix the flat, but some extra ones for emergency. While I was getting the patches, Mr. Ringling called the man over to the car (the six bright-eyed kids came too and clustered around the shiny Pierce Arrow) and told him he worked for the circus and said, 'when you and your family get to the showgrounds look me up. Ask for me at the red ticket wagon' and with that Mr. Charley handed him a card. He always carried these cards, but they had a pseudonym imprinted on them. When these cards turned up the boys on the circus lot knew whose they were.

"I was standing at the front door that afternoon about an hour before show time and was very surprised to see our highway friend and his children on the lot. Well, Mr. Ringling took that whole family to the side show, bought the kids pink lemonade and all other souvenirs, then he took them into the main tent and sat them down on the best seats in the house. The man never did know who befriended him. I saw Mr. Charley a short time later and commented on what he had just done. 'Fred', he said, 'I was a poor boy myself at one time. I never look down on anyone. It really did my heart good to do that.'

When Fred finished this anecdote he commented, "Charley Ringling was the grandest man in the world

BELOW LEFT—View of 1917 "range" wagon. On right is a 1948 view of the huge kettles used for cooking and the steam generator wagon No. 2. This generator provides steam for the dishwasher.

(Steve Albasing and C. P. Fox)

—I know, he was my boss for seven years."

As these six children watched the 1913 performance they were no more enthralled and amused than the children who saw the 1893 or 1953 shows.

The Ringling brothers realized that the circus amused people in all walks of life. Hollywood star and a pigtailed girl of 10, or Boy Scout and President of the United States—everyone is suddenly and mysteriously brought to the same level. Snobbishness, sophistication, class consciousness are lost, as children of all ages thrill to the most democratic of all entertainment —the circus.

A few years ago Professor Wm. Lyon Phelps of Yale wrote, "The circus is one of the greatest institutions in the whole world. It makes an enormous contribution to human happiness." It does so because there are so many aspects to a Ringling performance that everyone gets pleasure from watching it.

The circus is amusement—its purpose was aptly described by Alf. T. Ringling in their Red Wagon Annual for 1899 in this way:

"To be good, mankind must be happy. To wreathe the face of humanity in smiles for a time, to loosen the chains that hold man captive to his duties and return him to them better fitted for his obligations, is the mission of amusement and the one great desire of moralists is, and ought to be, that it be pure and wholesome.

"Amusement unfetters the mind from its environs and changes the dreary monotony of the factory's spindles to the joyous song of the meadow lark. It gives flight to the caged soul to tread in airy places. It softens the wrinkles of sorrow, makes smiles of frowns.

"This is the mission of amusement — and the circus, with its innocent sights of joy for the children and its power to make all men and women children again for at least one day, comes the nearest of any form of amusement to fulfilling this mission."

Quite frequently the management was accused of splitting the circus into two small segments after they left New York. The origin of this tale probably dates back to the days when the opposition would spread the following story. "We bring all of our circus performance to your town. We do not split it up for deceitful gains after playing the big cities."

It is possible, too, that the press agents thought that by denying such rumors, they would add stature to their circus in the minds of the populace. How else can one interpret the following notice that appeared in the Monroe, Wisconsin, *Sentinel* in 1884. The Ringling Circus was only a few weeks old—a forlorn and tiny troupe of acrobats and musicians they were as they toddled out into the great competitive circus world.

"In justice to Yankee Robinson and the Ringling Bros., we simply state that their great double, four shows in one, does not divide as reported. The entire show is in this city. It is the same show yesterday, today, and tomorrow. Don't fail to see the street parade and you will believe all we say—this notice is not paid for."

Ringlings never split their show, for the cost would be prohibitive. It would entail two big tops, two menageries, two sets of seats; in fact, two of everything, resulting in two circuses. In this day and age, it is difficult enough to keep one show functioning smoothly and to route it. For eleven years after the Baraboo brothers purchased the Barnum & Bailey show, they operated it as a separate entity. However, these were two distinct circuses—each with its own winter quarters, each with its own territory and performance. One of the reasons given for combining these two titles in 1919 was the difficulty in handling the two shows. So whether the circus is seen in Madison Square Garden, or Oshkosh, Wisconsin, the performance is identical.

The Ringlings have always been generous with their performances. The proceeds of the first show at the

RIGHT—Pies by the hundreds are baked in the ovens built into a wagon. (RB&BB)

BELOW is view of the dishwasher. The china comes out of machine steaming hot and sparkling clean. C. P. Fox)

ON LEFT is interior of the cookhouse as the dining tent is called.
(RB&BB)

Garden each Spring has, for years, gone to charities—such as Army Emergency Relief Fund, Navy Relief Fund, Polio Foundation, etc. In 1949, at a special Hollywood performance, in which scores of movie celebrities joined the acts (seats sold for $5 to $100), over $200,000 was given to St. John Hospital Guild. During World War II on opening night at New York and Boston, admission was by War Bond only. At subsequent performances throughout the country, a special honor section was set aside for War Bond purchasers. It is calculated that $100,000,000 worth of bonds were sold through special performances. In 1943 alone over 60,000 service men were given free passes through arrangements with the U. S. O.

Year after year in the 1890's and early 1900's, the circus put on a prodigious stage show they called a spectacle. On one side of the main tent was a huge stage. Partaking in these pantomime dramas were hundreds of people, horses, camels, and elephants. In 1901 it was *Joan of Arc*; in 1914 *The Queen of Sheba*. In 1917 *Cinderella*. Today these fabulous productions are no longer given, as this cumbersome and show-type of theatrical is out of step with today's competition and fast pace. Now the show does feature one or more production *walk arounds*, each with a given theme such as *Nursery Rhymes, Holidays*, or *Pantos Paradise*. People like John Murray Anderson, Albertina Rasch, Robert Ringling and John Ringling North, have produced, or helped to produce, these colorful numbers. The glorious and exciting costumes make these pageants the gay extravaganzas that they are. In the workrooms at winterquarters the costumes for man and beast are produced each winter. 20,000 yards of fabric of all kinds are used. 35 million spangles and sequins are sewn onto the silks and satins.

Every performance is held together with music and Ringlings have had some impressive and wonderful band leaders. In 1892 it was Wm. Weldon, followed by Prof, Ganweiler, the Great Liberati; and in 1915 the famous Richards. In 1919, the first year the Ringling Bros. combined their show with the Barnum & Bailey circus, Merle Evans took over the musical directorship. At the close of the 1955 season, after 37 years, and some 22,000 performances, Evans retired from the Ringling show.

The circus band is the key to a smooth running performance—it keeps time to dancing horses (not vice-versa), plays loud brassy music for the elephants such as *Entry of the Gladiator*, or it can swing into tangos and boleros for the performing big cats which they seem to enjoy. The aerialists smooth flowing action brings a lilting tune like the *Skater's Waltz* from the band. Clowns, on the other hand, respond to a fast tumbling—loud and hot jazz music.

This job is done with a band of 26 in recent years. Evans himself played the cornet. In addition, the band had four trombones, five clarinets, two French horns, three cornets, three trumpets, a piccolo, bass drum, snare drum, two baritones, two bass tubas, and a Hammond organ. The band wasn't always this size. In the wagon show days the Ringlings sported a band of eight horns and two drums, while in 1895 the Great Liberati had a 60-piece concert band. In 1920 Chas. Ringling, who was a musician himself, gave Evans a 36-piece band.

It was early in the 1942 season that the circus band

became enmeshed in a labor dispute and the Musicians' Union pulled the men off the show. For the balance of the season the circus performance struggled and limped along with canned music.

At the end of the last performance of the season the band swings into *Auld Lang Syne*, or *Home Sweet Home*, tunes that are sweet music, indeed, to all the circus personnel, for after some 400 performances everyone welcomes the end of the season.

Almost as thrilling as the Big Show itself were those two vital adjuncts to any self-respecting circus, the side show and the menagerie. The Ringling Brothers were fully aware of this, and back in 1892 their route book proudly proclaimed:

"Ringling Bros. Side Show is the only one in existence that carries a full complement of stage, scenery, and every other appurtenance necessary for a first-class theatrical exhibition. A glance at this tented palace would induce the compilers of Webster's Dictionary to insert the word, 'side show' in its pages. At present it is not there."

Today *side show* is in the dictionary.

The curiosities and performers that constituted the side show in that year were the Mastodonic Fashion Plate (fat lady); Lilliputian Princess; Living Skeleton Dude; Colossal Mexican Giant; Tattooed Man; Arabian Princess; Snake Enchantress; Arkansas Boy Giant; King of Dwarfs; Albino Family; Japanese Fantasiast; Magician; and Ventriloquist.

The side show, with its list of human oddities, always attracted large crowds. In 1954, an all-time attendance record for the side show was set in Philadelphia on May 29, when 21,976 people bought tickets. The lineup of attractions that brought in this crowd consisted of an armless and legless girl; Fireproof Man; Knife Thrower; Sword Swallower; Snake Trainer;

Magician; Musical Glasses; Dancing Fat Girl; Seal Boy; Tattooed Girl; Whip Cracker; World's Smallest Man; and Scotch Highlanders.

On the circus lot an annex was an exhibition in a separate tent of a special attraction which the patron was charged extra to see. The Ringling Circus has not resorted to the use of an annex for years. Before the turn of the century they did have a fascinating exhibit in an annex—a cinematograph. This forerunner of the movie projectors was developed from an Edison Kinetoscope peep show machine to the point where it was able to show public movies. The first New York showing by the Edison people was in June 1896. The next year the circus had one of these machines set up as an annex show. The tent was black and became known as the Black Top. This, of course, kept the interior of the tent dark enough for the projectoscope to show its movies.

The film was 35 mm and had only one pair of sprocket holes per frame, using a film speed of 16 frames per second. The hand cranked machine was of simple construction, but the banners in front of the tent said, "more wonderful than the inventions of the past 100 years—Edison's latest and greatest invention —actual cost $10,000." The movie shown this first year was *the Great Corbett-Fitzsimmons Fight.* The following year the banners headlined *The War Graph* showing in moving scenes *The Story of Cuba.* *Remember The Maine* was emblazoned over the entrance to the tent. The novelty of this attraction drew the crowds in droves.

The after-show, or concert, as it was sometimes called, was a special performance that was put on in the main tent immediately following the regular show. For 25 cents those who wished to watch this extra show could move into the reserved seat sections. The concert was usually made up of a wild west exhibition

THE RINGLING SIDESHOW bannerline sparkles on the midway at night—1949 at Milwaukee.   (C. P. Fox)

of trick riding, with a mixture of Australian bullwhip crackers and an amazing display of the art of lassoing. Ringlings on one occasion, had an expert lasso four horses that were thundering down the track at a full gallop. Generally, the wild west program spotlighted a famous cowboy movie star. Col. Tim McCoy head-lined the aftershow for a number of years in the '30's. In recent years the Ringlings have had not had a con-cert, feeling their 3-hour main show was enough of a session for circus patrons.

Any collection of wild animals is a menagerie; yet somehow the word seems to be used most generally in reference to travelling zoos of the circus. Ringling's menagerie has for years been considered one of the outstanding exhibits of the world's animals in the United States. It was the animal men[1] who could be credited with a menagerie's success, even under the most adverse of conditions. For years men like Charles Malloy, Charley Smith, John Sabo and today, Cecil Montgomery, have presented a rare collection of ani-mals. Robert Bean, Director of the famed Brookfield Zoo in Chicago, said, "Ringlings for many years had Charley Smith in charge of their menagerie. In this country there are few, if any, better animal men. Charley was tireless, intelligent, perceptive, and his perceptions amounted to a fifth sense." George Speidel, Director of the Milwaukee Zoo, felt that it was the im-maculate condition in which the animals were kept, plus their well balanced diet that resulted in the con-sistent way in which their big cats gave birth and cared for their young while travelling cross-country. The sleek coats and clear eyes were indicative of their splendid condition.

The menagerie was always displayed in a four or five-pole top of its own just inside the main entrance.

[1] A school teacher from a small town interrogated the hippo-potamus keeper for the benefit of her zoology class and the following conversation took place:
  School Teacher: "Where did you capture that hippo-potamus?"
  Keeper: "In the Baraboo River."
  School Teacher: "Where, pray, is the Baraboo River?"
  Keeper: "It is a large body of water that flows through the vast territory of the Sauk." (Baraboo, Wis. is in Sauk County.)
  School Teacher: "How did you capture him?"
  Keeper: "Hips cannot see by moonlight; therefore, they manage their foraging before the moon rises or after it has set. Sometimes they wander so far away from the water that the moon comes out on them before they can return. They are then absolutely helpless and fall easy prey to their captors who chain and rope the unlucky river horses and put a bandage over its eyes so that he remains under the impression the moon is still shining long after it has set. It is then securely enclosed in a stout box before the bandage is removed."
This story appeared in the Ringling Bros. route book for 1899 under the date of Oct. 9 at Hennessey, Oklahoma. Such fables were the stock in trade for most animal men who used them to defend themselves against the daily deluge of questions.

There was never any extra admission charge to see the animals. In 1954, however, the menagerie was dis-played in the end of the main tent. This move was made in an effort to cut down the number of baggage wagons by the elimination of the menagerie tent. It was not a successful move as far as the patrons were concerned. Then, too, the arrangement caused crowded conditions and was soon abandoned.

Among the rare and unusual animals that have been seen in the Ringling menagerie were Snow Leopards, a herd of Pigmy African Elephants, Ibex, Gigantic Sea Elephants, and Gorillas. This last species was best rep-resented by *Gargantua,* the 550-pound ape who proved to be one of the greatest circus attractions of all time. This magnificent beast was viewed by an estimated 40 million people, who witnessed some of his astounding feats of strength. Gargantua could rip a burlap bag to shreds as if it were a wet paper napkin. He was often seen to fold a new tire casing, not in half, but in quar-ters. He first joined the circus in 1938 and on Novem-ber 25, 1949, at Miami, on the last stand of the season, the great ape died.

Alf. T. Ringling had a keen interest in animals. Herewith is printed a letter he wrote on September 7, 1919, to Mr. O. D. Brandenburg, Editor of the Mad-ison, Wisconsin, *Daily Democrat.* (Alf. T. was con-fined to bed at his Oak Ridge, N. J. home at the time. He died later that year.) Many interesting facts of his character come to light in this letter.

"Would you think the Madison Zoo and Madison people would care to add trained animals to their col-lection? This I suppose would be a separate depart-ment to the Zoo and I suppose would necessitate an arenic building with seats, a ring and a stage, a price of admission to trained animals part of zoo and what is of great importance, additional expense?

"I have the needed animals and would be glad to present them free to the zoo. The list of trained ani-mals is as follows:—

1. Act of trained lions—4 Males, 1 Female
2. Act of trained Brown Bears—4 or 5
3. Act of trained White Horses—4 of them
4. Act of trained Shetland Ponies—about 10
5. One or two elephants added to one there now which would make a splendid act.

"The boys in the zoo could add to these a trained pig, goose, donkey, or whatever they happened to de-velop and I believe in a year or two the Madison Zoo would have something different and more popular than anything of the kind in this country. People from all over the state would be attracted and it seems like two or three performances ought to pay the expenses which, of course, would need to be moderate.

"I cannot help soaring a little on any subject I get

interested in and I feel that you will not mind it if I say that a building answering the purpose of a performing arena could be used in many other ways. One, in particular, has occurred to me and that is the production of tableaux and spectacles of certain dramatic limitations. Take the many Indian legends and historic Indian battles and episodes of Wisconsin—these alone would furnish hundreds of dramas.

"Now about the animals that might be an everlasting joy to Madison—and again they might be a terrible and continuous pain, I think you will know.

"If you can believe me, I am having a fine time in bed and there are days that pass so rapidly I wonder if I have not too strong a leaning toward actual laziness; but all new adventures have their charms and this one of lying in bed has its charms for me. You would laugh if you saw the bed covered with books, letters, and magazines, and in the back of my head a thousand things I am intent on doing while reclining at an angle of 45 degrees.

(Sgd) Alf.'

Today many zoos are doing just what Alf. T. suggested in that letter of almost 40 years ago—a show of trained animals. The St. Louis Zoo is an outstanding example.

The cost of the animals in the menagerie always intrigues the circus patrons. Today's prices for these beasts are eye openers. The prices listed below are for average display animals. Some specimens are worth more than others because of size, or other unusual qualities. Then, too, any animal that is trained to do an act immediately doubles, or even quadruples in value to the circus.

Camel	$1500
Zebra	1000 to 1500
Indian Elephant	3500
Kangaroo (Pair)	750 to 800
Oran-Utans	2500
Baboon	250
Python (20 Ft.)	500 to 750
Cheetah	1000 to 1300
Black Rhino	4500
Giraffe (Minimum)	3500
African Elephants	4500
Leopard	1000
Chimpanzees	500 to 1000
Okapi	7000

The gorilla Gargantua the Great was, undoubtedly, the costliest menagerie animal of all time, with the possible exception of Barnum's Jumbo. Gargantua's size and ugly contenance made him worth every cent of his $10,000 price tag. At today's prices, it is doubtful that the Ringling menagerie of recent years could be replaced for a half million dollars.

Not as glamorous as the big top, side show and menagerie, but just as essential, was the circus cookhouse, for a circus, like an army, travels on its stomach.

Ringling Hotel is here today and there tomorrow—and George Blood, for many years superintendent of the dining department, once said:—"I serve the same 1400 people every day, but in a different city; while the usual restaurant serves different people every day but in the same city."

This department had approximately 140 men, when the circus was under canvas, which included chefs, cooks, waiters, bus boys, machine operators, canvasmen, storekeepers, commissary clerks, and truck drivers. The cookhouse was first on a lot and first off. It was always there ready with "three squares" for all the personnel. Without a doubt, the finest food available was purchased and served in each city. Good food and a lot of it was one of the keys to the success of the show.

The dining tent itself was divided into two sections—one for performers and officials, the other for the workmen. The food served in both sections was identical. The tables were covered with red plaid cloths with a vast assortment of sauces and seasonings available on each. One of the very necessary and important pieces of cookhouse equipment was its own portable Cleaver-Brooks generator that produced steam and hot water for cooking and washing dishes.

The speed and dispatch with which this department prepared and served these robust meals under the most difficult of conditions was a never-ending source of bewilderment and awe to those who watched the circus come into town. Attached to the cookhouse was a wagon with built-in ovens, one with a built-in refrigerator, another was a general store where the circus crew could purchase cigarettes, gum, candy, shoe laces, razor blades, and other everyday necessities.

AN 1897 SEASON pass issued by Otto Ringling.
(W. H. Woodcock Collection)

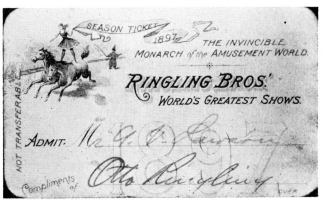

ABOVE—1894 ticket wagon with policeman standing dutifully by. (Sauk Co. Hist. Soc.)

LEFT—The vast crowd surges in to see the show—1894. (Sauk Co. Hist Soc.)

BELOW RIGHT 1953 front door in modern dress. This was the year the ticket wagons were lavender and other pastel colors, an innovation which brought a yowl of protest from old-timers. (C. P. Fox)

BELOW—1905 pink lemonade stand with sideshow banner line in background. (Leonard Roser)

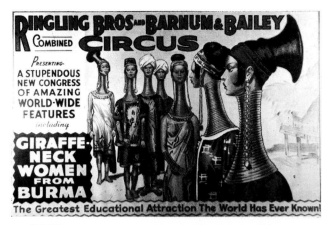

ABOVE is a lithograph that advertised "The greatest educational attraction the world has ever known."
(C. P. Fox Collection)

ON RIGHT is one of the Burmese girls featured by the circus in 1933.
(Atwell-Milw. Jour.-Wis. Hist. Soc.)

BELOW is 1894 sideshow bannerline advertising a "rooster orchestra" and the illustrations show roosters playing various instruments. The white-jacketed sideshow band boasted eight horns and a bass drum.
(Marion Dillon)

THE CIRCUS' entire sideshow troupe for 1933.   (Fred Pfening, Jr., Collection)

SIDESHOW BARKER persuasively speils out his pitch to entice the crowd into buying a 30c ticket. Circa 1940.
(Atwell-Milw. Jour.-Wis. Hist. Soc.)

RIGHT—1897 annex that displayed a cinematograph,
the forerunner of movie projectors. The great Corbett
and Fitzsimmons fight was shown this first year. The
tent used was dark canvas, called the "black top".
(Wis. Hist. Soc.)

THE UBANGIS were one of the most successful attractions the Ringlings ever had. This troupe of Africans was brought to America for the 1930 season.

(Eddie Jackson Collection)

LEFT is seen the poster advertising the women who had "mouths and lips as large as those of full grown crocodiles".

(Chas. Kitto Collection)

THE RINGLING MENAGERIE contains some of the most magnificent specimens. On right is a male Siberian Tiger. (RB&BB)

TYPICAL MENAGERIE SCENE (1929) when cages and dens of animals from all corners of the world were displayed in beautiful wagons as seen below.
(Robert Good)

BELOW: A spectacular sight in 1931 was this huge herd of 18 zebras. They were temperamental beasts and some had to wear muzzles to keep them from nipping the customers.
(Atwell - Milw. Jour. Wis. Hist. Soc.)

THIS IS AN 1895 COURIER advertising the "greatest gathering since the Deluge."   (H. H. Conley Collection)

THE TERROR

Tremendous New Educational Feature Awes Al G. Barnes and Sells-Floto Spectators

Continued

With a smirk of cruel calculation and a sadistic scowl of challenge on his huge bestial face, Gargantua The Great now defies civilization from behind the heavy, chilled steel bars of the strongest cage ever built.

Of triple reinforcement throughout, the twenty-foot cell-like prison on wheels in which he may be viewed with perfect safety, is an interesting and unusual exhibit in itself, combining all the known scientific devices for air conditioning and insulation.

Two outer enclosures of heavy, shatter-proof plate-glass surround the massive barred cage, the germ-filtered air of which is kept at an even temperature of 70 degrees Fahrenheit, providing protection against colds and pneumonia, which almost invariably have been the cause of death among these awesome anthropoid apes.

The country's leading experts have reproduced in the construction of the cage of The Big Show's dangerous captive, as far as humanly possible, the actual atmospheric conditions of far-off Belgian Congo's coastal region, the native habitat of Gargantua The Great and his mighty forebears.

STRIKING CONTRAST

So much like a horrifying nightmare vision of what man might have been, Gargantua The Great offers the most pernicious portrait study ever recorded by a camera lens.

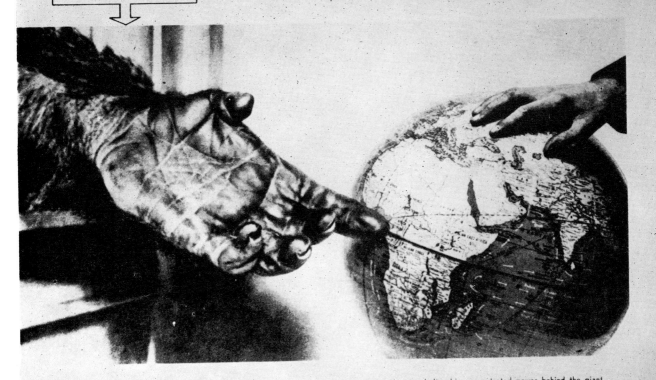

The massive hand of Gargantua The Great and that of a normal sized man, emphasize the almost unbelievable concentrated power behind the giant gorilla's forefinger which points to his approximate place of origin in the dim forests of western equatorial Africa.

A PAGE from a 1938 booklet about Gargantua. This was the year many Ringling acts went over to the Ringling owned Barnes-Sells Floto Circus.

(C. P. Fox Collection)

GARGANTUA, a marvelous specimen of a full grown gorilla, was probably the greatest circus attraction since Barnum's Jumbo. Below is shown a 1938 lithograph advertising the big ape—his first year on show.

(RB&BB and C. P. Fox Collection)

A PAGE from an 1895 courier telling about the towering, sky-reaching giant giraffe.   (H. H. Conley Collection)

THE GIRAFFE, which towers 15 to 18 feet, is one of the most attractive animals in the menagerie (1915). At one time Ringlings carried four of them. (Steve Albasing)

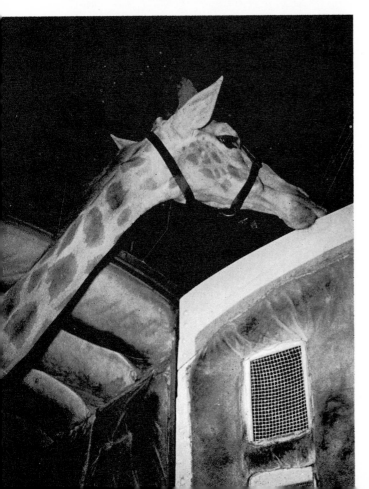

ABOVE—Each giraffe has its own special underslung wagon when traveling. (C. P. Fox)

LEFT—Each wagon is heavily padded to protect the ungainly looking beasts from injury. (RB&BB)

THE SNAKE THAT SWALLOWED HIMSELF

By H. B. HANMORE

Aguinaldo whetting his Appetite for his great Swallowing Act.

From photo taken by our Official Photographer of Aguinaldo Swallowing Himself

The big boa constrictors received from the Philippine Islands about five years ago were not taken with the World's Greatest Shows the season of '98, as early in the spring there had been an addition to the family and Pa and Ma Boa were extremely vicious and naturally too dangerous to take on the road. They were left in charge of competent attendants in winter quarters, and the Big Show was forced to dispense with them as attractions. In September, "Aguinaldo," the male head of the family was seen to be especially nervous. He had devoured two of his offspring on the afternoon of Sept. 20th, and it was feared he would swallow 'ma' if the pair was not separated. In this extremity the principal keep in charge wired for instructions and received orders on the 23rd of September to separate the big snakes at once. This was effected by placing a sheep in a shifting cage and moving it close up to the snake den and letting one of the monsters into the shifting cage. It happened that the female— "Lucrezia Borgia"—darted into the cage where the sheep awaited its doom. Before "Aguinaldo" had realized the situation the door was closed and the big serpents were effectually separated. "Lucrezia" spent no time in useless preliminaries but wound herself around the sheep in a twinkling, while her eyes fairly blazed in anticipation of the delicate morsel so unexpectedly provided. In a few moments the sheep was but an inanimate pulp, and "Lucrezia" plastered her with saliva and "took her in out of the wet."

"Aguinaldo" was not a silent but a very active and noisy witness of the little drama in which he was denied participation. He threshed around in the den and made frantic dives against the bars and tried every way to squeeze through. But bars in winter quarters are made to hold the choice specimens inside. "Aguinaldo" simply wore himself out while he staked in. How his wicked eyes burned with rage and ineffectual hate! He finally ceased his frantic efforts to break through the bars and coiled his horrid length in sinuous folds and his head dropped, his eyes closed and he gave himself up to reflection, while "Lucrezia," her appetite appeased by the choice delicacy she had partaken, stretched herself out in comfort, winked the other eye, and slept the sleep that a full stomach, an easy conscience and a good digestion affords.

"Aguinaldo" remained quiescent for an hour or more and then a miracle happened. His head moved slowly around towards his tail and he opened his ponderous jaws and the tail disappeared, and by degrees more and more of the body followed into that capacious maw. The attendants were paralyzed with wonder as they saw the monster's body disappearing within the cavernous depths of his interior. But, of course, there must be a limit! Naturally, when the lower part of the snake's body had disappeared the interior would be filled, and the employees silently waited the denouement, which they felt could not be long delayed, as the unswallowed

portion of the body was greatly distended, while the serpent's eyes were bulging as if they would burst from their sockets. He was plainly distressed and apparently surprised that the swallowing process had come to a halt.

"Aguinaldo" was in a quandary. He breathed with great difficulty and was suffering agonies. With one supreme, despairing effort he gave a final gulp and — DISAPPEARED! Disappeared as if the bottom of the cage had opened and swallowed him up. But the bottom of the cage remained intact. The attendants pressed with staring eyes against the bars. Nothing remained. The cage was empty. "Aguinaldo" **in his rage had swallowed himself!!! Nothing like it ever occurred** and probably never will occur again.

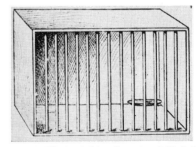

From Photo taken by our Official Photographer immediately after Aguinaldo had Swallowed Himself.

"Aguinaldo" has vanished like the baseless fabric of a vision and left no trace behind. "Lucrezia Borgia" is a widow with two fatherless boas on her hands—so to speak. Perhaps if she is left alone to bring them up by hand, unaided and without a father's care, she might gobble 'em whole. But good boas are scarce and "Lucrezia" has been separated from her remaining babes. She can have all the spring lamb or seasoned sheep she wants. The babies will receive every attention caculated to develop their growth in order that they may become useful snakes in their day and generation.

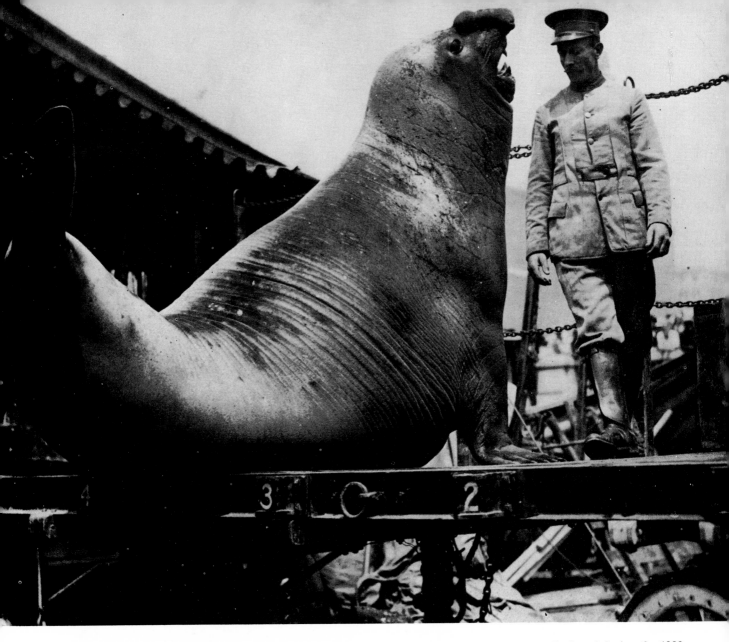

THIS HUGE SEA ELEPHANT was purchased from the Hagenbeck Zoo in Hamburg and displayed during the 1928-1929 seasons. It was carried in one end of a stock car when enroute. While on the circus lot it stayed on a platform wagon where it was watered and fed. This wagon was drawn by six horses around the hippodrome track, which enabled all patrons to see the Goliath. (Atwell-Milw. Jour.-Wis. Hist. Soc.)

ON LEFT is a circus poster advertising the monster.
(C. P. Fox Collection)

AN UNUSUAL INTERIOR VIEW of menagerie in 1933. The 40 elephants were lined up on right side of the tent.
(Fred Pfening, Jr., Collection)

ABOVE—Wagon No. 103 has an ominous imprint on the canvas "Wild Animals—Danger—Do Not Touch". This added great excitement to the scene. To each town Ringling brought a collection of wild animals equalled by only a few zoos of the country.

(Caterpillar Tractor Co.)

THE CIRCUS usually had a snake den in the menagerie. Above is the huge python being fed.

(Wis. Hist. Soc.)

RIGHT—This letter, from Henry Ringling North, Vice President of the circus, gives a good idea of the cost of the specimens displayed in the menagerie.

(F. J. Zeehandelar)

LOWER—The 1916 collection of ostriches.

(Steve Albasing)

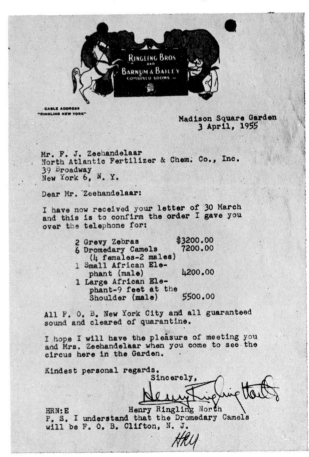

RINGLING BROS
AND
BARNUM & BAILEY
COMBINED SHOWS

CABLE ADDRESS
"RINGLING NEW YORK"

Madison Square Garden
3 April, 1955

Mr. F. J. Zeehandelaar
North Atlantic Fertilizer & Chem. Co., Inc.
39 Broadway
New York 6, N. Y.

Dear Mr. Zeehandelaar:

I have now received your letter of 30 March and this is to confirm the order I gave you over the telephone for:

2 Grevy Zebras	$3200.00	
6 Dromedary Camels	7200.00	
(4 females-2 males)		
1 Small African Elephant (male)	4200.00	
1 Large African Elephant-9 feet at the Shoulder (male)	5500.00	

All F. O. B. New York City and all guaranteed sound and cleared of quarantine.

I hope I will have the pleasure of meeting you and Mrs. Zeehandelaar when you come to see the circus here in the Garden.

Kindest personal regards.

Sincerely,

Henry Ringling North

HRN:E
P. S. I understand that the Dromedary Camels will be F. O. B. Clifton, N. J.

HRN

REPRINTED BELOW is a set of rules given to each circus employee. Hilarious to read now, the rules were deadly serious 50 years ago. The Ringling Brothers were obsessed with the idea of keeping their circus on a high plane.

SUGGESTIONS AND RULES
EMPLOYEES
RINGLING BROTHERS

The object of these rules and suggestions is not to limit the employees in the enjoyment of their rights, but rather to promote harmony and goodwill, and co-operate with our employees in conducting our institution in a business-like, high-standard manner.

The personal appearance and behavior of each individual is important, not only in so far as the relations of employee with employee are concerned, but equally as much for the impression we make on the public. We should want the "town folks" to feel that the "show folks" are real men and women and ladies and gentlemen as well.

Undoubtedly few of us would adopt a course opposite to some of the rules given; however, the rules are made to protect the majority against imposition by the few who might thoughtlessly annoy and disturb:

1. Be cleanly and neat in dress and avoid loud display.
2. Absence from work will not be permitted without making arrangement with your department head. If this is not possible and you are unavoidably absent, you must send information at the earliest possible moment in order that your place may be filled; and on your return, immediately give explanation of cause of absence. In case you should be ill and not able to leave the cars, you must immediately notify the head-porter, who will send a message to the show grounds.
3. No employees will be permitted to loan money to other employees and receive any profit from the transaction.
4. Gambling, especially in the cars or near the cars, on or near the show ground, is strictly prohibited.

IN THE CARS

5. No pet animals, revolvers, intoxicants or inflammables allowed in the sleeping cars. Candles must not be used in the cars; if an individual light is wanted, supply a "flash light" type electric. No others will be allowed.
6. No smoking in cars at any time.
7. Loud talking, singing, playing upon musical instruments, or disturbing noises in or near the cars must stop at 11 P. M.
8. Do not clean teeth at wash-bowls.
9. Cooking is prohibited in the cars.
10. Be considerate in using toilet rooms.

CAUTION—Look both ways; be careful in crossing railroad tracks or in walking upon same.

AT THE DINING TENT

11. No dogs allowed in the dining room during meal time.
12. Coats must be worn in the dining room at meal time.
13. When the "HOTEL" flag is up the meal is ready; when the blue flag is up the meal is over.
14. No food nor dishes can be taken from the dining room without permission.
15. Drinking glasses are thoroughly washed and rinsed. Do not waste water washing them at the drinking tank.
16. People bringing friends into dining room to eat will purchase meal tickets at the commissary wagon.
17. MEAL HOURS: Breakfast will be over at 9:15, excepting on late arrival of show. Lunch will be over at 12:45 noon.
18. People will remain outside the guard rope until the flag is raised.

TO PERFORMERS

19. Take the same care of company wardrobe as you do your own; do not sit on dirty boxes, pedestals, wagons, on the ground, etc., while wearing spectacle costumes.
20. Ladies must return bundled wardrobe to wardrobe mistress as soon as possible.
21. Gentlemen must fold costumes and place in proper location.
22. Do not bring liquors or intoxicants into the dressing rooms.

23. Remain outside of Big Tent until time for your act or assistance.
24. Do not take strangers or friends into dressing rooms without permission.
25. Cooking, making coffee will not be allowed in dressing rooms.
26. In going from dressing tents to dining tents do not pass through the menagerie or circus tents, and never pass through the main entrance.
27. Do not chew gum while taking part in spectacle.
28. Male performers are not to visit with the ballet girls. The excuse of "accidental" meetings on Sunday, in parks, at picture shows, etc., will not be accepted.
29. The use of alcohol or gasoline irons for pressing is strictly prohibited on show grounds or in the cars.
30. Do not lounge in wardrobe department of dressing rooms.
31. Do not practice or rehearse in main tent after 6:30 P. M.
32. Do not change position of trunks as placed in the dressing room.
33. Do not play ball in the main tent or "back yard."
34. Employees listed for Street Parade must be dressed and ready to "mount" at 10 o'clock A. M., unless notified to report earlier.
35. Do not run horses to "catch up" in parade—be on hand in time.
36. Do not sit "crossed-legged" on floats or tableaux wagons.
37. Button up coats, etc.
38. Absolutely, do not chew (gum or tobacco) or smoke in parade.
40. Report to the management at once any accident you may observe which may have been caused by the parade.
41. Do not loiter about the "front" of the show grounds.
42. Do not nod to friends or acquaintances who may be in the audience.
43. Avoid arguments with other employees. Be agreeable and promote harmony.

Since you have chosen to travel with the circus, it is evident that your success depends upon the success of circuses in general, and the one by which you are employed in particular. Therefore, the greater the success of the circus, and especially the part of that success to which you contribute, the better it is for you and the more valuable you will be in your profession.—Don't overlook this point—do your best — it is for you first and the company second.

All the foregoing rules and suggestions will also apply for the government of the Ballet Girls. In addition thereto the following especial rules are given for their guidance:

1. Do not dress in a flashy, loud style; be neat and modest in appearance.
2. You are required to be in the sleeping car and register your name not later than 11 P. M. and not to leave car after registering.
3. Girls must not stop at Hotels at any time.
4. You are not permitted to talk or visit with male members of the Show Company, excepting the management, and under no circumstances with residents of the cities visited.
6. The excuse of "accidental" meetings will not be accepted.
7. You must be in the ballet dressing room at 1 o'clock for matinee and at 7 o'clock P. M. for night performance.
8. You must not go into the big dressing room.

NOTE—If some of the rules seem harsh and exacting, please remember—experience has taught the management that they are necessary. It is intended to protect the girls in every possible way. Good order and good behavior are necessary, if you are to be comfortable and happy. The management urges each girl to live up to the spirit of the rules as well as to the letter.

TO CHILDREN, all circus acts are sensational and exciting. Here are seven superb examples of why the circus never ceases to thrill:

Left—Unus, balancing genius of the 1950's
Below left—The sensational Yacopi troupe.
Below—Helmuth Gunther—1953.
Right—The great Wallenda troupe of the 1940's.
Below right—The bicycle artists of 1953, the Frielanis.
Below right center—Everto, Swedish unicycle expert, 1955.

Below far right—Francis Brunn, 1949.

(RB&BB)

TOP—Panoramic view of the entire big top of 1920's.   (Atwell - Milw. Jour.-Wis. Hist. Soc.)

LEFT—Pat Valdo, onetime clown, for many years Ringling's director of performance.   (RB&BB)

BELOW are Fred and Ella Bradna. He was the dean of equestrian directors, and in the 20's she was a star equestrienne.   (Atwell-Milw. Jour.-Wis. Hist. Soc.)

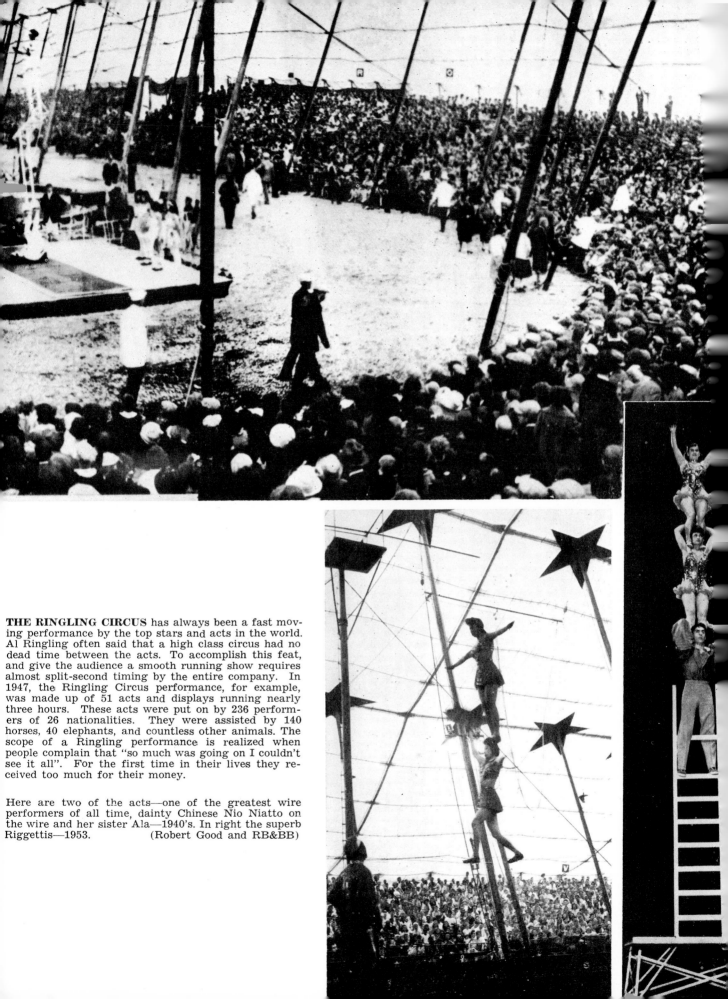

THE RINGLING CIRCUS has always been a fast moving performance by the top stars and acts in the world. Al Ringling often said that a high class circus had no dead time between the acts. To accomplish this feat, and give the audience a smooth running show requires almost split-second timing by the entire company. In 1947, the Ringling Circus performance, for example, was made up of 51 acts and displays running nearly three hours. These acts were put on by 236 performers of 26 nationalities. They were assisted by 140 horses, 40 elephants, and countless other animals. The scope of a Ringling performance is realized when people complain that "so much was going on I couldn't see it all". For the first time in their lives they received too much for their money.

Here are two of the acts—one of the greatest wire performers of all time, dainty Chinese Nio Niatto on the wire and her sister Ala—1940's. In right the superb Riggettis—1953. (Robert Good and RB&BB)

THE STORY OF THE HUNT TOLD BY LIVING MODELS AS WHITE AND SILENT AS THE SNOW

THE CIRCUS heavily advertises its sensational acts on lithographs or posters. Typical of this colorful form of art is (above) that depicting Ernest Clark doing the triple somersault—1940.
Above left—the somersaulting automobile, one of the most hazardous acts of all time.

Left center—The beautiful, never to be forgotten statue acts "as white and silent as the snow".

Below left—Lillian Leitzel, top performer of her day—1930's.
(Strobridge Litho. Co.)

RINGLING HORSES—Right above — Trainer, Charles Mroczkowski and his Liberty horse act of 1953. (RB&BB)

FAR RIGHT BELOW—Typical of many top-notch bareback troupes is the Loyal Repensky's.—1940's.
(Atwell-Milw. Jour.-Wis. Hist. Soc.)

RIGHT—Beautiful equestrienne Claude Valoise, 1950 season. (C. P. Fox)

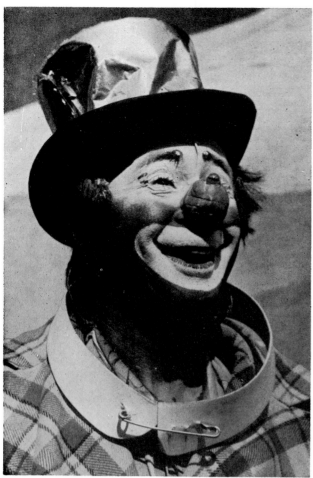

ABOVE—Paul Jerome   (RB&BB)

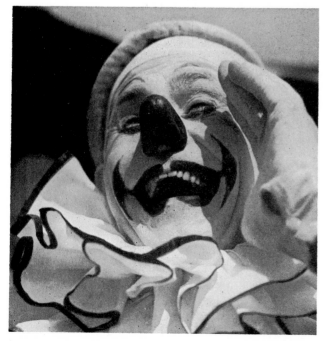

IN 1880 the Ringling Circus graduated from a wagon show to a railroad show. Their statement to the American people that year makes fascinating reading.

(Richard Conover Col.)

TO THE AMERICAN PEOPLE.

Again we come before you, submitting for your approval or condemnation the best efforts of our lives, embodied in our New and Monster Consolidation of Gigantic Railroad Shows. During the last half generation your several verdicts have been overwhelmingly in our favor, and the pride with which we contemplate the enormity of our present World of Wonders is not unmixed with gratitude to our millions of friends and patrons; for while we are conscious of having received honor and fame of that peculiar and lasting nature accorded to no others, we do not fail to see that not only to our own efforts, but also to that discriminating intelligence of a great and enlightened free nation, do we owe our advancement to the proud position of America's Representative Showmen. While we have labored on sturdily and incessantly with that measured tread which, seeming slow, yet gathers greatness with almost inconceivable rapidity. Your hearty support and uninterrupted patronage have been to us like a master's welcome, saying "Well done, good and faithful servant." And now, when we come before you with the fruits of years inculcated in one grand and culminating triumph, the grandeur and munificence of which we honestly believe cannot be duplicated on earth, we do so with a firm and unshaken trust in your support, which in the light of past events has ever been in proportion to the merit which craved it.

To emulate morality and make purity in amusement the guide to direct our projects, as well as integrity in business, have ever been our ideals of a perfect tented exposition; and we are gratified beyond words in being able to not only say that we have attained our ideal perfection, but to prove it with the convincing proof which a visit to our Great Moral Show will abundantly establish.

THE SHOW OF ALL NEW FEATURES!
BACKED BY UNLIMITED CAPITAL!

Larger Menageries, Finer Circuses, More Museum Features, Huger Hippodrome Spectacles and Classic Tournaments, Richer Oriental Pageants, Bigger Tents, More Massive Railroad Trains, More Elephants, More Horses, More Men, Women and Children, and a Bigger, Better, Richer, Grander Show THAN THE SUN EVER SHONE UPON BEFORE

250———HEAD OF HORSES———250
200———STAR PERFORMERS———200
80—STARTLING SENSATIONAL ACTS—80
75———EMINENT MUSICIANS———75
5—GREAT, GLORIOUS BANDS of MUSIC—5
7———OPEN DENS OF WILD BEASTS IN FREE STREET PROCESSION———7
10—ORDINARY MENAGERIES IN ONE—10
8———GRAND, COMPLETE CIRCUS COMPANIES———8
10—ACRES OF EXHILARATING SIGHTS—10
3 SPECIAL ADVERTISING CARS, HERALDING THE COMING OF THE GIANT 3 OF THE SHOW WORLD ON ITS OWN MONSTER TRAINS

1—TICKET ADMITS TO ALL—1

THE 1889 ISSUE letter-head showing the leased Van Amburgh name, which was well known in the circus world since mid-century.

SOLOMON AND THE QUEEN OF SHEBA

Produced under the Personal Direction of MR. AL. RINGLING

Time, 1000 B. C.   Place, Jerusalem

Scene I—THE GREAT JUDGMENT HALL
Scene II—THE STREETS OF JERUSALEM
Scene III—AT THE GATES OF THE HOLY CITY
Scene IV—IN THE PALACE OF THE KING

CAST OF CHARACTERS

SOLOMON	King of Israel	HANNAH	The True Mother
ZADOK		AZUBAH	The False Mother
ABIATHAR }	High Preists of the Temple	BALKIS	Queen of Sheba
BENAIAH	Captain of the Guard	OPODRUSA	
AZARIAH	A General	TOUMI }	1st Ladies in Waiting to the Queen
ZABUD	Chief Advisor to the King	BELVA	
AHISHAR	Master of Ceremony	AKBAR	Minister to Balkis
JEHOSHAPHAT	Master of the Tribute	HARMAK	Special Envoy of the Queen
ELIHOREPH }	Scribes to the King	AMENHAT	An Arabian Wonder Worker
AHIAH			

AND

The Princes, Governors and Nobility of Israel; Masters of Ceremony, Officers and Ladies of the Court, Envoys and Embassadors from Foreign Lands, Astrologers, Dancers, Entertainers, Court Musicians, Flower Girls, Priests, Incense Bearers, Coryphees, Soldiers, Prisoners, Slaves, Figurantes, Guards, Athletes, Arabian Courtiers, Necromancers, Sages, Camel Drivers, Trains of Visiting Dignitaries, Populace of Jerusalem, Etc.

PRODUCING STAFF

Entry and Pantomime Music Composed by	Mr. Faltis Effendi
Grand Ballet Music Composed by	Mr. J. J. Richards
Scenery Designed and Painted by	Sosman & Landis Co.
Costumes and Accessories Designed by	Mr. William Crowe
Costumes and Accessories Executed by	Henderson-Ames Co.
Ballet Dresses Designed and Executed by	Mr. F. Schoultz
Orchestra under the Direction of	Mr. J. J. Richards
Stage and Ballet under the Direction of	Mr. Ottokar Bartik

KANK SOLOMON AND THE
QUEEN OF SHEBA
IN ONE SCENE

All the first assembled multitude in places as directed below.

12 Property men as Tribes and People from Jerusalem with different object in their hands such as squares, Compasses, Trowels, etc., standing on quite high platform on highest part of same in back row and at left of Throne.

8 Property men as King's Warriors carrying Bows, Quivers, and Shields, standing on quite high platform on highest part of same in back row at right of Throne.

8 Property men as Hebrew Soldiers carrying round shields and spears standing on high platform on highest part of same in back row at left of Throne.

12 Grooms as Isralite Soldiers carrying spears, Bows and Quivers, Quivers in bunches strapped on their back, standing on quite high platform on highest part of same on back row at left and next to the Tribes and People from Jerusalem.

16 Cook House men as Soldiers carrying Battle Axes and War Clubs standing on quite high platform on highest part of same on back row at right of Throne and next to the King's Warriors.

12 Performers as Soldiers (Later Mounted) with spears and shields, standing on quite high platform on highest part of same on back row at left of Throne and next to Property men Hebrew Soldiers.

Hugh Melnotte	Ed. Nemo	John Tripp
Mr. Evans	Mr. Borsini	Mr. Borsini
C. LaMole	Mr. Rodrigues	Mr. Rodrigues
Mr. Jahn	Mr. Florimond	Mr. Fortune
Mr. Fred Stelling--Extra man in this section		

12 Performers as Solomon's Governors, each carrying a sword and banner with the name of the Province he represents printed thereon, standing on second steps of platform at right of Throne. These people to also carry swords.

Pete Mardo	H. D. Mack	Joe Hodgini
Mr. Bento	Young McCree	Ed. Rooney
Mr. Fortune	C. Nelson	R. Nelson
J. Mijares	Mr. Florimond	Paul Minno

2 Scribes with books on second steps of platform at left of Throne.

Julian TyDell   Mr. Raleigh Wilburn

1 Recorder with staff on second steps of platform at left of Throne.
Jules Turnour.

1 Captain of the Guards (Later Mounted) carrying sword standing on first steps in front of the Throne.

William Carroll)

YEAR AFTER YEAR, in the late 90's and early 1900's, the Ringlings put on a prodigous stage show they call a spectacle. On one side of the main tent was a huge stage. (See next page above.) Partaking in these pantomime dramas were hundreds of people, horses, camels, and elephants. In 1901 it was "Joan of Arc"; in 1914, "The Queen of Sheba"; and in 1917 "Cinderella." Left—The original typewritten script of the 1914 "Queen of Sheba" show, which gives an idea of the size and pretentiousness of these productions.
(Wis. Hist. Soc. and Steve Albasing)

WILLIAM WELDON and his 1892 band. There were no violins, harps, or cellos in this circus band, or in any other real circus band. Instead horns, horns and more horns supplemented this season with cannons, anvils, and sleigh bells. Music played at a Ringling performance includes about everything from rumbas, polkas, fox trots, to cake walks, waltzes, gallops and marches. All the music is geared to the acts, and the director who plays with his back to his band must watch the performance with a practiced eye. In the course of a three-hour show, over 200 cues are given to the director, which means he has to change the music, or its tempo over 200 times. For the wild animal acts there are nine cues alone as the tigers and lions develop their routine. Thus, once a season's score is decided upon, it is never changed. (Paul Luckey Collection)

ABOVE — Merle Evans, for 37 years Ringling's bandmaster. Above, right —Typical musical program—1923.
(Wis. Hist. Soc.)

MUSICAL PROGRAM
Ringling Bros. and Barnum & Bailey Combined Shows
MERLE EVANS, Bandmaster

1. Overture—Golden Dragon ....King	24. Overture—Norwegian Rhapsody ....Svendsen
2. Overture—Semiramide ....Rossini	25. Overture—Danish Festival ....Tschaikowsky
3. Overture—William Tell ....Rossini	26. Overture—Herodias ....Massenet
4. Overture—Hungarian Fantasia ....Tobani	27. Overture—Rigoletto ....Verdi
5. Overture—Second Hungarian Fantasia......Tobani	28. Overture—March Slave ....Tschaikowsky
6. Overture—Second Hungarian Rhapsody......Liszt	29. Overture—Ruy Blas ....Mendelssohn
7. Overture—Carmen Fantasia ....Balfe	30. Selection—Macbeth ....Verdi
8. Overture—Oberon ....Weber	31. Selection—Samson and Delilah........Saint-Saens
9. Overture—Il Gurarney ....Gomez	32. Selection—Faust ....Gounod
10. Overture—1812 ....Tschaikowsky	33. Selection—I Lombardi ....Verdi
11. Overture—Rienzi ....Wagner	34. Selection—Gypsy Life Fantasia.........LeThiere
12. Overture—Sunshine and Showers..........Flath	35. Selection—Apple Blossoms ....Kreisler
13. Overture—The Courts of Granada..........Chapi	36. Selection—Bohemian Girl ....Balfe
14. Overture—Dedication and Benediction from the Huguenots ....Meyerbeer	37. Selection—Aida ....Verdi
15. Overture—Fingals Cave ....Mendelssohn	38. Selection—Irene ....Tierney
16. Overture—Rakoczy ....Keler-Bela	39. Selection—Shuffle Along ....Sissle and Blake
17. Finale from 4th Symphony..........Tschaikowsky	40. Selection—Lucrezia Borgia ....Tobani
18. Overture—Tannhauser ....Wagner	41. Selection—Her Soldier Boy ....Romberg
19. Overture—Lohengrin ....Wagner	42. Selection—You're in Love ....Friml
20. Overture—Der Freischuetz ....Weber	43. Selection—Songs of Scotland.............Lampe
21. Overture—Maximillian Robespierre ....Litolff	44. Selection—Some Time ....Friml
22. Overture—Slavonic Rhapsody ....Friedman	45. Selection—The Barefoot Trail ....Wiggins
23. Overture—Sicilian Vespers ....Verdi	46. Selection—Sometime ....L. W. Lockwood

BELOW is Spader Johnson's famous Clown Band—1897.   (Wis. Hist. Soc.)

THE WILD ANIMAL ACTS are fraught with constant and real danger. The trainer must know and understand the temperament of each and every beast in the big cage. Here Alfred Court's Bengal tiger walks the tight rope. The big cats and bears can never be tamed, but through patience and understanding and persistence they can be trained. (RB&BB)

OPPOSITE TOP—DeJonghe's chimpanzee act—1955; and below the incomparable Clyde Beatty, for many seasons on the Ringling show. (RB&BB)

LEFT—One of Capt. Roland Teibor's seals—adept at balancing, they also learn to blow air through their nose into a series of horns and play "My Country 'Tis of Thee," not to please the audience, but to earn tidbits of fish. Below—Herta Klauser and one of her bears—1950. Below left—Two famous acts and Emil Pallenberg's bruins that skate, dance, ride bicycles and walk on stilts.

(R&BB and C. P. Fox Collection)

Elephants and Horses

Frank Braden, eminent vocabulist of the Ringling press staff, once said, "A circus without an elephant? Why that is just like a horse race without a horse!"

All circus elephants are called "bulls," whether male or female, and rarely does the show carry any males. They get too obstreperous and difficult to handle in their rutting season. An exception was Snyder, who started his career with the Ringlings and ended up on the Sells-Floto circus. He went berserk on the lot one day and in his rampage he wrecked a number of wagons and tents. When finally cornered he was mercifully shot to avoid further trouble. Snyder had the unusual distinction of siring five elephant calves —none of which lived more than a few months. In 1889 the Ringlings did advertise Fanny as an American born elephant—a great rarity.

On two occasions the Ringling Circus displayed genuine white elephants which are the rarest of rare attractions. In 1897 and 1898, Keddah was with the show, and 30 years later in 1927, Dr. Po Min brought Pawah (Mr. White) to the U. S. from Burma for one year's showing only.

Over the years, the elephants have been used for work as well as performing. The bulls are exceptionally deft at pushing wagons in soft or muddy lots. In 1939, the year after the circus disposed of its baggage stock, the elephant herd was called into its greatest working test. The big beasts were used to unload the trains, haul wagons to and from the lot, unroll the canvas, raise the poles, raise the canvas, and spot wagons, as well as perform. They really earned their keep in this transition period from horse power to tractor and truck power.

The ability of the elephant to pull recalls the time when the circus offered the U.S. Government 25 elephants for artillery service during the Cuban War in 1898.

Professor Lockhart, an Englishman who had a trained elephant act on the show in the 1890's wrote:—

"Elephants are selected for training when young. The bumps on their heads are taken into consideration, for the phrenology of the elephant head is a sure index to character. A flat, low narrow head belongs to a vicious low-bred dangerous elephant. On the other hand, well rounded bumps over the eyes, a high forehead, and straight well-set eyes indicate intelligence and docility. Educating an elephant is like educating a child. You must begin training in childhood if you want them to be perfect at maturity. Patience, perseverance, and pluck are needed to train elephants."

Stories are told of elephants' distrust for a flimsy bridge, and the big beast's caution has saved many a heavily loaded wagon from crashing through into the water. Ed Dougherty, who was with the show in the pre-railroad days, recalled that the elephants had a particular dislike for bridges with loose planks. Said he, "When the bulls refused to cross a shaky bridge, they were always taken down to the water's edge, and they quickly swam across the creek or stream."

In these mud show days it was customary to equip the elephants with leather or canvas shoes to keep their feet from getting sore. A 10 or 15-mile trek on a hard rubble road was tough on the calloused pads of the pachyderm's feet.

A hilarious tale about Mickey Mann, who was Ringling's first elephant man, still circulates in Baraboo. The story deals with the years when the show travelled overland from town to town. Mickey would draw a farmer into a conversation on the value of an elephant for plowing. "Why, one elephant could pull a three-bottom plow as easily as eight horses," he would say. He would then sell Babylon, one of the two elephant's the circus owned at the time, to the farmer. After the evening show, Mickey, the farmer, and Babylon would walk down the road to the farm whereupon the bull was settled down with a bale of hay. In the early morning hours, as the circus was moving down the road to the next town, Mickey would wait until he was opposite the barn in which he had put Babylon, then in his usual hoarse rumbling voice shout, "Come on, Babe;" whereupon the elephant would walk right through the side of the barn and join the plodding caravan—only to be sold again the next time Mickey could find a gullible farmer.

Almost as colorful as the elephant men were the

rare breed of circus teamsters who handled the big show's horses and Jim Hickey was, in the opinion of the Ringling teamsters, the most outstanding driver of them all. A small man of 150 pounds, he was handicapped by the fact that the toes of both his feet had been frozen off in his pre-circus days while driving a stage. How a man of this size could hold the lines and drive these big teams was, to many, miraculous. (On the circus the reins are always called lines).

Hickey was known as a man who could handle any team. He would get a string of horses to respond to his hands and calls like none other. So when the Ringlings put a 24-horse hitch of greys on to their No. 1 bandwagon in parade, Hickey got the job of driving them. This team was hitched four abreast and there were six such teams of four horses. As one fellow teamster put it, "that was a powerful lot of leather that mite of a man held in his hands."

Jim Hickey and his 24 were coming onto the lot after parade one day. The circus grounds being small and confined, Hickey brought his team to a stop to survey the lot and find out where to spot his huge bandwagon. Chas. Rooney, assistant boss hostler, rode up and pointed out the spot. Immediately Hickey realized that to get his wagon onto that spot would require a tricky "S" turn for his team. As he gathered his lines and collected his team, Rooney trotted up to one of the lead horses and made the drastic mistake of grabbing the bridle in an effort to help guide Hickey through the maze of wagons.

Now Hickey had a high tenor voice that could be heard a mile. Also, he was touchy about his ability to handle his team. To him, or any teamster, the greatest insult that could be inflicted was to have a hostler grab a bridle of a lead horse.

At the sight of Rooney's action almost 100 feet out in front of him, the furious Hickey erupted from his seat and in his clarion voice, which sounded all over the tented lot, screamed, "Here, you son-of-a-bitch, take the whole team," and with that he threw all the lines onto the backs of the wheelers, climbed down from the wagon and stalked off in indignation. Rooney had learned a lesson the hard way. These teamsters were a proud bunch!

Every teamster loved his horses and had the greatest admiration for them. Jim Traver, in talking about his team said, "They were the best horses that ever looked through a collar." Although he did recall one morning, early in the spring at LaCrosse, Wisconsin.

"They were fresh colts—first year out—I had my hands full all the time. This particular morning I was pulling the hippo den to the lot and I fell asleep. As we approached a corner, my team, following the wagon ahead, turned, but being young and green, they cut the corner too close, and the front wheel of the wagon

ONE OF RINGLING'S BLACKSMITHS—theirs was an indispensable job on the circus. (C. P. Fox)

went up over the curb and broke off a fire hydrant. I was rudely awakened by a huge jet of water cascading all over me. If this team had been into the season a few more months this never would have happened, as a well broke team would have had sense enough to swing wide enough for the wagon to clear the curb."

Spencer Alexander, known on the lot as Old Del (he came from Delavan, Wisconsin) was Boss Hostler for many years. Here was an outstanding horseman who kept his men on their toes. All horses had to be well groomed and cleaned every day. Any Ringling teamster will recall his booming voice, as he strode into one end of the horse tent calling out, "By God, get them harnesses cleaned, shine up the brass, curry those hosses, brush out those manes and tails!" Old Del had a keen eye trained on each horse—he knew a sick horse was deadweight around a circus lot. As he put it, "around here I want a sound horse and one that will try to jump through his collar when the going is tough."

On the parade days the teams were assigned to a float, den, or bandwagon . . . the same one each day throughout the season. For example, John Winn drove the 10-horse team on the No. 1 Bandwagon. He had one bad eye and wore a black patch over it. When parading in Mobile, Alabama, one of the crowd standing on the curb was heard to remark, "Man alive, look at that man driving all them hosses—and he has only one eye. How many could he drive if he had two eyes."

Jim Traver drove the hip den in the parade. He had his troubles with the hippopotamus, who was determined to move up to the front end of the den. With this great massive weight bearing down on the front wheels it was extremely difficult for the wheel team to turn the wagon. Traver equipped his brakeman with a long pole that had a spike inserted in the end. This prod, when poked through the front window of the cage, persuaded the hippo to stay at the rear of his den during the parade.

The Ringlings were always, and still are, proud of their horses, which are exceptional, rather than average examples of horseflesh. Their never ending quest for superb horses brings to mind the personal experience of Vernon Kraft back in 1911. Kraft worked for a livery stable in Blanchardville, Wisconsin. The stable had a magnificent Percheron stallion that had unusual style and beauty. However, through poor handling he had become so vicious and mean he could not be used for breeding any more. No one dared to handle him, much less work him and the stable owner could not sell him, as everyone in the countryside knew his reputation.

One day a Ringling horse buyer arrived in town. When shown the mean stallion the buyer purchased him because of his beauty—but at a bargain price because of his disposition. The livery owner gloated to his friends at the deal he had made. Shortly, a Ringling stock car was shunted onto a siding and two men rode over to the livery to get their stallion. It was immediately apparent that these men were experts.

Before the stud knew what was happening, they had a twitch on his nose, then a new halter on his head, equipped with a simple martingale to keep the stallion from wildly tossing his head. Next, they deftly put a strap around each leg just above the hoof. To each strap was fastened a short piece of light chain.

ASHVILLE, N. C.—1908—an eight-horse hitch pulling a pole wagon from train to show lot.
(Wis. Hist. Soc.)

They then introduced into the box stall a small terrier they had brought along. The dog began to worry the stud, who flayed his own legs with the short chains each time he kicked.

No matter which way he kicked, or with what leg, he inflicted this punishment on himself. Within 15 minutes the stallion was subdued and docile. While one man removed the leg straps, the other stood at the stallion's head talking to him quietly. He then mounted the stallion and rode bareback to the rail siding, leaving the livery owner standing with mouth hanging open, realizing that he had practically given away his magnificent Percheron.

The Ringlings had deep feelings for their horses. Wm. Prielipp, Al Ringling's chauffeur says, "If Mr. Al ever saw a man kick, or beat a horse, he was fired on the spot."

Alf T. Ringling, in the 1895 route book, with an uncanny vision of the future, wrote:—

"A circus without horses would be like a kite without a tail. The noble horse is an adjunct as absolutely necessary to the show as the rudder is to a ship. It is indeed doubtful if there would have ever been a circus had there never been a horse. With the circus, the horse is a necessity in every department. The most important of all the horses with the show are the ring stock, or bareback horses. A way might be devised for transporting the show from the railroad cars to the grounds. Horseless vehicles might be contrived to do this work in a horseless age. A parade might be made without the horse and could be dispensed with in many respects where he seems, by habit and custom, indispensable. But no contrivance run by steam, electricity, or naphtha could be invented to take the place of the live white horse running around the circus ring with a rider on its back. The old-time cry of the clown, 'bring out another horse' could hardly be paraphrased into 'bring out another motorcycle,' with any degree of satisfaction, even if the rider could do his tricks upon some such horseless horse."

In 1951, carrying on the tradition of the finest possible horses, Henry Ringling North purchased 12 colts from the King Ranch in Texas. These perfectly matched Bay stallions performed as a trained liberty group during the 1955 season. The circus has since received its second and third shipments of colts from the King Ranch at a cost of $1300 each. Within the next few years, the U.S. public will be thrilled by the appearance of 36 beautiful Bay stallions performing at the same time—12 in each ring.

At winterquarters one will find many old equine troupers out on pasture. Too old to perform, these ponies, hackneys and saddle horses will live out their days under the Sarasota sun.

ABOVE—Bareback horses ready for ring—note white powdered resin on their backs.　(C. P. Fox)

UPPER LEFT—1953—Roberto de Vasconcellos, master of the high school.　(RB&BB)

LOWER LEFT—1944 Albert Ostermaier and his horse, Doheas.　(RB&BB)

BELOW RIGHT—1897—the one and only Silver King being carried on the shoulders of 12 men.
(Sauk Co. Hist. Soc.)

ABOVE AND RIGHT—Comical two-headed horses and gorgeously robed horses await their turn to parade in "walk around" on hippodrome track.   (C. P. Fox)

THE CHICAGO LOT in early 1930's showing draft stock. These wagons are loaded with seats and will be pulled into the big tent as soon as it is up.   (Atwell-Milw. Jour.-Wis. Hist. Soc.)

NORWOOD, OHIO—1916, Jim Hickey, one of Ringling's finest drivers, is shown here with a 24-horse hitch of matched gray Percherons on the No. 1 bandwagon. Hickey held six lines in each hand. An assistant sat behind him to keep the leather from twisting as it slipped through his fingers. When the team swung wide around a corner, as much as 10 feet of lines would pull through his fingers and, as the team straightened out, this leather had to be pulled back through his fingers by the assistant so Hickey could always be driving a collected team. The bobbing red plumes on the horses heads were 18 inches high.

(Harry Simpson Collection)

BELOW—Franz Ackerl's Lippizan beauty—1950.
(C. P. Fox)

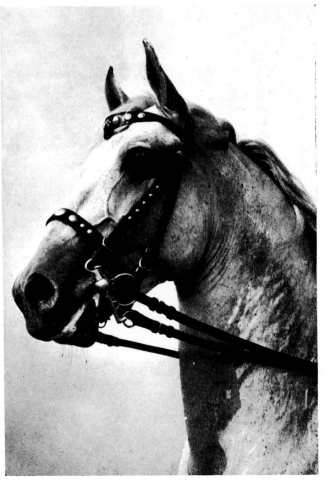

ABOVE—1915—Eagle Jack and horse Tess that performed without a halter. (Steve Albasing)

LEFT—A page from a 1900 courier advertising John O'Brien's famous 61-horse act. (H. H. Conley Collection)

BELOW—1922—Jorgen Christiansen and his famous black stallion troupe. (Atwell-Milw. Jour.-Wis. Hist. Soc.)

ABOVE—1946—horse tents. In case of rain or wind the canvas side wall will be erected. (C. P. Fox)

BELOW—1954—Circus vet J. Y. Henderson, Henry Ringling North, circus Vice President, and Charles Mroczow- ski, horse trainer with 12 King Ranch stallions.
(RB&BB)

RICCOBONO'S GREAT FEAT OF HORSEMANSHIP WITH THE WHIRLING TABLE

HE PULLS OFF COAT

HE TAKES OFF BOOTS

The Worlds Greatest Triumph of Animal Training

HE TAKES OFF TROUSERS

HE TAKES OFF THE QUILT

THE GOOD-NIGHT HORSE
HIS WIFE AND FAMILY

THE GOOD-NIGHT HORSE HIS WIFE AND FAMILY

RICCOBONO'S COMPANY OF EQUINE ACTORS

America has never before seen an example of animal training that can approach this wonderful act. A horse wearing boots, pants, coat, vest, hat and everything else, even to a watch and fob, comes home to his family, dines and reads the newspaper. When the clock strikes ten he pulls off his boots, lights the candle, goes to his bed, removes his pants and other clothing, blows out the candle, draws the covers down, gets into bed, pulls the covers over him and closes his eyes. And then his wife, with the true instinct of her sex, as soon as she hears him snore, deftly goes through her lord's pockets.

A WONDERFUL TROUPE OF HIGH SCHOOL HORSES

Decked with silver-woven trappings and flowery garlands, going through all the intricacies of the quadrille and moving in a harmony of motion that delights and astounds, is another achievement of triumphant equestrianism to be seen with the great Ringling Bros. Circus. POST GRADUATE PONIES, TRICK HORSES, AND EVEN MULES OF HUMAN REASONING POWER, lend much additional interest to the TRAINED HORSE FEATURES OF THE GREATEST SHOW ON EARTH, IN WHICH ONE HUNDRED BEAUTIFUL EQUINES APPEAR.

THIS 1907 COURIER PAGE said the circus had "post graduate ponies, trick horses and even mules of human reasoning power."

(H. H. Conley Collection)

ABOVE—Elephants being used for heavy work in early 1940's. Pulling up the first, or King pole, c a u s e d these beasts to lean into their harness.
(C. P. Fox)

C I R C U S ELEPHANTS are in their prime between 25 and 45 years of age. Their life expectancy is about that of a human being. If, occasionally, an e l e p h a n t reaches the age of 60 or 70 years, it is not of much value to the circus for performing or work.
(RB&BB)

BELOW—1955 — the elephant baby carriage act which was a big hit.
(C. P. Fox)

ABOVE—The Ringling elephants ponderously walk from menagerie tent in background to the big top to prepare for their entrance to the performance—1950, Madison, Wis. (C. P. Fox)

WHEN GOING TO THE CIRCUS the first sight of the elephants is in the menagerie where the entire herd stands side by side all ready and willing to beg peanuts. (Atwell-Milw. Jour.-Wis. Hist. Soc.)

BELOW is the Ringling herd in 1944 during the performance.   (Robert Good)

ABOVE—Prof. Lockhart, an Englishman, had a great elephant act on the show in 1897.

(Fred Terbilcox Collection)

LEFT—With a spangled robe on its back and girl in tights on its head, this huge elephant is ready for the grand entry march.

(Atwell-Milw. Jour.-Wis. Hist. Soc.)

BELOW—Pigmy Africans in profile with an Indian, shows difference in the two species of elephant.

(C. P. Fox)

BOTTOM—A team of four bulls moves a heavy wagon onto lot in Miilwaukee, Wis.—1939.

IN 1916 Ringlings changed the name of Jenny, whom they acquired from the W. B. Reynolds Show many years before, to "Big Bingo". Jenny had grown into an unusually large elephant, so gigantic, in fact, that the circus sought to capitalize on her size. Above is an actual photo of her.

Below is a lithograph that said her height was 11½ feet. She was displayed standing on a platform to give an added illusion of height.

(Atwell, Milw. Jour. - Wis. Hist. Soc.)

BELOW RIGHT is an actual photo of an elephant claimed to have been born in Baraboo, Wisconsin. It was named Baby Boo. Circa 1901.

(Joe Burke Collection)

ABOUT WHITE ELEPHANTS.

THE RAREST OF ALL THE ANIMAL KINGDOM, AND THE MOST EXPENSIVE TO BUY.

EVER own a white elephant? It isn't the easiest thing in the world to get hold of, in the first place, and once you've got him, he becomes somewhat of a responsibility and care. Not that he is any more delicately constructed than black elephants, but you will imagine that he is more susceptible to colds, and all sorts of troubles—because he will cost you so much money that you can never quite forget his extreme.

For more than four years special agents of the Ringling Brothers' World's Greatest Shows scoured India and Burmah, looking for what has generally been believed to be a mythical animal. One was exhibited in the United States many years ago, but he was so palpably a fake that the amusement-going public laughed at the showman who exhibited him and took it as a good joke. It has been a matter of history, however, for years, that white elephants did exist in the Orient. That they were simply albinos, was generally understood by naturalists. Albinos are in all animal tribes, to a greater or less extent, therefore why should not an albino elephant be found? The idea that there is anything sacred about a white elephant is a pure fallacy, to be sure, although the Brahmin and Buddhists believe that a white elephant is the reincarnated spirit of a defunct priest of the temple, and respect him accordingly.

The agents of the Messrs. Ringling found three white elephants in various temples in Burmah, but the matter of their sale or purchase would not be listened to for a moment. The natives would as lief sell their great god Buddha. A fourth was heard of in the remote interior, and was said to be the property of a

KEDDAH, THE SACRED WHITE ELEPHANT.

59

Portuguese trader. After months of weary journeying, the trader was found and also the white elephant. He was a pure albino, about seven years old, and at the present time stands about five feet high. His eyes are of the usual pinkish hue, noticeable in all albinos; his skin is very soft for an elephant and is of that peculiar light mouse-color, of the prevailing stylish spring Fedora hat—not pure white, but nearly so.

Keddah, for that is the white elephant's name, lives in regal style now. The matter of his purchase in Burmah, and his subsequent transportation to the coast and thence to San Francisco, would make an interesting tale. He is about one-quarter as big as big "Baldy," who is the captain of the herd of twenty-five elephants carried by the Ringling Brothers, but in dollars and cents he is worth as much as several "Baldies." He rides in regal style, in a massive white chariot, weighing five tons, and elaborately ornamented inside and out. When on exhibition in the menagerie he is dressed in full Burmese regalia, and is attended day and night by two of the most experienced keepers procurable. But he eats peanuts and popcorn just the same as cheap elephants and he'll eat all he can get. When feeding time comes he has the best of everything, but, like all other elephants, steals as much more as he can from his brethren. He is the cutest, prettiest, most entertaining elephant ever exhibited anywhere, and is the pet of all who see him. As a menagerie feature he has proven the best drawing card it has ever had, and his name is upon every tongue, on show day, wherever the big show goes.

ELEPHANT TRAINERS AND KEEPERS.

THESE PAGES from 1897 route book describe the purchase of the Ringlings white elephant Keddah.

(Sauk Co. Hist. Soc.)

KEDDAH was with the circus in 1897 and 1898. She died in October 1898 after her railroad car caught fire and she was severely burned.

(H. H. Conley Collection)

IN 1927 the Ringlings had a white Burmese elephant named Pawah. Shown here is the elephant with Dr. Po Min who brought the sensational beast to America. (Atwell, Milw. Jour. - Wis. Hist. Soc.)

LEFT is the lithograph describing Pawah. The word "Pawah" means "Mr. White." (C. P. Fox Collection)

Rolling Stock

The wagon is the backbone of the circus. Into these red wagons (the commissary and dining department vehicles are green) is loaded all of the fantastic array of equipment in a completely orderly fashion each day of the season. One way to comprehend the vast complexity of the Ringling Circus is to peruse the list of wagons and their contents. Here are the vehicles used in the 1955 season[1]:—

Wagon No.					
	1	16 feet long		-	cookhouse equipment
"	2	12	" "	-	steam boiler
"	3	19	" "	-	cookhouse ranges
"	4	20	" "	-	cookhouse supplies & refrigerators
"	5	14	" "	-	dining equipment
"	6	19	" "	-	dishwasher
"	7	19	" "	-	cookhouse ranges
"	8	20	" "	-	dining tent & equipment
"	9	19	" "	-	general repair dept.
"	10	14	" "	-	menagerie supplies and equipment
"	11	17	" "	-	ringstock & wardrobe tents
"	12	14	" "	-	elephant trappings & equipment
"	29	18	" "	-	band & sound equipment
"	30	17	" "	-	ringstock wardrobe
"	31	29	" "	-	animal act arenas
"	38	17	" "	-	big top stakes
"	43	42	" "	-	big top center poles
"	44	30	" "	-	big top quarter poles
"	48	18	" "	-	midway concession stands
"	49	18	" "	-	popcorn plant
"	57	23	" "	-	aerial act rigging
"	60	20	" "	-	concession supplies
"	61	19	" "	-	property men's equipment
"	64	17	" "	-	wardrobe
"	70	12	" "	-	ticket office
"	71 - 81	12	" "	-	menagerie animal dens
"	82	21	" "	-	rhinoceros cage
"	83	18	" "	-	giraffe wagon
"	85	21	" "	-	hippopotamus cage
"	86	19	" "	-	giraffe wagon
"	87	18	" "	-	baby tigers
"	92	18	" "	-	tigers
"	93	18	" "	-	lions
"	94	23	" "	-	polar bears
"	97	28	" "	-	gorilla cage
"	102	19	" "	-	candy tent concessions
"	103	17	" "	-	snack diner
"	104	16	" "	-	commissary & timekeeper
"	105	18	" "	-	power control equipment & light dept. office
"	108	15	" "	-	dual stakedriver
"	109	19	" "	-	midway power plant
"	111	17	" "	-	big top power plant
"	112	17	" "	-	big top power plant
"	114	17	" "	-	lights & equipment
"	115	19	" "	-	sideshow front & front door equipment
"	116	19	" "	-	sideshow office & supplies
"	117	17	" "	-	ringstock equipment & blacksmith shop
"	118	19	" "	-	ticket & publicity office
"	119	21	" "	-	sideshow front & sideshow tent
"	120	21	" "	-	sideshow front & sideshow equipment
"	121	17	" "	-	tickets & mgr.'s office
"	122	17	" "	-	tickets & legal dept.
"	123	20	" "	-	tickets & gen. mgr.'s office
"	124	16	" "	-	tickets & office
"	125	22	" "	-	male performers wardrobe
"	130	14	" "	-	train loading light plant
"	131	21	" "	-	special equipment
"	134	27	" "	-	female wardrobe
"	135	17	" "	-	performing dogs
"	136	18	" "	-	veterinary's office & equipment
"	137	16	" "	-	ringstock trappings
"	141	20	" "	-	wardrobe trunks & personnel mgr.'s office
"	142	20	" "	-	special equipment
"	143	20	" "	-	wardrobe trunks
"	145	20	" "	-	special equipment
"	146	20	" "	-	special wardrobe

Sanitation Wagon No. 1 - 27 feet long - Men's toilets
Sanitation Wagon No. 2 - 27 feet long - Ladies' toilets
[1] Complied by Edward A. Lester.

This totals 79 wagons. In addition, there were 28 portable seat wagons, each 35 feet long and weighing 35,000 lbs. when loaded.

The vast amount of equipment listed above does not take into consideration the great array of powerful Mack trucks used for carrying canvas, pulling wagons, and hauling water. Nor does it include the collection of Caterpillar tractors equipped with hoists, winches, and cranes to meet any situation. The Ringling Circus is self-sufficient and must always help itself when a breakdown occurs, or a muddy lot bogs down the

IT WAS IN THE LATE 30'S that the transition from horses to tractors and wagon wheels to pneumatic tires took place. (Caterpillar Tractor Co.)

1915 SCENE when heavy bales of rolled up canvas were loaded by hand. (Steve Albasing)

1947 SCENE showing some of the motive power used by the circus. (C. P. Fox)

wagons. David Blanchfield is superintendent of motive power. He graduated to this job, having been a teamster prior to 1938. He is a key figure in keeping the circus rolling. The following is a complete list of the motive power used by the big show in 1955:

Mack Truck No. 233 - 20 feet long - water for cookhouse, menagerie, shop & performers buckets

"	"	234 - 20	"	"	- water for midway
"	"	235 - 20	"	"	- wrecker
"	"	237 - 20	"	"	- water for horses
"	"	238 - 20	"	"	- water for elephants
"	"	239 - 20	"	"	- water for big top spray
"	"	251 - 31	"	"	- big top rigging & side poles
"	"	252 - 31	"	"	- ½ of big top canvas
"	"	253 - 31	"	"	- ½ of big top canvas
"	"	254 - 31	"	"	- menagerie tent
GMC	"	241 - 16	"	"	- welding equipment
Halftruck		250 - 20	"	"	- stakedriver
GMC Truck		3 - 19	"	"	- sanitation
Willys Truck		1 - 12	"	"	- dump truck
"	"	7 - 12	"	"	- light stakedriver

Caterpillar Tractor B-1 Model D-4 - canvas hoist
"	"	B-2	"	- stakepuller
"	"	B-4	"	- used at runs
"	"	B-5	"	- stakepuller
"	"	B-6	"	- used at runs
"	"	B-7	"	- crane
"	"	B-8	"	- crane
"	"	A-2	"	D-7 - used at lot
"	"	A-3	"	D-7 - used at lot
"	"	A-5	"	D-7 - used at lot
Wheeled Tractor	B-9	"	D-6 - used as a pull-up at runs
"	"	C-4	"	- used at trains
"	"	C-5	"	- used at trains
"	"	C-6	"	- used at trains

Willys Jeep No. 3 - power take off for erecting seat wagons
" " 4 - power take off for erecting seat wagons
" " 5 - tire repair
" " 6 - Supt. Blanchfield
GMC Bus No. 1 - 31 feet long - 36 passenger - for hauling personnel between lot & train
" " 2 - 31 " " - 36 passenger - for hauling personnel between lot & train
Chevrolet Station Wagon - 17 feet long - Miscellaneous services

In 1935 the management started to equip the wagons with pneumatic dual tires. Gone is one of the most traditional of circus heritages—the wooden spoked wheel, webbed with colorful wood panels, heavy steel rim, and glorious white, blue, and red strippings, known as sunburst wheels. Then, with the passing of the baggage horse in 1938, the circus began to rebuild its wagons. The removable tongue gave way to a shorter one of steel construction, hinged to fold up against the front of the wagon. All of the wagons are

LEFT — 1938 — a crawler type tractor pulling a heavily loaded seat wagon into the big top. (Caterpillar Tractor Co.)

now built of steel and very few have springs. Those that do are the gorilla cage, giraffe dens, ticket and office wagons. Most of the wagons are built at winter-quarters where they are designed and constructed for their special uses. One of the most interesting vehicles in many a year was the new office wagon ordered in 1956. It was to be plush and comfortable, costing $35,000. The wagon never toured with the circus, as the following year the show went into arenas, giving up rail travel after 67 years, in favor of trucks.

In 1948 the management purchased 28 specially built seat wagons. These wagons, which cost $10,000 each, put a tremendous dent in the man-hours needed to set up the seats. Formerly, 250 men struggled for two and a half hours to erect the bleachers and chairs. With the new setup 15 men do the job in an hour.

Unnecessary weight is the bane of the existence of all circus managers. The wagons can haul just so much of a load, and if equipment is unnecessarily heavy it means more wagons; thus, more railroad cars. Early in the game the Ringlings realized the necessity of trimming useless weight from all paraphernalia. So sensitive were they about unnecessary heavy loads that when they purchased the Barnum & Bailey show in 1907 this was one of the first criticisms they had of their new acquisition. This circus was notorious for having

heavy and cumbersome equipment. It caused delays and required more time to put up the show, more men to do it, and more wagons to haul it. So, when the purchase was consumated, Otto entrained for Mc-Alister, Oklahoma, where the Barnum show was playing. On Oct. 12 he sent in this report:—

"To Ringling Bros.
The property here has been kept in fine shape and I find cars, horses, baggage wagons, etc. in most excellent condition. The seat stuff is entirely too heavy, with no more seating capacity than we have. They use four jack wagons instead of two; five blue plank wagons, instead of three. Their blue seat stringers are heavier than our grandstand stringers. Their reserved seat stringers are heavier than our blue and reserved seat stringers combined and, of course, their grandstand stringers are also very heavy, and their jacks are ridiculously heavy, and the back jacks of their blue seats are fully two feet shorter than ours, making their blue seats rotten.
(Sgd) Otto R."

On the circus, unnecessary weight is like a gigantic unseen ball and chain. It slows every move and motion—it is like a plague. The Ringlings knew this shortcoming of their newly acquired property and immediately took steps to cope with the massive problem. The Barnum & Bailey show was soon *ringlingized* from big top to bottom.

Circus Logistics

From Fortune Magazine

FORTUNE magazine for July 1947 said:—"The Next-Greatest Show On Earth is the feat of transporting the Ringling troupe." This article, entitled CIRCUS LOGISTICS, is probably the most exact and clearly written description of this phase of the circus ever published.

The editors of FORTUNE have given special permission to reprint this article verbatim:—

"Circus Logistics"

The only permanence of the circus is its impermanence. Leaving New York after a long April stand in Madison Square Garden, Ringling Brothers and Barnum & Bailey Combined Shows, Inc. annually hauls its "Greatest Show on Earth" on a tour of some 18,000 miles that ends in Sarasota, Florida, late in November. During this perambulation the Ringling show may play in as many as 150 communities, which is merely another way of saying that the Big Show habitually solves a problem in logistics that is complicated enough to muddle the most competent colonel of roving Marines.

Each time the circus leaves a city it tears itself down and packs itself on four railroad trains. On arrival at the new town in the early dawn of the next day, it reverses the process so neatly that when the new-town customer arrives on the new lot a few hours later, he

feels at home. To him the circus looks exactly as it looked last year. The hardened Ringling employee has the same feeling. To him the circus of that moment looks not only as it looked last year, but as it looked last month and last week. It looks also, he has no doubt, just as it will look next week, next month, and next year.

To demonstrate the constant movement of the circus, and to explain its illusion of stability in the midst of that constant movement, it is only necessary to detail a typical twenty-four hour cycle of circus life—such a cycle as the one that might begin tonight in the town of Imaginary, Wisconsin.

At 8:00 p. m. of this pleasant summer day in Imaginary, Wisconsin, the circus is poised to produce its evening version. The lot, conveniently close to town, is a tight-packed acreage, offering ticket buyers excitingly non-Wisconsin sights, sounds, and smells. Dominating is the gray canvas dome of the largest single tent in the world, the Big Top. When the show begins in a few minutes, on its oval track around three rings and two stages, there will be a "straw house"—circus talk for a sellout.

Late arrivals, jostling in at the main entrance gate, find themselves on the midway. On the left side of this short, broad avenue are the ticket wagons, selling reserved seats for $3 and general admissions for from 80 cents to $1.50. On the left too are brightly lighted booths where hard-faced men with rasping voices peddle almost anything that is both edible and indigestible. They also sell a line of cheap, but not cheaply-priced, souvenirs. On the right is the side-show tent, its not too horrific contents advertised by a row of glaring posters and by a strident spieler on a platform.

Late-comers probably pass up the side show, display their tickets to takers at the front gate or marquee, and push on into the menagerie tent. Here they meet the satisfactory, muffled roar of a lion, the pungent, not-unpleasant wild-animal smell, the sight of monkeys and elephants; of Boston, the baby giraffe; of Gargantua, most publicized of all giant gorillas. They might linger a while trying to get a decent glimpse of Gargantua in his badly-lighted, glass-enclosed cage, but the blare of the Merle Evans twenty-eight-piece circus band, as it begins its two-and-a-half-hour marathon of brass, hurries them to their seats under the bright lights and dark shadows of the Big Top.

To most, the circus means no more than the places just enumerated—the midway, the side-show tent, the front gate, the menagerie, and the Big Top. To many others there is much of interest to be seen on the rest of the lot. Some of the non-spenders lack the price of a ticket; some maintain that the finest spectacle offered by the circus is outside the big tent and free of charge. As these specialists, known as "lot lice," wander along the sides of the main tent or stand gawking in the growing dusk on the fringes of the back yard, they are looking at a circus that, while already vanishing, is well set up.

Much earlier today, Lloyd Morgan, circus man in charge of layout, arrived in Imaginary to find a rarely satisfactory piece of ground. The property, a comfortable mile from the railroad siding, was an eighteen-acre rectangle with one of the short sides on a main highway. The turf was almost level, requiring no grading. The soil was damp but firm; there would be neither dust nor mud. Vital water mains were handy.

After a brief look, Morgan knew he could use a straight-away, or—as he would have called it—a "Yankee Robinson" circus layout. He placed the main entrance gate in the middle of the narrow side of the lot facing on the highway. This, to many circus performers, at once became the "Eighth Avenue" side. Circus actors, wherever they may be, are apt to orient themselves by thinking of the Big Top as New York's Madison Square Garden. Thus, when standing on Eighth Avenue and facing the front door of the main tent, the Forty-ninth Street side is to the left, the Fiftieth Street side to the right, the Ninth Avenue side at the far end. Many of the circus workers who travel with the show under canvas, on the other hand, have never laid eyes on Madison Square Garden. These refer to the area about the entrance as the "front yard" and call the opposite end of the lot the "back yard." To them, for technical reasons, the Forty-ninth Street side is called the "short side," the Fiftieth Street side is named the "long side." By the use of either set of these terms, a man or an object can readily be pinpointed, no matter where the show is playing. These terms, also, give circus employees a comfortable sense of permanence in the midst of motion. Morgan spotted the Big Top so that its long sides paralleled the long sides of the lot. All in all, he spotted some forty-three tents, including the numerous canvas-walled chemical toilets known as "donnickers."

Even on such a big lot as this one in Imaginary, the operating circus is crowded. In addition to the tents, there are the 191 big, bright-red circus wagons that carry the show. There are the eighteen trucks and fourteen tractors that move the wagons. Tonight—it is exactly 8:17 p. m. when the show begins—there are also on the lot 900 animals, about 1,400 circus em-

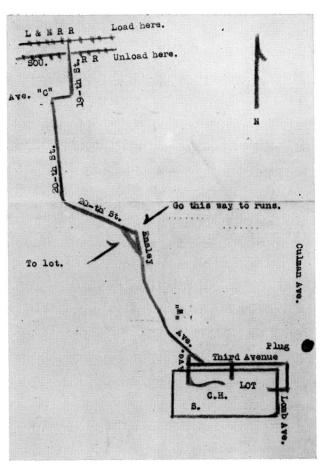

LETTER on far left from the "24-hour" man to the Boss Hostler illustrates to what extent the show went to insure smooth operation on circus day. Mr. Knudson tells him all details and on back of letter (above) draws a map of route to lot—nothing is left to chance. —1938 season. (Mike Tshudy)

ployees, approximately 10,000 customers. The size and the busyness of the place at this moment give it an air of permanence. Actually—even though it is barely dark and the show will run for two and a half hours—the Ringling Circus, for some time, has been quietly melting away.

The Outside Fades

The big cookhouse, the first tent to be set up early this morning, has long since vanished with its crew of 130 and its fourteen red wagons. Already waiting to be reloaded on the trains, also, are the specialty or service departments, which during the day functioned as blacksmith, cobbler, commissary, and harness maker. There is activity everywhere. Men are setting out and lighting ball-shaped kerosene flares. From a distance there comes a roar of tractor motors starting. As elaborate floats come out of the main tent at the conclusion of the "Spectacle," each is pounced on by a crew of three and swiftly laced into a canvas cover. Almost immediately the "Spec" wagons will be on their way to the trains. In the back yard, an elephant effortlessly pushes one of the heavy circus wagons with his head. A clown stands in the brightly lighted entrance of the dressing top, his face chalked white.

But the wise lot louse, who wants to get the most for his nothing, knows that the best free show of the moment is at the Eighth Avenue, or "front-yard" end of the Big Top, where a swarm of men is at work tearing the menagerie tent to pieces. He steps along the side of the Big Top under a web of guy ropes, passing "Clown Alley"— a narrow canvas lean-to where the clowns keep their props during the show— and the performers' side entrance, the "Forty-ninth Street Connection." When he gets to the menagerie tent the side walls have already been stripped away and the goings on inside are his for the looking.

The most impressive thing about any part of the circus teardown is the imparted sense of an urgent necessity for speed, and the sight of many men simultaneously doing many things without many orders. In the menagerie tent at this moment, men are taking away the overhead lights. Others are swathing seventeen wild-animal cages in canvas. The observer steps back to avoid being trodden on by a llama, which in company with a donkey is being walked away. The tent is shrill to the sound of whistles, as "cat handlers" direct the snarling small yellow tractors. Three quick whistle blasts cause a "cat man" swiftly to back his tractor up to a wagon. One blast stops him. Two doubles and he is away, pulling the $25,000 air-conditioned cage of Gargantua and his mate. A work elephant, with two men manipulating his dragging chain, begins to pull down the side poles that support the perimeter of the roof. The tent is emptied when forty-odd performing elephants, solemnly absurd in clown costumes, march away into the big tent. (When they emerge again, at the other end, thirty-two of them will keep right on walking the long mile to the train.) The last light goes out, and in a few moments the overhead canvas comes billowing down. The menagerie tent is no more.

Emotionally satisfied but physically hungry, the spectator takes himself over to the midway for a hot dog. He is just in time, for the "grab joints" and the "juice joints," concluding that they have squeezed the last dime from the last customer, are ready to leave. Across the way, the side show, too, is collapsing into its five wagons. In a matter of minutes the entire front section of the circus will be rolling down the road.

The show ends at precisely ten-forty-five, but for twenty minutes there has been a pool of interest between the Big Top back door and the door of the main dressing tent. This deeply shadowed area, edged by silent spectators, has become more and more crowded. Clowns and midgets streaming from the arena at the

end of a "clown break" cause an eddy in the double line of well-mounted, brightly costumed girl riders who are waiting to enter. An elephant, hitched to a prop wagon, edges forward to place his head against the canvas of the back door. Behind him follow the nineteen other wagons that will take away the contents of the Big Top. A tractor backfires as it drags away a packed trunk wagon.

A few minutes later, a burst of applause marks the end of the concluding high-trapeze act. Over the loudspeaker the master of ceremonies says "Goodnight, and thank you." The sudden silence of the band is almost as painful as its previous long-term noise. Two elephants move stolidly through the back entrance of the Big Top, pulling wagons. There begins a metallic clashing that will continue deafeningly until 6,000 chairs have been folded. The Big Top is on its way down.

Imaginary, goodby

Urgency is again the keynote, but now the urgency seems more intense. The big audience may think it files out of the tent in its own time; actually it is shoved. Ushers nag the slow-of-foot. The two lead elephants progress massively down either side of the track, only a half step behind the last of the crowd. At the end of seven minutes the 10,000th ticket holder steps out into the Wisconsin dusk, and in those seven minutes, work has been done.

Six hundred men toss themselves at the job of tearing out the insides of the Big Top. In addition to the standard gang of laborers, electricians, prop and rigging men, the teardown crew sucks in ushers, drink and peanut butchers, ticket takers, midway concession men, clowns, midgets—almost every male on the payroll who is not busy elsewhere. These men work with an intense, concentrated energy totally out of proportion to salaries or other personal benefits offered them by the show. Asked to explain, circus men shrug. "It's a disease."

The biggest job in stripping the tent is to remove the chairs and the framework they stand on. The framework consists first of plank platforms that hinge in the middle. (Since they fold with a slap, they are called "bibles.") The bibles rest on forty-foot alloy I beams called "stringers," and the stringers rest on jacks. The metal chairs are all folded in a space of seven minutes, and the end of their clamorous closing is a relief.

Ring makers and side-wall men are breaking away the heavy ring curbs into sections. Propmen tear at the performers' stages. A youth nimbly runs up a twenty-foot ladder leaning against one of the tent poles. He unties a big electric-light so that it swings free, comes rapidly down, runs with his ladder to the next pole, sweatingly repeats the job. Flying rigging is lowered and is tucked into canvas bags. The side walls of the big tent are disappearing. Electricians begin to uproot and reel in the four miles of cable that have supplied light to a darkening arena.

On the main track bibles are being loaded on a wagon. Two men gruntingly hand one up to a stripped-to-the-waist giant Negro, who lightly tosses it behind to add to his neat stack. Stringers and jacks are being lugged into the outside darkness. Elephant and manpower combine to take away the smaller of the poles supporting the twelve-plus tons of Big Top canvas. At eleven fifty-five the main tent is stripped.

It stands vastly and dimly empty, with a lone workman beside each of the six towering main poles. Since more than half of the smaller poles have been removed, the canvas sags. A single, last light is blotted out, and from the canvas boss—invisible at the edge of the tent —comes the softly spoken order, "Let her go." The last half hitch is loosened in the main falls holding the canvas to the peaks. At the same time, the bases of the sixty-one standing poles are jerked free. The Madison Square Garden of the sticks begins its impressive collapse.

It takes forty-five seconds for the deflation of the Big Top balloon, which gives the six pole rigger men time to get out from under. (These men seldom fall, but if one does he carries a sharp knife to slash himself free.) On the outside, teams of colored canvasmen are waiting. Even before the tent is flat on the ground they throw themselves at the heaving fabric, slipping, grabbing for hand holds, as they try to hasten the descent. When they finally reach the bases of the center poles they begin to work rapidly outward, unlacing one piece of the great cloth pie from the next. Working again from the inside out, they compete in folding and rolling the segments into bundles for loading. The winners take pleasure in jeering the defeated. Tonight, the job of separating and packaging the eighteen canvas pieces of the Big Top takes exactly ten minutes.

Still standing are the six towering main poles of the Big Top, and the meticulous job of lowering them one by one begins at once. At the same time, the 486 stakes that anchor the guy-line ropes of the big tent are being pulled. These four-foot wooden spikes, about two feet of which show above-ground, are yanked in pairs by a tractor dangling two chains from a boom. Workmen loop the chains around the stakes. The tractor heaves; the stakes resist—finally dangle free. They lie where they fall until a workman called "Whitey" (he has palsy) collects them in his little wagon hauled by Sheba, the donkey.

The last free show of the night on the circus lot is the leveling of the last Big Top main pole, called "No.

1." Because none of the other poles are standing, its entire weight is held by a rope and cable angling from the peak to the ground. On the ground end the rope weaves through a maze of stakes that act as tether, hovered over anxiously by George Smith, the circus general manager, and the canvas boss, Leonard Aylesworth (wearing dirty cotton gloves). As the rope is slowly let out, the strain on it is so great that it smokes, and must be doused with water. But in four minutes the No. 1 pole is safely horizontal. It is exactly 12:24 a. m., which means that one hour and thirty-nine minutes after the evening show ended, the Ringling Brothers Circus is about ready to say goodby to Imaginary.

The Squadron, and two brothers

Tonight the Big Show will travel slightly more than 100 miles from Imaginary to a one-day stand in Shortstop, Wisconsin, on four railroad trains made up of forty-eight double-length flat cars carrying red wagons, eleven stock cars for animals, and twenty-six coaches for employees. The first of these trains is called the "Flying Squadron." The other three are labeled the "second section," the "third section," and the "fourth section."

The principle guiding the make-up of the trains is that the Squadron must carry the equipment and personnel required to lay out the lot, as well as to make the lot livable for those who follow. On it, therefore, will be the cookhouse and staff, Lloyd Morgan with his layout equipment and crew of thirty, and the various specialty shops and personnel. To provide its own motive power it will take trucks, tractors, work horses, a car of elephants, the menagerie, and the front door. The basic ingredients of the second section are the side show and the canvas and poles of the Big Top. Section three lugs the contents of the Big Top. All other loadings are matters of the convenience of the moment; generally speaking, anything can be placed on any train. (Since performers and top executives are last to be needed on a new lot, their sleeping coaches comprise the fourth section.)

The trains leave and arrive in one, two, three, four order, but the loading seqence is one, three, two, four. The reason is that the Big Top contents are ready for the train before the Big Top itself, but cannot be used the next day until the main tent has again been set. The contents, therefore, are loaded first on section three. When the Big Tent arrives at the siding it is loaded on section two and departs in advance.

Ray Milton, the train boss, has the tricky task of loading the flatcars with circus wagons and other rolling stock. The trickiness of the job lies in the fact that it is never done by rote; i. e., wagons are not spotted at the same place on the same car night after night. While loading by the numbers would make Milton's life less worrisome, he cannot take advantage of it. For any one of many reasons a wagon might be—often is—late in reaching the siding; this would immediately stall such a loading program. Milton is forced to fill his flatcars, not by a prearranged plan, but by juggling wagons according to their length.

The largest circus flatcars measure seventy and seventy-two feet and have two feet less of loading surface. If Milton is not to leave a wagon or two behind when the trains pull out, he must use almost every available foot of space on every car. To aid him in solving this puzzle, each wagon is plainly marked on all four sides with its number and loading length. Milton stands in the light of a flare at the end of the train and calls the numbers of the wagons he wants loaded. When two seventeen and two eighteen-foot wagons have been hauled up the chute and spotted by the little "cats" that ride the ties alongside the train, Milton has a tidy carload. He will get the same result with three seventeens and a nineteen. A special problem is presented by the sixty-foot Big Top mainpole wagon. But the hood of a jeep will fit under its rear overhang, and the jeep body fills the remaining ten feet of space. There are many such loadings.

In Imaginary, tonight, the loadings go smoothly, so that the Squadron puffs out of the siding at ten-thirty. It is followed by the second section at one-thirty, the third at two-thirty, and the fourth at about three-thirty. In some twenty hours since it arrived early this morning the Ringling Circus has set itself up, torn itself down, reloaded and departed—all for five hours of show time. Tomorrow morning the only physical remnant of the circus in Imaginary will be the so-called "twenty-four-hour-man." He will see to it that the lot is cleaned up to the satisfaction of the city fathers, and will take care of all bills and complaints before he leapfrogs ahead of the circus to another town.

Circus life is wearying

The night train ride—in this case from Imaginary to Shortstop, Wisconsin—is not so much an interlude in the lives of the thousand-odd circus employees as it is a normal, integral part of their daily lives. Each worker has his assigned place on the train, and by this stage of the tour has established some sort of traveling routine.

Just another day

The weather holds good this morning, in Shortstop, Wisconsin, and if the crowd of five hundred that gathered at six o'clock to greet the Squadron arriving from Imaginary can be taken as an omen, this will be another fine circus town. Jim Haley and John Ringling North, President and Vice President of the show —their private cars are still on the roll with section

four—reflect that there still seems to be plenty of loose money around in spite of all the talk of coming depression. They wonder if they could possibly get another of those rare but pleasureable things, a sellout. Their layout man, Lloyd Morgan, is not quite so content.

When Morgan and his crew arrive on the scene of today's operation they find a scowling twenty-four-hour man superintending the dumping of a carload of cinders to fill in holes and to smooth out unevenness of the ground. The lot is probably the worst of the season, for in addition to being tough, dusty, and littered with rubbish, it is far too small. But Morgan merely says a small prayer of thanks that he is not ankle deep in mud and goes to work. There is no chance for a "Yankee Robinson" layout here, so he spots the Big Top so that it will be a continuation of

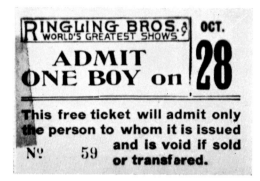

TO CHILDREN all over America, circus day is one of exciting sights, sounds, and smells. Countless boys have worked for a free pass (see above) and found doing the work a greater thrill than watching the performance.   (C. P. Fox)

170

CHILDREN strain for a peek at the wild animals. (Atwell, Milw. Jour. - Wis. Hist. Soc.)

the midway. There is no room between the two for the menagerie, so it is left untented but enclosed by nine-foot side walls on the Fiftieth Street, or long side.

After a survey Morgan drives flagged stakes to mark the sites for the six main poles of the Big Top. (At the beginning of the season these flags were fifty-six feet apart, but because the rope lacing the canvas sections together has since stretched, they must now be placed at intervals of exactly fifty-eight feet, six inches.) A pile driver mounted on a truck begins to nail down the circle of stakes around the main tent.

By eight-thirty the big cookhouse has been erected at a far corner. Its own live steam generator is passing on hot water to an automatic dishwasher. Diesel oil fires are burning in two big ranges built into red wagons. Food is being cooked. The "hotel" flag has been raised to the peak, which means that the cookhouse is already serving the first of the forty-two hundred meals it will provide that day. Performers and executives eat in one half of the tent on long trestle tables, workmen in the other. The food is the same for both, and it is good.

By this time the over-small area is already swarming with citizens of Shortstop. Hundreds of children are underfoot, or are climbing on the menagerie wagons in an attempt to get a peek inside. The elders have

brought lunches and are prepared to spend the day. They settle down under trees at the edge of the lot, producing pipes or needlework. The circus, accepting their presence as an inevitable evil, gets on with the job.

The main poles are Oregon fir and stand sixty feet tall. They taper from a diameter of ten inches at the base to nine at the peak. (Although not one of these $1,900 sticks has ever broken, two replacements are purchased each year.) The most ticklish job is raising the No. 1 pole, for the reason that little leverage is available. Its base is placed on a heavy plank known as a mud block to prevent sinking into the ground, and against stakes to stop lateral slipping. From the peak of the pole, which has been lifted onto a wooden horse, a rope passes along its length, through a block at the front-yard end, and on to an elephant. As the pole rises, guy-line cables stretched from the peak to short and long sides keep it from falling sidewise, and another toward the back yard snubs it at the vertical.

When the No. 1 pole has been raised and secured, a rope from its top provides leverage for the easier raising of pole No. 2, and so on. It takes about twenty minutes to raise all six poles this morning, and during that time all of the smaller tent poles have been laid on the ground in their proper positions. On top of them the 226-man Negro canvas crew, with the assistance of kids, is unrolling and lacing together the sections of canvas. When Leonard Aylesworth arrives—wearing the typical circus boss's uniform of shirt sleeves, panama hat and big black cigar—the huge oval of canvas lies smooth and flat. The crew stands, spaced and waiting along its perimeter.

"Way up over your head," is Aylesworth's first command. He speaks in an ordinary conversational tone, but the grapevine carries his order almost instantly to the entire crew. At once the 122 side poles spaced along the edges are raised upright so that the canvas now resembles a great flat saucer. An elephant moves in under the shadows of the canvas at the Eighth Avenue end. His driver hitches him to a two-and-one-half-inch hawser that runs through a block and tackle at the peak of No. 1 pole and down again to the 280-pound iron baling ring that will raise the roof. "Go ahead on one," says Aylesworth, no louder than if he were asking for a match. The elephant moves out toward the light and the canvas at No. 1 pole moves up about fifteen feet. "Hold one." The elephant halts and another moves in to the base of pole No. 2. "Go ahead on two." The canvas at the second pole begins to rise. "Hold two." Aylesworth ducks his head and moves into the darkness of the low-hanging tent. "Go ahead on three . . . go one . . . hold three . . ."

The low-voiced chant continues and the canvas continues its rise on all six poles, revealing an interior that, in the deep shadows, seems even vaster than it is. (The Big Top measures 544 feet 6 inches, lengthwise, and 244 feet 10 inches in the other direction.) It is a place of straining ropes and sweating men. "Catch four," remarks Aylesworth and his command can be heard in echo as it is belayed to the faraway elephant driver. In a moment the rope on No. 4 pole is made fast.

When all the heavy baling rings have reached the pole peaks and their lines have been secured, Aylesworth is through giving orders other than to his foremen. He stays in the tent merely to keep an eye on the business of setting quarter poles.

The Big Top canvas is held from the ground by the side poles at the perimeter. It is prevented from oversagging toward the center by two concentric ovals of red and blue quarter poles. The red quarter poles, thirty-four feet tall, are placed sixty feet in from the outside walls, and the forty-two foot blue quarter poles, twenty-five feet closer, will line the edge of the main track. All are raised or "set," by combined man and elephant power, as follows:

A crew of workmen, with a foreman directing, seize one of the heavy sticks and lift it into the air high enough so that it can be grasped by an outsize pair of wooden tongs. The gang divides to man both of the twelve-foot handles, and there begins an upward and outward heaving motion with the object of pushing the iron spike at the end of the pole through a hole in the canvas. This "stabbing" is accomplished in time to a rhythmic chant, which, according to the foreman, runs, "Pick it up. Walk it forward, easy. Lift it up. Shoot it home—hard!" But to the casual listener the words are unintelligible.

When a quarter pole has been stabbed home, the crew leaves, on the run, for the next. Its place is taken by an elephant, whose driver loops a chain about the base of the slanting pole. The elephant, casually reaching for a wisp of grass with his trunk as he moves, pulls it to an almost vertical position, lifting the tent roof at the same time. When all of the quarter poles have thus been placed, the Big Top is technically set. As Aylesworth ambles from the tent, teams of colored men—in time to another meaningless chant—are swaying as they tighten, or "guy out," the ropes holding the side poles. Coming in are the jacks, stringers, and bibles that will hold the arena seats.

A Cycle Ends

Meanwhile much has been happening on the rest of the lot. The blacksmith shop has been set since early morning and is now repairing a broken axle. The commissary is selling a pair of stout gloves to a workman. The doctor's tent and the barbershop are open. On the midway, orange drinks and live chameleons are being audibly peddled. In the performers' dressing tent near the back door of the Big Top many of the actors are quietly pursuing their anything but private lives.

The main dressing tent is the closest approximation of home for the men who use one half of it and for the women who occupy the other. Their small boxlike trunks, placed on the bare ground every day in the same position, hold all of their professional and many of their personal belongings. In the men's side a juggler is sitting on a trunk writing a letter in pencil. A high-wire man, stripped, is taking a bath in a bucket of water. A clown has set up a portable coat rack and mirror. Sitting on a folding chair, he is rummaging in his open box.

Over on the women's side, a young bareback rider is washing clothes in a bucket of water. Show girls are reading or gossiping in the only sort of privacy they have. As time goes by, the tent begins to fill. Finally, as the clothes washer picks up her soggy bundle, there comes the clear sound of the first bugle—another afternoon performance will begin in forty-five minutes. She sighs and walks outside, to hear a brief, but readily understandable, exchange of talk:

PLUNKIE (morosely): What's the name of this burg?

POLER (with a grunt): Who the hell cares?

Winter Quarters

In *Historical Sketches of Sauk County* (Wis.) published in 1891, an article on the Ringling Bros. Circus of Baraboo pointed out the phenomenal rise in a few short years of the brothers. The article ended by saying, "Thus the proverb is verified *from little acorns mighty oaks are grown.*"

This is a poignant observation, as winterquarters, whether in Baraboo, Bridgeport, or Sarasota, are not just a group of buildings in which the glamorous circus of the summer hibernates through the winter. Quite on the contrary, this long homestand is a beehive of activity. For it is here that plans for a bigger and better show are put into effect. Days, weeks, and months of designing and planning are feverishly executed by all the craftsmen in the employ of the circus. A circus attains all its growth and new polish while it is in winter quarters, but remains static while out on tour.

Baraboo, Wisconsin, was the Ringlings' winterquarters from their first year, 1884 to and including the winter of 1917-18. At the end of the 1918 season the circus moved into the quarters of their other great circus, Barnum & Bailey, in Bridgeport, Connecticut. It was in 1927 that John Ringling moved his winterquarters to Sarasota, Florida, where he had acquired a vast amount of land.

Because of its fascinating aspect, a town that winters a circus soon develops a sense of pride and admiration for the show and showpeople. Baraboo was a characteristic circus town. On April 28, 1894, the *Baraboo News Republic* ran a typical story, excerpts of which are:—

"Circus day is here. A day which in brilliance of display and magnificence of turnout, excels even that national holiday—the Fourth of July. For 11 years the five Ringling Bros. have offered Baraboo and the surrounding country a day of more than usual pleasure. The proprietors of this mammoth amusement enterprise occupy their time in the winter preparing for the future, instead of looking back upon the past. Thus, it is that they are better as they grow older, and the work of the past winter is no exception, rather a more concerted effort on their part to make theirs the leading show on earth. Today is Ringling day—"

When a community winters a circus, as Baraboo did for so many years, its effects are felt in many ways becoming ingrained in its people and its way of life. One typical such episode showed up in the minutes of a City Council meeting in 1895. It seemed the Ash street bridge over the Baraboo River was not safe. Complaints had been received, so the mayor appointed a comittee to investigate the bridge's condition and report back with their findings. Their report was terse:—'The Ringlings just hauled all their wagons over the bridge on the way to loading tracks; thus, in our opinion, the bridge is safe'."

With their vast conglomeration of wild animals, the Ringlings had a problem of disposing of the bodies when age, accident, or sickness caused one to depart from this world. To solve this dilemma, they made a deal with Jack Rooney, who owned a 40-acre farm a few miles out of town on County Trunk A. It was a sandy plot of ground where the animals could be quickly and easily buried. One cannot help but think of the bewildered consternation of a Paleontologist if, in the distant future, he should stumble onto this unorthodox graveyard and find the bones of an African Zebra, oryx, baboon, Asian buffalo, and tiger, a Polar bear from the Arctic, all in the same field.

All animals were not buried here, many of the rarer specimens being sent to museums. Herbert L. Stoddard recalls that in 1910 he and George Shrosbree prepared the hide and skeleton of a huge bull hippo to take back to the Milwaukee Public Museum. It took them a week to accomplish the job. Stoddard later acquired a zebra, hyena, antelopes, and an Asiatic elephant for the museum.

HENRY MOELLER—Circus wagon builder.
(C. P. Fox)

TOP VIEW shows Baraboo winterquarters on Water Street—circa 1913.

BELOW—Wagons draw up in cornfield at end of season waiting to be repaired and refurbished.
(Steve Albasing)

George McFarland, who worked for the show in the 1900 era as a blacksmith, said that one of the first things done when the show hit Baraboo was to wash, repair, and oil all the harness. This was a tedious and fantastic chore, as there were some 700 sets to be renovated. McFarland likes to tell of the Swede who applied for a job at winter quarters. Ole, as he was called, was hired by the Animal Department and his first task was to clean out a cage containing six lions. The superintendent gave Ole a long-handled scraper for reaching through the bars and then went off about some other business.

In a few minutes he heard the den of lions putting up a tremendous growling and roaring. Rushing back he could not see his new man—then to his horror found Ole inside the wagon calmly scraping it out. The six lions were cowering in the corner, growling and gruffing at the intruder. The superintendent, ashen white, finally talked Ole into slowly backing out the door. When he was advised that no man had ever been in that cage before, the Swede answered, "Ya, and how should I clean it?"

After all wagons and equipment were put in their proper places at the close of each season's tour, the circus paid off all the workmen in gold coins. Many a Baraboo citizen remembers these days. The men made three stops—the first was at the barbershop for a shower, shave and haircut; the second at a clothing store where they bought a new outfit from skin out;

and third, the taverns. Payday at the end of the tour was a big day for all the town. Included was bonus money which was withheld each month through the season by the management. This was done, by agreement with the employees, to encourage them to stick with their jobs throughout the season. If they quit their job along the route they forfeited the bonus.

In Baraboo's Walnut Hill and St. Joseph's Cemeteries the names on the headstones read like a circus hall of fame, for they are final resting place for many of the Ringlings and scores of troupers. With a deep interest in his ancestors who formed the great circus, Henry Ringling North made an annual trek to Baraboo when the circus was under canvas. As soon as the show got to its Wisconsin stands, Mr. North drove to Baraboo, picked up his cousin, Henry Moeller, and together they would visit the cemetery. North cautioned Moeller—"Spare no expense to keep these family lots in order."

Many troupers settled in Baraboo. Then, too, with the influence of the circuses' presence, many local citizens toured with the show. It is astounding how many citizens, who had no show people in their ancestry, came to be outstanding stars. Typical examples are the three Rooney Brothers. Hugh had five children who became equestrians and acrobats. John had four children who became animal men and hostlers. Mike had four children who became bareback riders.

In Baraboo, Wisconsin, the circus was housed in buildings that lined both sides of Water Street. The site was only a few blocks from the downtown district. The citizens became accustomed to having a veritable jungle of beasts on their doorstep. Roars, trumpeting, cries, screams and calls of all description were part of the circus pattern, as were the exotic smells that emanated from the area. Animal escapes, runaway teams of new horses might cause some consternation, but the sight of 30 elephants trouping through the residential district was a daily occurrence. Teams of camels or zebras, six, eight, or 10-horse hitches pulling massive wagons over the streets caused hardly a head to turn.

Henry Moeller was one of Baraboo's most stalwart citizens. Hanging in his office was a sign that typifies his wonderful philosophy of life—"Men who know it all are not invited." He and his brother, Corwin, worked for their father, Henry Sr., operating the Moeller Carriage & Wagon Co. To them fell the job of furnishing the enterprising Ringling boys with vehicles. In the early mud show days, Henry said they always carried them on the cuff until the tour began and the circus started to make money. The Ringlings were so poor that they could only afford common farm wagons that the Moellers fixed up with seats, racks or high sides. None of them had tops—a piece of canvas served as a roof.

One fascinating anecdote that seemed to be typical of the Ringling frugality in these early days was recalled by Henry Moeller:—

"I think it was the Spring of '87. We had purchased two old democrat wagons and had fitted them out with seats for the performers. Al Ringling came bustling into the shop this day and announced he had three more performers lined up and we were to arrange for the necessary seats. I told Al that we would have to put an extension on one wagon, or build a completely new body. Al told me he couldn't afford to do that, so between us we figured how to place the first and second seat back to back and then put the third seat at the rear. Al said, 'that's fine, just the thing. It will be a tight squeeze, but that's fine, do it.'"

The thriving young circus showed its stature by increasing in size and scope year by year. In the late '80's they began to buy wagons from slipping competitors in the East. With each purchase, all equipment was shipped into the Moellers, who rebuilt the vehicles to the Ringling's specifications. Each succeeding year the Moellers built more and more baggage and parade wagons, carriages, coaches and carts. Their ledgers for 1916 show they charged $425.00 for an electric light wagon. The beautifully made Cinderella coach cost the Ringlings $175.00, and a new stage coach for the 1917 show was $165.00. Year after year, as the circus came in off the road, the Moeller shops would recondition the wagons. They underwent the roughest of treatment during the summer tour— on and off railroad cars, to and from lots, through mud, sand, clay; always with tremendous loads.

During the winter of 1912-13, for example, the Moeller shops repaired 31 cages, 16 floats and bandwagons, two calliopes, two ticket wagons, and nine miscellaneous wagons, or a total of 60 vehicles. They were paid $2917.84 to do this work, which took from early November to early April. On January 12, 1913, the huge United States bandwagon was drawn up to the wagon shop. Herewith is a detailed list of repairs done, which was typical of that required for any of the wagons:—

24 hours on repairing carving	$ 9.60
36 feet lumber for new floor	2.16
repair seats on top of wagon	2.12
1 Pr. long 5" wide brake shoes	1.50
straighten up and set 2 brake beams	.75
1 new wheel shoe plate	.75
straighten up front gear	1.00
1 new No. 85 wheel, tire 7/8" thick, 4" wide	35.00
extra panels between spokes	4.00
bolts and general tightening up	1.25
repair pole—2 iron bands	.50
1 new end forging for evener	.40

$59.03

Dan Schilling, a woodcarver, who worked for the Moellers, had the rather technical job of replacing ears, noses, faces, and even breasts, that were knocked off the allegorical carvings on the parade wagons. His was a delicate profession, indeed.

Moeller says that as the opening day would draw near there were always some last minute requirements and the Ringlings demanded immediate service. Henry tells, as a great joke on himself, about the time a last minute order for a wagon caused him an unexpected train ride. The wagon was finished and was being painted when a six-horse team arrived to get the vehicle. Orders were to take it directly to the rail yards where the trains were being loaded. Henry said, "there was nothing for me to do but grab my paint

STREET SCENE downtown Baraboo in spring when new teams were hitched up and broken to work together. Circa 1916.   (Joe Burke Collection)

RINGLING HOTEL on Water Street in Baraboo where winter employees stayed. Circa 1915.
(Steve Albasing)

pot, brush, and climb onto the wagon. When we reached the yards the wagon was immediately loaded and then I continued to finish painting it. When the train pulled out I still had the back end of the wagon to finish, so kept right at it. By the time my job was done we were six miles out and approaching Devils Lake. As the train slowed for a grade I threw off my paint pot and jumped. I had to wait for the next freight to get back to Baraboo."

The Ringlings owned the buildings at the Barnum & Bailey winterquarters at Bridgeport, Conn., but the land on which they stood was leased. This, coupled with the fact the Ringlings were toying with the idea of combining the titles into one huge show, started a discussion of either moving the Barnum & Bailey show to Baraboo, or the Ringling Bros. show to Bridgeport.

At the end of the 1918 season there were only four of the original seven brothers still living—John, Henry, Charley, and Alf T. So undecided were they as to where to winter the circus that, as the end of the tour drew near, Ralph Peckham, traffic manager, was ordered to contract with the railroads for transportation to both Baraboo and Bridgeport. When the brothers took a final vote Henry and Charley voted to send the Ringling show to Baraboo. This left the vote 50-50, so status-quo was the order and the Ringling Circus entrained for Baraboo from Waycross, Georgia, their last stand. When the show trains were about halfway to Wisconsin, Henry Ringling suddenly died. This immediately changed the picture, as now

ABOVE is the Al Ringling theatre that Al built in Baraboo. It is a showpiece even today.   (C. P. Fox)

LEFT—Charley Ringling's home in Baraboo. After he moved to Sarasota he sold it to his brother Henry.   (C. P. Fox)

BELOW LEFT is the $100,000 red sandstone mansion Al Ringling built in Baraboo in 1911.   (C. P. Fox)

BELOW—this historical marker was erected on outskirts of Baraboo by the State Historical Society of Wisconsin in 1956. The community is proud of its heritage. Shown in photo is Stuart Lancaster, a grandson of Charley Ringling, who was elected Vice President of the circus in 1957.   (C. P. Fox)

the vote was two for Bridgeport and one for Baraboo. John and Alf T. immediately ordered the circus trains turned around and sent to Bridgeport. Baraboo never wintered the circus again.

The following Spring the Ringlings combined their two shows into the great combine known today as the *Ringling Bros. and Barnum & Bailey Circus.* Very probably, the combining of the titles was a decision long discussed. With the scarcity of help and wartime rail restrictions, putting out one show simplified the task, as compared to trying to run both titles as separate entities.

Baraboo has never been the same since it lost the circus, but the town is so steeped in circus lore and history that the city fathers, under the guiding hand of the State Historical Society of Wisconsin, have formed the Circus World Museum. The old Ringling winterquarters are to be renovated and on July 1, 1959, will become a historical museum and research center for one of America's greatest traditions—the Circus.

In 1929, John Ringling purchased the American Circus Corporation (five circuses). These circuses all wintered on a large farm on the outskirts of Peru, (pronounced Pay-Roo by circus people) Indiana. These winter quarters, which were included in the deal, were never used by the Ringling Bros. Circus. They did, however, prior to 1938, ship all their baggage horses to this farm for the winter, as northern climate was a good conditioner for the horses and, of course, there was plenty of good timothy hay and oats readily available.

The Sarasota winterquarters had been built up into one of the show places of Florida. Until 1958 when the quarters were closed, tourists flocked to the home of the circus to watch rehearsals, see the horses, zoological gardens and feed the elephants. Visitors were overwhelmed by the magnitude of the circus' home. They saw $400,000 worth of wagons and cages, $200,000 worth of elephants, $60,000 worth of horses and ponies, $98,000 worth of props and rigging—truly a huge operation.

Since the Ringlings have been in Sarasota, they have maintained their own wagon makers, wheelwrights, blacksmiths, forge shops, welding shops, carpenter shops, etc. Their paint shops alone yearly consume a huge supply of materials:—

  5½ tons white lead
  810 gals. blue enamel
  562 gals. red enamel
  498 gals. silver enamel
  225 gals. varnish
  157 packs gold leaf
    6 barrels asphaltum
  10 barrels turpentine

BARNUM & BAILEY winterquarters in Bridgeport, Conn., which the Ringlings used from 1918 through 1926. (Steve Albasing)

INTERIOR showing wagons being painted. (Circus World Museum)

LOWER—Two views of the winterquarters of the American Circus Corp. in Peru, Ind. John Ringling purchased the corporation in 1929 and, along with it, these quarters. The circus shipped their baggage stock to Peru each winter where hay was plentiful and the climate conditioned the horses for the coming season. (C. P. Fox)

ABOVE—View of winterquarters, Sarasota, Florida, in 1953. Large white building right of center is sail loft and menagerie. Oblong building on extreme left is a training barn. Square corral is stable. (RB&BB)

LEFT—Wardrobe storage. (C. P. Fox)

CREW repairing a flat car. (RB&BB)

TOP—Paint shop —1930.

LOWER RIGHT — 1954—Osmond Osmondson, for many years Ringling's sailmaker and canvas expert.

LOWER LEFT— 1954—all wagons are repainted and lettered each winter.

(RB&BB)

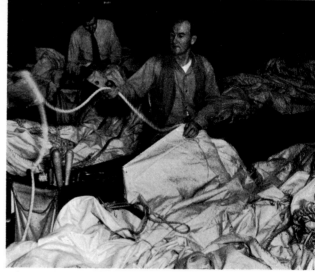

FEVERISH WINTER ACTIVITIES. Top—costume department. Above—sail loft. Left—carpenter shop.
(RB&BB)

10 barrels boiled oil

100 gals. steel car surfacer

57 gals. shellac

Henry Ringling North, who has an intense love of animals, in December 1955 announced the circus was planning an all year-round zoological garden at Sarasota. Some 80 acres of the circus grounds would be developed into a park, modeled after the Hamburg, Germany Zoo. This plan recalled one of a similar and even more pretentious nature that the Ringlings had in 1899, when they spoke in great detail of the "breeding farm for wild animals" they were planning. The story said they had secured control of three of the Florida keys, totalling 6,000 acres in size. It was the Ringling's plan to raise animals in as near natural surroundings as possible and to supply not only their own menagerie "but furnish animals to all prospective purchasers at a profit." The animal farm did not keep pace with the fertile minds of the five Baraboo brothers —it did not materialize.

Unexpected problems develop when a town like Sarasota was suddenly expected in 1927, to winter this great circus. One of the more unusual was the sudden overcrowded condition of tiny St. Martha's Catholic Church. It simply could not handle the influx of parishioners, even though the usual two Sunday masses were increased to five, so it was decided to build a new church. To help pay for the church the Ringlings put on a one-ring circus every Spring for five years on the lot next to the church, the circus furnishing the equipment, animals and personnel— $20,000 was raised and the new church was built in 1940. In gratitude, one of the beautiful stained glass windows was dedicated to the Ringling Bros. This window was reproduced on the Circus' 1943 Christmas card.

TOP—During one of their sojourns in Baraboo, Mr. and Mrs. August Ringling, Sr. and their boys lived in this house on Ash Street. The porch and right wing were added to this humble home since the Ringlings lived there.   (C. P. Fox)

SECOND—John Ringling's home in Sarasota. It was built in 1925 and 1926. It is estimated that the house and furnishings cost $1,500,000.
(Ringling Museum)

THIRD—Chas. Ringling's home in Sarasota built next door to brother John's. This marble mansion was built at a cost of $800,000 in the twenties. The music room had a $40,000 pipe organ. Soon after it was finished one of the top magazines contacted the architect suggesting that if Mr. Ringling would give them $1,000 they would feature his new home in an elaborate story. Chas. Ringling wrote his architect: "I don't see why we should pay $1,000 to display your good taste and mine."   (C. P. Fox)

BOTTOM is a view of the courtyard of the John and Mabel Ringling Art Museum in Sarasota. It was built in the late 20's at a cost of nearly two million dollars to house John Ringling's personal collection of art, including the most important collection of Peter Paul Rubens in America. The contents are valued at more than 10 million dollars.   (Ringling Museum)

Today, with the circus showing in arenas and coliseums, the exciting and pulsating winterquarters is closed and all but abandoned.

Epilogue

Epilogue

THE TENT IS FOLDED

In 1929 John Ringling purchased the American Circus Corporation (five circuses), borrowing $1,700,000 against his personal note to do it.

The stock market crash and the ensuing depression year began to tell on John Ringing. In 1932 he defaulted on his loan, and the bank moved in Samuel Gumpertz to actively manage and watch over the Ringling Circus.

Thus, for the first time in its great history, a Ringling was not at the active helm.

In 1936 John Ringling died. John Ringling North, as an executor of his uncle John's estate, took the necessary steps to bring the circus back into family control. He arranged, with the Manufacturer's Trust of New York, to loan the John Ringling estate $950,000. This was in 1937. Thus, when the bank was paid the balance of the 1929 loan, Gumpertz resigned and John North became president of the circus. He held this position until 1943. By this time the $950,000 had been paid off and the circus was again controlled by the family and free of debt.

Due to a shuffling of voting stocks, John North was voted out of his job in 1943 and his cousin, Robert, became President. In 1947 John North purchased the bulk of Mrs. Aubrey Ringling's stock (widow of Richard Ringling, who was Alf T. Ringling's son), and thus controlled 51% of the voting stock. He again became president of the circus. With this job he acquired the balance of the four and one-half million dollar debt from the Hartford fire claims. By 1954 John North had wiped out this debt.

Mr. North's efforts during the past ten years to gradually modernize and streamline his show went beyond the mechanical aspects of running the circus. The switch from horse power to trucks, sunburst wheel to pneumatic tires, and bleachers to seat-wagons were all accepted by the public. Sharp, however, was the press in its criticism of the use of pastel colors and the ballet girls in skimpy costumes.

The 1956 season was beleagured from the outset by labor trouble, high costs of operation, rain and muddy lots, a blowdown, accidents and elephant stampedes.

1941, MRS. IDA RINGLING NORTH (sister of the seven Ringling Bros.) and her sons. John Ringling North (on right) and Henry Ringling North, President and Vice President. Mrs. North died in 1950.   (J. J. Steinmetz)

These difficulties were compounded by the shortage of old-time "know-how" employees. While showing at the Boston Gardens that year, two unions, which had failed to organize the circus employees, went into the circus business themselves to harass the Ringlings.

(In an Associated Press release of Aug. 29, 1958, Senator McClellan, Chairman of the Senate rackets investigating committee, developed testimony that the idea of the Union Circus was to follow Ringling Brothers from town to town across the nation and split the circus-going crowd. The Unions gave up the venture after losing $16,000)

As the show moved west it began to bog down like a sluggish colossus, amid claims and counterclaims as to why.

On July 16 at Pittsburgh, John North announced tersely, "the tented circus as it exists today is, in my opinion, a thing of the past"; and with that the Ringling Bros. and Barnum & Bailey Circus ended its season and returned to winterquarters.

This trend of thought was not a sudden impulse on John North's part. As long ago as 1951 he commented that the day of the tented show was drawing to a close.

The nation's press mourned the Ringling demise. *Life* magazine, " . . . a magical era had passed forever." Washington, D. C. *Sunday Star,* " . . . and with it died just a little bit of America." Pittsburgh *Post Gazette,* "it looks like kids in the future won't know the circus, the thrill of greeting it at dawn—the sideshow, the walk thru the sawdust." *Newsweek,* "goodby to the gallant and gay." Washington *Daily News,* " . . . tumbled a world of excitement marking the end of a golden era in the history of entertainment." The Pittsburgh *Post Gazette* ran a Hungerford cartoon showing Uncle Sam with hat in hand and tears streaming down his cheek standing before a gravestone inscribed, "Here lies Ringling Bros. and Barnum & Bailey Circus."

Such was the tone of the nation's press, except for *Billboard* which administered a verbal spanking to the Ringling management:

"The one thing that forced closing was decimation of the once efficient organization that always before overcame those obstacles and more.

"The combination that left the show short on business and short on know-how was ineffective advertising, inability to move an unnecessarily heavy show, and uninformed and indecisive management fearful of arbitrary policies."

It will be recalled that prior to their first circus in 1884 the five Ringling boys put on their acts in halls; so with the 1957 season their show is back in "halls," only on a tremendous scale. Mr. North hired Art Concello as his General Manager to organize the "arena" season.

JOHN RINGLING NORTH, President of Ringling Bros. and Barnum & Bailey Combined Shows, Inc. Circa 1952. (RB&BB)

In the Spring of 1957 the Ringling show had its usual successful engagement in New York's Madison Square Garden. From there the circus went to mediocre business in the Boston Gardens.

Ringling agents were busily lining up other arena dates to build up a full route. Trouble developed when it was found that 40 percent of the arenas were too small for the circus, either in seating capacity, area to show, door clearance, or storage space for horses, elephnts, floats, etc.

Special rigging was designed and built for all aerial displays. A new rubber floor mat was put to use as a means of giving performers and horses good footing.

Under this new type of operation the circus figured on a daily cost of operation (*nut* in circus lingo) of $7,500 as compared to the $26,000 while under canvas. The payroll was cut to 300 people, including 175 performers.

The 1957 version of Ringling Bros. and Barnum & Bailey incorporated other vast changes. The show moved on four or five railroad-owned baggage cars, plus a fleet of a dozen or more circus-owned semi-trailer trucks. All performers rode regular raiload Pullmans. The show operated without menagerie or side show once it left the Boston Gardens. It was nothing but a "suitcase circus," as one press agent candidly put it.

A mid-June meeting of the owners of the circus resulted in the election of Stuart Lancaster (a grandson of Charley Ringling) to vice president. Lancaster had been heading up the fight of the minority group to gain control of the show. Lancaster insisted the circus could be operated successfully and at a profit under canvas. He had the opinions of many old-time circus men to back him up. "Let's give the circus back to the children" was the reasoning of Lancaster's group.

1957 was a hard and rough year on the Ringling Circus. It hurt the prestige of this great title immeasureably. It was rough on the performers and other personnel. At one period during late summer and fall the circus was showing only 58 percent of the time, and paydays came only when the circus was playing a stand.

Financially the season was dismal—resulting in a loss of $250,000. The Ringling circus in an arena or coliseum or ball park, just didn't draw crowds as did the tented circus.

Here are a few interesting comparisons:
San Diego - 1957 arena $32,000 gross for 4 days
San Diego - 1951 tent   50,000 gross for 2 days
Los Angeles - 1957 arena $73,560 gross for 6 days
Los Angeles - 1951 tent   167,279 gross for 7 days
Phoenix - 1957 arena $18,525 gross for 3 days
Phoenix - 1951 tent   38,832 gross for 2 days

El Paso was a rough stand. For three days the show took in $6,586, but had expenses of $19,286.

The 34-day stand in Mexico City was only a little better than break even. Receipts were $165,780, and expenses $154,339.

Lancaster and his mother, Mrs. Charles Sanford, took positive action in the form of a twenty million dollar lawsuit filed on September 6, 1957 against the Norths and Concello. The suit charged that over the past ten years the defendants had cost the circus up to $20,000,000 through mismanagement.

On February 25, 1958 the circus announced that it was closing winter quarters by the first of April and selling all surplus animals.

After the 1958 New York engagement the circus, now a truck show and without tents or menagerie, sent its animals to Pawtucket, R. I. on a lend-lease agreement. Included were seven cages of assorted animals, two giraffes, a rhino, a hippo, two tigers and a baboon. Under the arrangement the city will keep the animals for ten and one-half months of the year, sending them to the Garden for six weeks each spring.

On June 7, 1958 Stuart Lancaster and his mother resigned as circus officials. On July 16, two years to the day after the circus folded its tents for the last time in Pittsburgh, Lancaster opened a crusade to "return The Greatest Show On Earth to the American public." His group called itself "The Ringling 49'ers" because the minority group holds 49 percent of the circus stock.

The "arena" circus, meantime, continued its second season and financially, it was reported, did better. There were particularly successful stands at Atlanta and Omaha, although the long tour of Mexico was again far from profitable.

Thus, the Ringling Bros. and Barnum & Bailey Circus headed toward its 75th anniversary, May 19, 1959, on the controversial note of a tented or tentless circus.

How would the original Ringling Brothers have coped with this situation? Would they have favored a circus under the canvas, or under the sky?

"The show is over—the races run—

"All out and over" rings the cry.

The lights are lowered, one by one,

The crowds depart—"good night, good bye."

(From 1909 Barnum & Bailey Program)